1985

Long Term Care of the Elderly

Volume 157, Sage Library of Social Research

RECENT VOLUMES IN . . .
SAGE LIBRARY OF SOCIAL RESEARCH

Long Term Care of the Elderly

Public Policy Issues

Charlene Harrington
Robert J. Newcomer
Carroll L. Estes
and Associates

A. E. BENJAMIN, Jr.
PHILIP R. LEE
DOROTHY P. RICE
ROBYN STONE
JUANITA B. WOOD

MARJORIE P. BOGAERT-TULLIS
LYNN PARINGER
CAROL E. SATTLER
JAMES H. SWAN

Ida VSW Red, Coordinating Editor

Volume 157
**SAGE LIBRARY OF
SOCIAL RESEARCH**

 SAGE PUBLICATIONS
Beverly Hills   London   New Delhi

*To Maggie Kuhn, Lillian Rabinowitz, and Tish Sommers,
whose personal courage, social vision, and
national contributions have inspired the work of the
Aging Health Policy Center and the authors*

For information address:

SAGE Publications, Inc.
275 South Beverly Drive
Beverly Hills, California 90212

SAGE Publications India Pvt. Ltd.
C-236 Defence Colony
New Delhi 110 024, India

SAGE Publications Ltd
28 Banner Street
London EC1Y 8QE, England

Printed in the United States of America

Library of Congress Cataloging in Publication Data
Main entry under title:
Long term care of the elderly.

(Sage library of social research; v.157)
Includes index.
1. Long-term care of the sick—United States—
Addresses, essays, lectures. 2. Long-term care of the
sick—Government policy—United States—Addresses,
essays, lectures. 3. Long-term care of the sick—
United States—Finance—Addresses, essays, lectures.
4. Medicaid—Costs. I. Harrington, W. Charlene.
II. Newcomer, Robert J. III. Estes, Carroll Lynn,
1938-   IV. Series.
RA644.6.P83 1984   362.1'6   84-17754
ISBN 0-8039-2214-0
ISBN 0-8039-2215-9 (pbk.)

FIRST PRINTING

CONTENTS

TABLES

FIGURES

PREFACE

There is a dynamic tension within the health care field. It has been spawned by a continuing rise in health care costs, service cutbacks, and cost shifts from one level of government to another and to the public; a reduction in health care access among those with low incomes; and an awakening recognition that the current health care delivery system cannot meet the needs of the future without reforms. Particularly vexing are questions relating to long term care. Relatively few public or private insurance dollars are being expended on long term care. Yet these needs are rapidly expanding, and there is a wide consensus that new forms of care, particularly noninstitutional care, are needed.

Much has been learned in the past ten years concerning benefits and other consequences of the incremental attempts to reform aspects of the health care system. More will be learned from innovations and other strategies beginning to be put in place. Nevertheless, a fundamental issue remains to be addressed: Can and will public policy move forward in the long term care area before some control over the acute care system has been achieved? In our view, this is not an either/or question. For too long, health care policy has been fragmented, focusing on one dimension at a time and ignoring the dynamic interrelationship among acute and long term care services. A recent change in Medicare illustrates both the narrowness of public interventions in health and aging and the cross-cutting interaction between acute and long term care. The case in point is the change in Medicare hospital reimbursement, from a retrospective cost-based reimbursement to a prospectively determined rate. Rates under this new system (known as diagnosis-related groups or DRGs) are based on patient diagnosis and are more or less the same for all patients with a given diagnosis. How well this system will work remains an open issue for now, but the purpose of the policy shift is to place incentives in the reimbursement system to constrain hospital costs. Since hospitals are the major locus of medical care spending, such a strategy seems rational. The bad news is that this reform neglects the spillover consequences for either the sick elderly or the community delivery system of the constrained hospital placements under the DRG system. Key questions raised are: What percentage of patients will transfer into nursing homes, receive home care, or go without necessary care as a result of this and other policy shifts to contain costs? Will the public and private insurance money saved on hospital costs be reallocated to cover the costs of substitute care? If reallocations are to occur, how will they be implemented in the current delivery system, given that hospitals are paid largely by private insurance and Medicare; nursing homes by Medicaid and private out-of-pocket expenditures; and home care by out-of-pocket or in-kind support?

This book is designed both as an introduction to the existing literature on long term care issues and as an empirical assessment of the policies to date. Its goal is to provide a basic foundation of knowledge for aging advocates, professionals, and policymakers. The book is particularly designed for faculty and students in public health, public policy, sociology, anthropology, social welfare, and the health professions. Those who are planning or conducting research in long term care will find the data and analysis useful.

The study of public policies in long term care and their impact on the aged has occurred at a time of general economic instability, during which the country has faced recession, unemployment, inflation, high interest rates, and other financial problems. These problems, in turn, have contributed to cutbacks in health and social services and general adoption of cost containment as a top priority in government. In this austerity context, issues of quality, appropriateness, and access to services have of necessity been viewed as less important by policymakers than cost containment.

The manner in which long term care services are provided in the United States is shaped by federal policies, particularly in the Medicaid, Social Service Block Grant, and Supplemental Security Income programs. These basic federal requirements and recent budget constraints have had dramatic effects on state medical assistance and human service programs.

While recognizing the importance of federal policies, this book focuses primarily upon state policies and the broad discretion of states, in the implementation of health, income, and social service programs that represent the essential basis of long term care for the elderly. State policies for eligibility, benefits, utilization controls, and reimbursement affect the expenditures for institutional and community-based service, as well as who receives these services. It is these policies that have the most direct impact on services for the aged.

The existing emphasis on public policy and financing of acute care and nursing home services, with little support for community-based alternatives for the frail elderly, has shaped the type and nature of services available. The rapid growth of proprietary ownership has also been a dramatic trend in all types of long term care service delivery. Hospitals, board and care facilities, and community-based services are becoming increasingly recognized for their importance in long term care.

Public policymakers are seeking new approaches to controlling costs for long term care while improving quality and access. A key ingredient for policy formulation is knowledge of the existing system and in public policy. It is our belief that this book will contribute to a greater understanding of current policies and their potential impact on the aged, thus serving as a foundation for redesigning the long term care service delivery system.

Organization of the Book

This book is organized to present the current issues in public policy for long term care. Chapter 1 begins with an overview of the social, political, and economic factors influencing long term care policies. Current trends in health care expenditures for the major programs that provide long term care services are described. Chapter 2 presents the demographic trends for growth of the elderly in the United States and the problems of disability and health care needs of the elderly. The chapter outlines future projections for health care service needs if the current utilization and service delivery patterns are continued.

Chapter 3 describes the effects of state policies on long term care, based upon data from eight states on the Medicaid, Social Service, and Supplemental Security Income programs. Three chapters present empirical data developed in studies of specific policies in the Medicaid program between 1978 and the present time; these studies include an examination of the equity and incentives in state Medicaid eligibility policies (Chapter 4), state Medicaid cost containment approaches (Chapter 5), and Medicaid nursing home reimbursement policies

(Chapter 6). The following three chapters focus on the effect of state policies on service delivery—Chapter 7 describes institutional long term care services; Chapter 8 discusses board and care facilities, and Chapter 9 examines new initiatives in community-based long term care. The role of private nonprofit organizations in the delivery of community-based long term care is discussed in Chapter 10. Chapter 11 provides an economic framework for assessing the impact of Medicaid policy changes in long term care. The final chapter (12) presents proposed solutions to the current long term care problems described in the book. This final chapter presents issues under debate and recommendations for changing the existing long term care system.

This research is drawn from a series of longitudinal studies conducted by the authors in the Aging Health Policy Center and in the Department of Social and Behavioral Sciences, School of Nursing, University of California, San Francisco. These studies address various aspects of the organization, financing, and delivery of long term care and provide an assessment of both the policy shifts emerging in the 1980s and the long-range impact of public and private responsibility for the elderly.

Acknowledgments

Many individuals, agencies, and private organizations have in some way supported and contributed to the research, analysis, and preparation of this book. The intrepretations and commentary are those of the authors and should not be attributed to any other individuals or sponsoring agencies.

We are particularly grateful to the federal agencies and private foundations that have supported the research on which this book is based. Our research on long term care, and particularly on Medicaid, Social Services, and Supplemental Security Income (SSI) has been supported by two federal agencies. The National Center for Health Services Research supported a four-year study of the Correlates of Long Term Care Expenditures and Utilization in Fifty States (Grant No. HS04042) and the Health Care Financing Administration provided grant support for a three-year project on Long Term Care and the Impact of State Discretionary Policies (Grant No. 18-P-97620/9). Both of these studies have been important in describing the effects of federal policy changes and budget reductions on states during a time of fiscal crisis. The Commonwealth Fund has given support to the work of Dorothy Rice on the burden of illness for the elderly. The Pew Memorial Trust has generously supported the study of public policy, private nonprofit sector, and the delivery of community-based long term care for the elderly. This research has been influential in broadening our view of both public and private sector policies and policy impacts. We also appreciate the grant funds from the Pew Memorial Trust for health policy training both for Pew fellows and faculty who have contributed to the writing of this book. We would also like to acknowledge the assistance of faculty of the Institute for Health Policy Studies, University of California, San Francisco.

Our faculty colleagues in the Department of Social and Behavioral Sciences, the Department of Family Health Care Nursing, and in the School of Nursing have contributed greatly to our efforts by support, encouragement, and needed resources.

The research staff of the Aging Health Policy Center contributing to our work includes more than ten professional staff and research assistants. The primary efforts have been by Ida VSW Red in serving as editor and coordinator of this book. We would also like to acknowledge the research efforts of Lenore Gerard, Victoria Peguillan-Shea, David Lindeman, Alan Pardini, Marjorie Bogaert-Tullis, Carol E. Sattler, and Pat Fox. Patricia Saliba has made vital contributions in the coding and management of the data sets for all the studies reported here.

All the authors of this volume personally owe a great debt to Norton S. Twite and Susan Churka-Hyde for the production of the manuscript. We would also like to thank Nancy DeMartini, Elaine Benson, and Stephanie Wilkinson for managing the affairs of the Center while we prepared this book.

San Francisco   Charlene Harrington
                                                     Robert J. Newcomer
                                                     Carroll L. Estes

CHAPTER 1

SOCIAL, POLITICAL, AND ECONOMIC BACKGROUND OF LONG TERM CARE POLICY

Carroll L. Estes
Philip R. Lee

Long term care is a multibillion dollar service enterprise. It involves not only public sector government agencies at the federal, state, and local levels, but the private for-profit and nonprofit sectors as well. The definition of long term care is "a range of services that addresses the health, personal care, and social needs of individuals who lack some capacity for self-care" (Kane and Kane, 1982, p. 4). Thus, the long term care product is the service provided to those suffering from chronic physical or mental illnesses, mental retardation, or other severe disabling conditions. It also includes the professional and paraprofessional jobs, research, and capital generated through the provision of long term care. Long term care is financed through both public and private sources. Long term care seems to be a problem that has eluded any significant remedy, not only because of conflicting legislative authorities, providing different financing mechanisms, the fragmented organization and delivery of services, and the influence of organized interest groups on policy, but also because a comprehensive solution to long term care has not been sought.

The public policy debate has often framed the problem in the form of discrete issues arising from government crises in meeting the long term care cost burden or in providing quality of care with government financing services provided largely by the for-profit sector. Long term

Authors' Note: We wish to thank Lenore Gerard and Charlene Harrington for their invaluable assistance in preparing this chapter. The data and analyses that form the basis of the ideas in this chapter have been supported by the National Center for Health Services Research (Grant No. HS 04042), the Health Care Financing Administration (Grant No. 18-P9762019), and the Pew Memorial Trust.

care became a public policy issue only after attention was called to the skyrocketing costs of institutionalization of the very old and sick in nursing homes and the allegations and investigations of fraud, corruption, and even criminal abuse of patients (Vladeck, 1980; 1981; U.S. Senate, 1974–76). From a political perspective, long term care did not evolve as a result of rational planning for the needs of America's older citizens. It evolved piecemeal and as a byproduct of a health and social welfare system in crisis.

The increase in the number of older Americans has aroused public expectations of the health and welfare system for long term care services far surpassing the demands anticipated by policymakers twenty years ago at the passage of Medicare and Medicaid. The historical state role in caring for institutionalized dependent elderly populations has gradually shifted to a shared federal-state role, primarily as the result of legislation enacted in the 1960s and 1970s. Although the states continue to play the primary role, reliance on the federal government is present in terms of the fiscal incentives to provide services with federal/state financing and also in terms of a broader assurance of minimum standards in terms of eligibility, scope of benefits, and reimbursement of providers.

In addition, voluntary private charitable agencies have played a major role in the past by filling the service gaps left by state and local government welfare agencies. Today these providers, grouped together under the rubric of the private nonprofit sector, play a major role in providing health and social services at the local level. Whether through state and local public agency contracts or through direct city or county grants, fully forty percent of the support of this private nonprofit sector is derived either directly or indirectly from federal dollars (Wood and Estes, 1983; see also Chapter 10).

Long term care has emerged as a salient issue because there is a broad and growing population in need, a diversified but unbalanced financing system, and increasingly less ability to pay for long term care on an individual out-of-pocket basis because of rising costs (particularly for medical services). Moreover, the heavy burdens of long term care have touched not only the poor, but also millions of middle-income families and individuals for whom the high cost of caring for a chronically or acutely ill elderly person can lead to impoverishment and the necessity of relying on public resources. While public financing (i.e., federal and state) of the personal health care costs of the elderly has dramatically increased since 1965 as the result of

Medicare and Medicaid, high out-of-pocket costs continue to be borne by individuals and families (Fisher, 1980). Medicare covers approximately 38 percent of the older person's medical care expenses. The remainder must be paid either by private plans, Medicaid, or out-of-pocket. In 1984, elderly Americans will average more than 1,500 dollars out-of-pocket costs, thus spending about 15 percent of their annual incomes on health care (U.S. House, 1984).

To deal with the problem of long term care financing, the problem of the rapidly rising costs of health care must be resolved. A broad approach to controlling health care costs associated with long term care (e.g., nursing homes, hospitals, physician services) would necessitate changes to control overall costs in the entire health care industry. Such changes may, in the long run, "be necessary to maintain the level of services provided by Medicaid and Medicare" (U.S. CBO, 1984, p. 64). In the broad view, the problems of long term care mirror the problems of the American medical care system and of the welfare system—two dissimilar and reluctant partners engaged in the long term care enterprise. Further, the business of long term care operates in a pluralistic, competitive market where corporate interests as well as newly arrived entrepreneurial interests must be assured of profitable investment. Various actors within the long term care enterprise as well as organized advocacy groups seek short-term solutions to address their particular interests. These interest-group pressures give way slowly to an accommodation of incremental change, but there are few coalitional efforts aimed at providing a comprehensive continuum of care that cuts across the barriers of age, social class, disability, and race characterizing many who are dependent on others for daily assistance.

One of the most significant actors in the long term care policy arena is state government, which pays half of the nursing home bill (through the federal-state Medicaid program) and which has broad discretion in the management and provision of long term care services. As the major payers for nursing home services, state governments have a great deal of power over the market (Hill, 1981). Complicating the long term care picture is the current trend toward decentralization and the reassertion of the principles of state and local responsibility under new federalism aimed at preserving and extending states' rights and responsibilities. Any history of long term care must take into account these countervailing trends, values, and fiscal realities. The division of power and authority and the inequities in the revenue-generating capacity of the different levels of government also present inherent problems for a decentralized policy, such as current U.S. long term care policy (Estes and Gerard, 1983). The barriers created by fragmentation in policies and programs dealing with separate, components of long term care are not easily surmountable.

Historical Trends

What is commonly called the long term care dilemma can be understood more fully by an examination of the victories, contradictions, and accommodations rooted in past and present public policy. It is within this broader political and social environment that programs related to long term care developed incrementally, involving major political conflict over the legitimate function and role of the state. The enactment and implementation of major programs related to the development of long term care policy begins with the emergence of the modern welfare state during the American depression when the country had undergone economic hardship and changing views on the proper role of government. The landmark passage of the Social Security Act of 1935 laid the conceptual groundwork by addressing retired workers' need for an adequate and secure income. Although four-generation families may not have been envisioned by the framers of the social security legislation some fifty years ago, in an important way all future generations, young and old, would be affected: first, in terms of public expectations about what government can or should do for American workers who face voluntary or involuntary retirement; and second, in terms of establishing a federal role in protection against the risks of economic loss through social insurance principles. Today, it is recognized that the goal of an adequate income is an inextricable part of sound health and long term care policy (Ball, 1981).

It took the passage of thirty years and a major world war before income security was joined by health care for the elderly as a major national issue. There were, of course, individuals who suffered from chronic illness but they did so privately and at their own personal expense, since there was no major effective legislative concern at the federal or state level until the implementation of Medicare and Medicaid in the mid-1960s. The first major national treatment of chronic illness and long term care issues was undertaken in the mid-1950s by the Commission on Chronic Illness (Morris, 1981), but little public policy action followed until the enactment of Medicare and Medicaid. The major effort in health politics was centered on the debate for national health insurance, which was defeated (Estes, Gerard, Zones, and Swan, 1984).

Three historical trends are of particular importance in understanding the long term care dilemma: the predominance of the biomedical, acute care model; the welfare approach to dependency in youth and old age; and, finally, the politics of decentralization.

BIOMEDICAL ACUTE CARE MODEL

The biological and biomedical models of aging have contributed to the perception of old age as an individual problem—i.e., independent of social structure (Estes, 1979). In this biological view, aging is seen largely as a medical problem that occurs as a result of the individual physiological and chronological decline and decay that occur with chronological aging. This biological view not only fails to take into account social factors in individual host-resistance to disease, it also fails to deal with the problems of disease and again within the population (Syme, 1983).

The bias toward medical care in the allocation of public resources for the elderly has resulted in the "medicalization" of services, as exemplified in the high proportion of publicly financed health expenditures allocated to hospital and physician coverage, as opposed to community, in-home and other social services. In the process, however, long term care has been accorded a low priority because physicians and hospitals find such care less professionally or economically rewarding than acute care. As a result, health care financing and delivery is adapted to respond primarily to acute or catastrophic illnesses such as heart attack, cancer, and stroke, which are common diagnoses for hospitalized elderly persons. The system, however, is not adequate for those chronically ill individuals in need of a continuum of long term care services and supports, particularly for those needing assistance to cope with the tasks of daily living for an extended period of time.

For some who suffer from serious functional physical or cognitive impairments and who have inadequate resources to remain in their own homes, the biomedical model offers institutional care through nursing homes. As the de facto long term care policy, nursing homes have been required to perform multiple functions—custodial care, acute illness care, rehabilitation, chronic care, and terminal care—

without the resources to perform these tasks. Alternative policies for the provision of income maintenance, housing, and social supports have not been implemented because the dominant medical model has consumed resources that otherwise could have supported such policies. When a primary medical diagnosis of physical or mental disability is combined with a social diagnosis of poverty and loss or social supports, individuals are vulnerable to institutionalization and the state is likely to incur increased costs. Many states provide varying alternative remedies such as income supplements or board and care home placement. The major underlying problem is a lack of economic resources that would enable individuals and their families to secure access to appropriate treatment or management at the lowest cost. Even when there are moderate means to seek appropriate care, either the necessary support services may not be available or the cost over an extended period of years far exceeds the financial resources of the average retiree.

WELFARE APPROACH

During the early years of American social history, the major issues confronting the state were the unemployment, poverty, and illness that created conditions of dependency. Whether these social and physical conditions occurred late or early in life, the treatment was the same. The American state and local welfare system was decentralized and thus variable, but cohesive, in its application of the principles set out by the English Poor Law system from the seventeenth century (Williamson, 1982). The welfare system shunted the poor, old, and sick into workhouses, almshouses, or institutions for the mentally ill or dying that were little more than warehouses. For the aged who were poor all of their lives, this treatment was only a continuation of the differential treatment of workers in a class-based market economy (Estes, Gerard, Zones, and Swan, 1984). In the early years of the republic few survived to suffer the indignities of old age. Today, with a growing proportion of the population surviving to old age, the residual of the Elizabethan poor laws remain imbedded in public attitudes and public policy. Those who must look to state government for long term care have fallen heir to a welfare heritage developed to deal with the dependency associated with conditions of illness, poverty, or age.

Long term care policy is the stepchild of traditional welfare policy, which has been developed and instituted by state and local government to deal with the poor. Because most individuals cannot afford the full cost of needed long term medical or social maintenance, government policy has focused primarily on the provision of institutional long term ca, e for the poor and, increasingly, for those who are impoverished late in life by the rapid depletion of their private assets. The goal of public policy has been to manage this group in the most politically efficacious and least costly way, rather than to redress the underlying social causes of dependency.

DECENTRALIZATION

The delegation of major fiscal and political responsibility for the poor to the states has been maintained over the course of American history. Nevertheless, in at least two earlier periods of U.S. crisis (the 1930s and the 1960s), unprecedented federal intervention was extended to areas that had been previously considered the responsibility of state and local government or of the private sector. That occurred at least partly as a consequence of the depression of the thirties, which "created a broad consensus that the federal government must assume responsibility for maintaining prosperity, as well as for protecting individual citizens against the inevitable insecurities of life in a market economy" (Tobin, 1981, p. 11).

During both the depression in the 1930s and the period of heightened consciousness regarding civil rights, social justice and poverty in the 1960s, at least three arguments have justified the evolving federal role—that federal funds make possible: (1) an equalization in the level of public services among states and localities with vastly different resources; (2) a level of services required in the national interest; and (3) reflection of the superior capacity of the national government to collect taxes in contrast to states (Hale and Palley, 1981). In addition, services such as public education and health care were deemed to benefit the society as a whole and not just the individual who may receive the service. Government intervention in the financing of health care for the poor and the elderly were seen as appropriate governmental functions. Health care was not to be left to the market forces of supply and demand, and the individual's ability to pay.

However, even with the passage in 1965 of the Medicaid program establishing some uniformities and extending the federal-state partnership, the states have had important discretion in setting eligibility standards and in determining the scope of health and social services through the federal-state Medicaid and social service programs. Decentralization and state discretion in these programs have contributed to a variety of highly state-dependent and state-variable approaches to the support of long term care—varying primarily in terms of the stringency of eligibility for Medicaid coverage and state expenditure and utilization patterns under the program.

When former President Nixon employed decentralization through new federalism programs like revenue sharing in the 1970s to curtail the growth of federal programs, pressures for underwriting program expansion were transferred from the federal to state and local governments (Estes, Armour, and Noble, 1977).[1] This transfer of responsibility has exacerbated both state and local fiscal and tax pressures, creating a hospitable environment for the taxpayer revolts that emerged in the late 1970s and early 1980s. The Reagan administration's new federalism initiatives and domestic spending cuts in programs for the poor have raised new questions about the role of government, the individual and family, and the private sector in underwriting the cost of health and other long term care services for the elderly (Estes and Gerard, 1983).

These decentralization policies have been accompanied by a fragmentation and diversification of programs in many social problem areas. Policies concerning long term care illustrate how national policy goals may give way to more autonomous and variable state and local policy choices. Under new federalism, such choices involve the complexity of multiple programs under several political and geographic jurisdictions, as the number of decision-makers, authorities, and subgovernments acting at their own discretion complicate a focus on particular targets of intervention.

Further, under the broadly defined and decentralized enactments in which Congress only vaguely specifies its intention, the resultant ambiguity provides opportunities for political actors, vested interests, and active organizations of health professionals to shape large segments of health and social policy outside of the public legislative process and through the less visible implementation and administrative processes (Lowi, 1969). An important issue for long term care policy is the degree to which increasing decentralization of programs for the poor, aged, and disabled has, or will, foster politically motivated rather than need-based priorities and allocations. Certainly in the past, one result of decentralization has been the wide variation among states in eligibility and benefits for the poor, elderly, blind, and disabled in their health (Medicaid), social service (block grant) and income (Supplemental Security Income) programs (Estes, Newcomer, and Associates, 1983).

Issues concerning the organization, financing, and delivery of long term care have become more complex with inflation, recession, government fiscal crises and a federal administration committed to decentralization and domestic spending cuts. These conditions have not only created pressures to redefine the relationships between levels of government and between the public and private sectors, but have also threatened to choke off public financing for the desired and needed alternatives to institutional long term care. The willingness of states to underwrite the increasing costs of long term care is threatened by mounting pressures for state-level policies of retrenchment in the face of rising fiscal constraints on state governments.

Demographics

Demographic factors raise questions not only about economic effect (i.e., the use of resources to support the retired vs. the productive working sector), but also the effect on individuals and families who provide informal support, and on the health and welfare system which provides formal support (see Chapter 2). The explosion of the "fourth generation" has had a major impact on the scope and cost of long term care. The concept of the fourth generation refers to the demographic boom of the very old and is attributed not only to greater longevity but also to earlier marriages and earlier childbearing, which reduces the average span in years between generations (Townsend, 1979). In the twenty-five-year period since 1960, the population 75 years of age and over has nearly doubled (Vladeck, 1980; 1981). By the year 2000, this group is expected to increase from a current 38 percent of the elderly population to 45 percent (Rice and Feldman, 1983; see also Chapter 2).

The fourth generation is not merely an interesting piece of demographic data but rather signifies social and economic transformations in American life since the turn of the century. Particularly noteworthy is the observation that the majority of the very old will be women, unmarried or widowed. It is estimated that for every nursing home resident there are three people of equal functional impairment living in the community (Kane and Kane, 1981). The distinguishing difference correlates to economic and social factors—low incomes, marital status, and age. For example, widows and widowers have been found to be up to five times more likely to be institutionalized than were married persons; and those elderly who were never married,

11¼, 365

divorced, or separated have been found to have up to ten times the rate of institutionalization of married individuals (Butler and Newacheck, 1981). In addition, many women who traditionally performed the care giving role needed to sustain dependent family members can no longer meet this responsibility, alone, over an extended period of time (Brody, 1979).

Programs and Policies
Related to Long Term Care

Until the 1965 Medicare and Medicaid legislation, there was no significant federal policy which uniformly assured both coverage and access—regardless of state or residence or ability to pay—to needed health care services. The predominant practice was to pay for health care either privately, out-of-pocket, or through voluntary charitable associations and state or local social welfare agencies.

MEDICARE AND MEDICAID

The enactment of Medicare and Medicaid ushered in the current era of long term care policy. In neither program, however, is long term care policy explicitly addressed. On the contrary, although these two programs emerged from the same heated political environment, Medicare and Medicaid have distinctly separate ideological origins. Appealing to the fervor of the states' rights movement, along with the federal share incentive, government-financed health care for the poor gradually gained approval (Levine, 1984) with the passage of Medicaid legislation. Medicaid continued the traditional decentralized welfare approach to the poor resulting in highly variable, and politically vulnerable, policies at the state and local levels. Being "on the dole" was (and still is) the stigma attached to the unemployed welfare population (especially mothers and children) who were (and are) dependent on the state and local government bureaucracy.

Medicare, on the other hand, was won on a platform of "earned right" to health care protection free from the stigma attached to dependents of the state under the earlier welfare system. Enacted in 1965 as Title XVIII of the Social Security Act, Medicare was designed to provide health insurance to most individuals aged 65 and over and to disabled persons under 65 who meet certain criteria, and special treatment to certain workers and their dependents. Medicare is federally administered and financed for all persons eligible for Social Security payments, without respect to income.

Today, there are 27 million elderly and 3 million disabled eligible beneficiaries on Medicare. In 1983, total outlays exceeded 57 billion dollars. The program has two components. Part A (the Hospital Insurance Program financed with Social Security Trust Funds through employer and employee contributions) covers inpatient hospitalization, limited skilled nursing care, and home care that is medically necessary. Beneficiaries must pay deductibles before Medicare will reimburse for services; they also must pay copayments for those services over the reimbursement limits. Part B (the Supplementary Medical Insurance Program for physician services, outpatient therapy, medical equipment, and home health visits) is a voluntary program financed through federal revenues and monthly premium charges for enrollees (Muse and Sawyer, 1982).

Medicare is limited in terms of the reimbursement policies and types of services covered. Both Parts A and B require beneficiaries to pay various deductibles and coinsurance charges. Medicare does not cover long term care services, out-of-institution drugs, dental care, eyeglasses, hearing aids, and other important services. Of the total Medicare expenditures for 1981, almost three-quarters were spent on hospital services and one-quarter on physician services. Medicare expenditures were negligible in covering nursing homes (less than 1%), home health (1%), and other services (4%) in 1982 (U.S. HCFA, 1982). The limitations of the Medicare program, particularly in relation to the care of the chronically ill and disabled, resulted in Medicaid's becoming the primary vehicle for the payment of long term care services in the form of nursing home costs.

When Medicaid, Title XIX of the Social Security Act, was enacted in 1965 to provide federal matching funds for state programs, it was designed as a third-party insurance program to pay for medical care for eligible low-income families and individuals of all ages. From the conception of the Medicaid program, eligibility has been tied to state welfare policy. Although more than half of the nation's poor do not meet stringent state eligibility requirements, Medicaid is the principal health care insurance provided for the poor. Federal regulations require that state Medicaid programs provide hospital inpatient care, physician services, skilled nursing facility care, laboratory and x-ray services, home health services, hospital outpatient care, family planning, rural health clinics, and early and periodic screening. In addition, states may provide up to 32 other optional services including intermediate care, prescription drugs outside the hospital, dental services, and eyeglasses (Muse and Sawyer, 1982).

Although federal contributions account for almost half of the nationwide Medicaid expenditures, this program has become a dominant factor in state finances (U.S. CBO, 1981), and is often the largest item in a state budget (Freeland and Schendler, 1981). Since 1975, the state role in financing Medicaid has become increasingly problematic because state fiscal capacity has not kept pace with program growth. Medicaid expenditure increases have been one-third to one-half higher than the growth rates of state revenues (Bovbjerg and Holahan, 1982).

Recent changes in federal budgetary allocations limiting the growth of federal expenditures under Medicaid have marked a significant turning point in the history of the state Medicaid program. Program changes have increasingly taken the form of service coverage limitations, more stringent eligibility policies, and a variety of efforts to reduce the volume and cost of services. The total number of recipients peaked nationally in 1976; there has been a decline in recipients since (Newcomer and Harrington, 1983; see Chapter 3). Federal policy changes and the deteriorating fiscal condition of many state governments since 1981 have stimulated consideration of multiple program changes that will affect long term care.

SOCIAL SUPPORT

Federal income, health, housing, and employment programs proliferated after the enactment of social welfare legislation commencing with the Social Security Act of 1935. There was, however, little concerted effort to increase the role of the federal government in providing for the elderly or for other individuals whose needs for support and independence did not fall neatly within the parameters of the medical or welfare models of care. However, with passage of the Older Americans Act (OAA) in 1965, the federal role expanded. This Act included several global objectives relevant to long term care—an adequate retirement income, the best possible physical and mental health, suitable housing, and full restorative services for those who need institutional care. These goals exceeded both the authority of the entities created by the Act (state and area agencies on aging) and the small federal appropriations (never exceeding $900 million). The contribution of the Old Americans Act has been in raising the visibility of old age as an individual and social problem, and the support of a geographically dispersed "aging network" of planning and coordinating agencies and service providers (Estes, 1979). What distinguishes this program from others providing social services is the fact that there is no means-testing. Thus, all elders are eligible for the limited pool of available community-based services provided under the Older Americans Act.

In 1975, under the Nixon administration's new federalism initiatives, a comprehensive social service program was enacted through the passage of Title XX of the Social Security Act. Eligibility was limited to those in need according to state standards, but within certain federal limits. Between 1975 and 1981, the ceiling on federal Title XX funds was raised from 2.5 to 2.9 billion dollars, and the level of state funding also increased (Lindeman and Pardini, 1983). In 1981, the Omnibus Budget Reconciliation Act (U.S. PL 97-35) provided for a significant restructuring of the Title XX program. The Social Services Block Grant (SSBG) replaced the Title XX program, with the primary effect being reductions in both federal funding (by 21%) and federal regulatory authority.

HOUSING

Housing is an essential—although largely ignored—dimension of long term care (Meltzer, Farrow, and Richman, 1981; Newcomer, Lawton, and Byerts, in press). Age is an important factor in maintaining adequate and affordable housing since retirement often reduces disposable income by one-half to one-third. Older Americans pay a larger proportion of their incomes for rent than other age groups. For example, approximately 2.3 million elderly households spend over 35 percent of their incomes on housing. Forty-one percent of elderly renters with incomes below poverty level spend over 45 percent of their income for rent (U.S. Senate, 1983a, p. 299).

The federal role in housing has mainly addressed the needs of the severely disadvantaged—particularly black and hispanic—who have a greater probability of being inadequately housed. In addition to federal subsidized housing to low-income households (Section 8, Housing and Community Development Act, U.S. PL 93-383), there is federal financing for housing construction for older persons (Section 202), and grants to public housing authorities to provide nutritional meals and supportive services to partially impaired elderly and handicapped persons (Congregate Housing Services Act, U.S. PL 95-557; see U.S. Senate, 1983a). However, the federal role in housing is limited not only by inadequate funding but also by a narrow restriction of program focus and authority. There is a lack of integration of housing with the health and social needs of older persons who are vulnerable to institutionalization. This vulnerability could often be offset by preventive measures in the form of a supportive living environment with technological or structural modifications to assist in leading a dignified and independent life in the community. The resource of property can be quickly and unexpectedly eroded with the onset of chronic illness requiring long-term social and medical maintenance costs. A broad sector of middle-income retired couples with serious chronic illness have been faced with the grim choice of either divorce (i.e., separating personal property of spouse) or state-imposed "spend-down" of income and assets to poverty level in order to receive long term care under the Medicaid program (see Chapter 3).

The importance of relating housing to long term care (not only in terms of available supply, but also structural or technological modifications) is often realized too late, when the functional independence of an individual has been threatened and families can no longer cope. For some individuals who are able to engage in planning for old age, the continuing care retirement community (CCRC) is an appealing (if not always affordable) concept. In the United States today there are about 275 of these communities where some 90,000 elderly people live independently in their own apartments. It is common for individuals to sell their homes and to use the homeowner equity for a CCRC down payment. What is unique about these communities is the health care guarantee, providing insurance against the cost of long term care, as well as supplementing Medicare and private coverage for acute health care costs (U.S. Senate, 1983b).

Overall, public policy has fostered a piecemeal approach to housing needs, with incentives toward a privately developed and publicly financed nursing home industry. It has been suggested that the multibillion-dollar nursing home industry has functioned as a substitute for the lack of adequate income, suitable low-cost housing, and community social supports (Scanlon, Difederico, and Stassen, 1979). Based on narrowly targeted services and eligibility under the federal-state Medicaid program, nursing homes have by default become the dominant long term care policy. The valuable resource of home ownership is threatened by this policy.

SUPPLEMENTAL SECURITY INCOME

Income is another important factor affecting both ability to privately purchase long term care services and eligibility for publicly financed programs. Key among resources available to low-income persons, and a state determinant of Medicaid eligibility for long term care, is the Supplemental Security Income (SSI) program. The SSI program, passed in 1972 and implemented in 1974, was significant in providing a guaranteed minimum income for the poor who are aged, blind, or disabled. The program federalized state welfare payments and instituted national standards of income and resources. In December 1982, of a total of 3.9 million people receiving federally administered SSI payments, 2.2 million were disabled, 1.5 million were aged, and 77,000 were blind (U.S. SSA, 1983). Many states provide a supplementary payment to eligible individuals in addition to the basic federal SSI payment. Since most aged SSI recipients are poor and very old, this program has been extremely important in helping a vulnerable population to maintain marginal independence in the community.

The SSI program is also important in long term care because of its relationship to Medicaid eligibility and domiciliary care. The law provides automatic Medicaid eligibility for SSI beneficiaries (aged, blind, and disabled) unless states choose to adopt more stringent standards based on 1972 Medicaid eligibility (as 15 states had done by 1982). The law also permits states to provide additional payments to SSI beneficiaries to cover the costs of congregate housing or domiciliary care. Because states vary in their coverage of institutional care (both types and numbers of categories) and in levels of supplementation, SSI policies may affect Medicaid caseloads and expenditures, as well as the development of particular segments of long term care services (see Chapter 3).

Cost of Long Term Care

The health care system has been described as the nation's third largest industry, with a labor force of over 7.5 million people. Total national health expenditures have reached alarming levels (Gibson,

Waldo, and Levit (1983). A few facts illustrate why policymakers and the public have become increasingly concerned (Gibson et al., 1983).

- In 1982 total national expenditures for health care were 322 billion dollars, or 1,365 dollars per person.
- Share of GNP for health expenditures rose from 7.9 percent in 1972 to 10.5 percent in 1982.
- Almost 15 percent of 1982 federal tax dollars went to the health care industry; up from less than 1 percent in 1965.

The problem of health care costs is not of recent origin: they have been rising at a rapid rate for the past thirty years. Increased health care costs have been reflected not only in aggregate national expenditures, but also in per capita health care expenditures and in the rapid increase in the cost of health insurance premiums to employers and others who must purchase them. Medical care costs have continued to rise at a rapid rate, even as the rate of inflation in the rest of the economy has decreased. According to the U.S. Department of Labor, the cost of medical care in the United States rose more than twice as fast as all other prices during 1982. The consumer price index for medical care increased 11 percent in 1982, while it rose only 4.3 percent for all services and 3.9 percent overall.

The increases in national health expenditures by type of service are shown in Table 1.1. Expenditures for hospital services comprised 47 percent of total expenditures for personal health care in 1982. Expenditures for hospital care increased by 288 percent between 1972 and 1982, compared to a 158 percent increase in the gross national product for the same time period (Gibson et al., 1983). Thus, the increase in expenditures for hospital care has been a major contributor to the large increase in total health care expenditures between 1972 and 1982. Nationally, while less money was spent on nursing home services (9.5% of total health care expenditures in 1982) than on hospital or physician services, expenditures for nursing home care nevertheless increased by 320 percent between 1972 and 1982—more rapidly than any other health care service. An analysis of the cause of these increases in total personal health care costs (between 1981 and 1982) shows that the largest percentage gain was for general inflation (51%), but medical care price inflation (in excess of general inflation) was 27 percent. Only 8 percent of the increases were accounted for by population increases and 14 percent by other factors (Gibson, Waldo, and Levit, 1983).

TABLE 1.1   National Personal Health Care Expenditures by Type of Service, 1972-1982

	Expenditures (in $ billions)			% Increase 1972-1982
	1972	1978	1982	
Hospital care	34.9	75.7	135.5	288.3
Physicians' services	17.2	35.8	61.8	259.3
Nursing home care	6.5	15.2	27.3	320.0
Drugs and medical sundries	9.3	15.4	22.4	140.9
Eyeglasses and appliances	2.3	4.1	5.7	147.8
Dental services	5.6	11.8	19.5	248.2
Other health services	4.4	8.7	14.7	234.1
Total U.S. personal health care expenditures	80.2	166.7	286.9	257.7

SOURCE: Adapted from Gibson et al. (1983).

General expenditures for medical care have increased for all payers, but the increase has been higher for the government than for either private health insurance companies or patients paying out-of-pocket in the decade between 1972 and 1982, as shown in Table 1.2. Federal and state public expenditures increased by 78 percent between 1978 and 1982, with the greatest increase for federal Medicare expenses, primarily because of the rapid increase in hospital costs (Gibson, 1979; Gibson et al., 1983).

State policymakers have cause for concern because Medicaid expenditures have been growing more rapidly than inflation. From 1972 to 1982, the Medicaid program grew from 8.5 billion to 34 billion dollars (a 300% increase) (Gibson et al., 1983). Medicaid is funding a growing percentage of total personal health spending (11.7% in 1982) and represents a growing proportion of many state budgets (Harrington, Newcomer, Estes, and Lee, 1984) (see Chapter 3). State and federal Medicaid dollars together paid for about half of the publicly financed national nursing home expenditures of 27 billion dollars in 1982 (Gibson et al., 1983). Although the public costs of the Medicaid program escalated at a rate of 11.5 percent between 1981 and 1982 (Gibson et al., 1983), the number of Medicaid recipients did not increase nor did the utilization rates of services (see Chapters 3 and 4). Thus, price increases are the key factor in expenditure increases, while population growth, improvements in quality, or complexity of care are negligible factors.

The effects of these cost increases for middle- and low-income individuals is equally important. Individuals who pay for health care

TABLE 1.2   Personal Health Care Expenditures by Source of Funds, 1972-1982

| | (In $ billions) | | % |
	1978	1982	Increase
Patient direct payments	55.3	90.4	63.5
Private health insurance	45.4	76.6	68.7
Government	(65.0)	(115.7)	(78.0)
Federal Medicare	24.9	50.9	104.4
Federal Medicaid	10.2	16.9	65.7
Federal other	11.4	15.9	39.5
State Medicaid	8.1	15.5	91.4
State other	10.4	16.5	58.7
Philanthropy and industrial inplant	2.2	4.2	90.9
Total personal health	167.9	286.9	70.9

SOURCES: Adapted from Gibson (1979) for 1980; adapted from Gibson et al. (1983) for 1982.

costs have paid more than the general increase in the consumer price index. Table 1.2 shows that individual patient direct out-of-pocket increases were 64 percent between 1978 and 1982. For the elderly, the direct out-of-pocket costs are particularly high.

Public expenditures for long term care services are a sizeable proportion of total public spending for the aged, although national statistics are not fully available. Public nursing home and home health expenditures are shown in Table 1.3. In 1982, the total health spending for nursing home services was 15 billion dollars and only 1.6 billion dollars for home health. Medicaid and private individuals paid for 62.7 percent and 43.6 percent, respectively, of total 1982 nursing home costs; private insurance and philantrophy, 1.5 percent; Medicare, 1.8 percent; and other public programs, 4.8 percent (Gibson et al., 1983; U.S. HCFA, 1984).

Many long term care projects are funded out of federal research and demonstration project funds and state Medicaid demonstration projects. Accurate statistics on social service block grant funds spent on long term care services are also not available, but states estimated that about 21 percent of total program funds benefited the elderly (U.S. Senate, 1982). Some portion of the total 3.5 billion of state

TABLE 1.3 Public Long Term Care Expenditures in 1982, by Source

Health Sources	1982 Expenditures (in $ billions)		
	Nursing Homes	Home Health	Total
Medicare	.5	1.1	1.6
Medicaid	13.3	.5	13.8
Other public	.8	NA	.8
Veterans Medicare	.5	NA	.5
Total	15.0	1.6	16.7

SOURCES: Adapted from Gibson et al. (1983); and U.S. HCFA (1982).

and federal dollars spent in 1982 for the aged were spent on social services, which include in-home support services. Other home care and demonstration project funds are provided by state and federal funds from the Older American's Act. As noted above, the nonmedical/social services funds for long term care are only a small percentage of those financed by Medicare and Medicaid.

The factors of cost and demographics—especially the increasing numbers of those over 75 years of age—have made long term care a salient political issue. From a policy perspective, cost and demographic factors raise complex and difficult choices which, in varying degrees, have an impact on each major economic and social institution of American life—government, family, and industry. The medical cost factor must be considered in terms of highly inflationary expenditures affecting government budgets. But it is also crucially important to consider the actual allocation of expenditures and the overall effect of meaningful policy choices which, in turn, affect individual choice for those seeking care. Historically, there is disproportionate weight given to medical care in the financing and provision of services for the elderly. Brody (1979) reports a 30-to-1 ratio in public dollars allocated for medically oriented service expenditures compared with health/social service expenditures for the long-term support of the health of the elderly. The gap between public funding for health versus social service dollars had widened by 1982 to approximately 40 dollars to one dollar. The reimbursement structure of Medicare and Medicaid, the two major programs providing health care for the elderly, are biased toward institutional medical services. The Medicare dollar is largely absorbed by the acute care treatment of older persons undergoing catastrophic illness at the terminal stage (Davis, 1982), while the Medicaid dollar for elders is absorbed by nursing home institutional care (see Chapter 4). In both programs, an enormous sum of public dollars is consumed by medical institutions serving a small percent of older people in crisis. Efforts aimed at meaningful change in the values and structure underlying long term care may be precluded by the states' short term budgetary goal of cost control as well as by federal restrictions on domestic social spending.

Conclusion

The designers of a comprehensive long term care strategy will face the formidable obstacles of a system focused on biomedical acute care, a welfare approach to need, and decentralized responsibility and authority in the provision of care. Many positive professional and community efforts have been directed toward a more comprehensive and humane long term care system of services. Koff (1982) and others (Brody, 1979) envision a long term care system in which institutional and community-based services are integrated and appropriately utilized in a continuum of care (see Chapter 9). There are, however, no systemic or systematic links between the myriad of health and social services emerging as alternatives to institutionalization, nor between the acute and chronic care systems (Palmer, in Vogel and Palmer, 1983).

For older Americans, public policy reflects an emphasis on end-stage life cycle management. Intervention comes late, often at the stage of personal crisis, when the individual is socially, financially, or physically dependent on others. Approaches to long term care in the United States rely almost exclusively on health service strategies designed to provide assistance to individuals only when a health-related problem has progressed to the point where it results in substantial functional physical or mental impairment. This service strategy emphasis and the disproportionate resource allocation to it have eclipsed the much-needed consideration of the linkage of income, family, and housing policies to these services. However, there is an emerging policy interest in treatment not only of the effects of chronic illness, but also of causal factors such as income, nutrition, housing, and poverty. The need for broad solutions is illustrated, for example, by the fact that the percentage of persons reporting functional impairments is twice as high among the poor as among those with adequate incomes (U.S. DHEW, 1980).

This newly emergent policy interest is slow in implementation, but there has been progress in such areas as nutrition and life-style intervention efforts as well as in service efforts like adult day health, social centers, and home health. These new directions at the federal, state, and local levels have been initiated as much by the focus on cost control as they have by professional and community-wide goals of accessible, appropriate, and humane levels of care for America's older citizens. The policy dilemma of the 1980s is to achieve an equitable balance between these dual interests.

Note

1. Even though President Nixon established a decentralized federal revenue-sharing system, one of his major accomplishments was to federalize the Supplementary Security Income (SSI) program in order to establish minimum welfare benefits. See later discussions on SSI in Chapters 1, 3, and 4.

References

Ball, M. "Rethinking National Policy on Health Care for the Elderly." In *The Geriatric Imperative.* Ed. A. R. Somers and D. R. Fabian. New York: Appleton-Century-Crofts, 1981.

Bovbjerg, R. R., and J. Holahan. *Medicaid in the Reagan Era.* Washington, DC: Urban Institute, 1982.

Brody, S. J. "The Thirty-To-One Paradox: Health Needs and Medical Solutions." In *Aging: Agenda for the Eighties.* Ed. J. P. Hubbard. Washington, DC: National Journal, 1979, pp. 17-20.

Butler, L. H., and P. W. Newacheck. "Health and Social Factors Affecting Long-Term Care Policy." In *Policy Options in Long-Term Care.* Ed. J. Meltzer, F. Farrow, and H. Richman. Chicago: University of Chicago Press, 1981, pp. 38-77.

Davis, K. "Medicare Reconsidered." Paper presented for the Duke University Medical Center Seventh Private Sector Conference on the Financial Support of Health Care of the Elderly and the Indigent, Durham, NC, 14–16 March 1982.

Estes, C. L. *The Aging Enterprise.* San Francisco: Jossey-Bass, 1979.

Estes, C. L., P. K. Armour, and M. L. Noble. "Intent Vs. Implementation." Paper presented to the Gerontological Society, San Francisco, CA, October 1977.

Estes, C. L., and L. Gerard. "Governmental Responsibility: Issues of Reform and Federalism." In *Fiscal Austerity and Aging.* By C. L. Estes, R. J. Newcomer, and Associates. Beverly Hills, CA: Sage, 1983, pp. 41-58.

Estes, C. L., L. E. Gerard, J. Zones and J. Swan. *Political Economy, Health and Acting.* Boston: Little, Brown and Company, 1984.

Estes, C. L., R. J. Newcomer, and Associates. *Fiscal Austerity and Aging.* Beverly Hills, CA: Sage, 1983.

Fisher, C. "Differences by Age Groups in Health Care Spending." *Health Care Financing Review,* 1, No. 4 (Spring 1980), 65-90.

Freeland, M. S., and C. E. Schendler. "National Health Expenditures: Short-Term Outlook and Long-Term Projections." *Health Care Financing Review,* 2, No. 3 (Winter 1981), 97-138.

Gibson, R. M. "National Health Expenditures, 1978." *Health Care Financing Review,* 1, No. 1 (Summer 1979), 1-36.

Gibson, R. M., D. R. Waldo, and K. R. Levit. "National Health Expenditures, 1982." *Health Care Financing Review,* 5, No. 1 (Fall 1983), 1-31.

Hale, G. E. and M. L. Palley. *The Politics of Federal Grants.* Washington, DC: Congressional Quarterly Press, 1981.

Harrington, C., R. J. Newcomer, C. L. Estes, and P. R. Lee. "Comparative Study of Long Term Care in Eight States." Working paper. San Francisco, CA: Aging Health Policy Center, University of California, 1984.

Hill, L. "Challenge for the Nursing Home Industry: Growing Burdens and Shrinking Resources." Unpublished paper presented at George Washington University, Washington, DC, 1981.

Kane, R. A., and R. L. Kane. *Assessing the Elderly: A Practical Guide to Measurement.* Lexington, MA: Heath, 1981.

Kane, R. A., and R. L. Kane. "Long-Term Care: A Field in Search of Values." In *Values and Long-Term Care.* Lexington, MA: Heath, 1982.

Koff, T. H. *Long-Term Care: An Approach to Serving Frail Elderly.* Boston: Little, Brown and Co., 1982.

Levine, P. B. "An Overview of the State Role in the United States Health Scene." Chapter 10 in Litman, T. J., and Robins, L. S., eds. *Health Politics and Policy.* New York: John Wiley & Sons, 1984.

Lindeman, D. A. and A. Pardini. "Social Services: The Impact of Fiscal Austerity." In *Fiscal Austerity and Aging.* By C. L. Estes, R. J. Newcomer, and Associates. Beverly Hills, CA: Sage, 1983, pp. 133-155.

Lowi, T. *The End of Liberalism.* New York: Norton, 1969.

Meltzer, J., F. Farrow, and H. Richman, Eds. *Policy Options in Long-Term Care.* Chicago: University of Chicago Press, 1981.

Morris, R., Ed. *Allocating Health Resources for the Aged and Disabled.* Lexington, MA: Lexington/Heath, 1981.

Muse, D. N., and D. Sawyer. *The Medicare and Medicaid Data Book, 1981.* Washington, DC: U.S. Health Care Financing Administration, Office of Research and Demonstrations, 1982.

Newcomer, R. J. and C. Harrington. "State Medicaid Expenditures: Trends and Program Policy Changes." In *Fiscal Austerity and Aging.* By. C. L. Estes, R. J. Newcomer, and Associates. Beverly Hills, CA: Sage, 1983, pp. 157-186.

Newcomer, R. J., M. P. Lawton, and T. Byerts, Eds. *Housing an Aging Society.* New York: Van Nostrand Reinhold, in press.

Rice, D. P., and J. J. Feldman. "Living Longer in the United States: Demographic Changes and Health Needs of the Elderly." *Milbank Memorial Fund Quarterly/Health and Society,* 61, No. 3 (1983), 362-396.

Scanlon, W., E. Difederico, and M. Stassen. *Long-Term Care: Current Experience and a Framework for Analysis.* Washington, DC: Urban Institute, 1979.

Syme, S. L. "The Social Environment and Disease: Towards a Proper Epidemiology." Paper presented at the 16th Annual Meeting of the Society for Epidemiologic Research, Winnipeg, Canada, June 17, 1983.

Tobin, J. "Reagonomics and Economics." *New York Review of Books* (December 3, 1981), 11.

Townsend, P. *Poverty in the United Kingdom.* Berkeley, CA: University of California Press, 1979.

U.S. Congressional Budget Office (CBO) *Medicaid: Choices for 1982 and Beyond.* Washington, DC: U.S. CBO, 1981.

————. *Reducing the Deficit: Spending and Revenue Options.* Washington, DC: U.S. Government Printing Office, 1984.

U.S. Department of Health, Education, and Welfare (DHEW). *Income and Resources of the Aged.* Washington, DC: U.S. Government Printing Office, 1980, 1982; 1983a.

U.S. Health Care Financing Administration (HCFA). Medicare and Medicaid Expenditures Statistics. Unpublished data. Baltimore, MD: U.S. Department of Health and Human Services, 1982.

————. Medicaid Program Data Branch. *National Medicaid Statistics: Fiscal Years 1975 to 1982.* State 2082 Tables data tape. Baltimore, MD: U.S. Department of Health and Human Services, 1984.

U.S. House of Representatives. Select Committee on Aging. "Impact of the Proposed FY 1985 Budget on the Elderly." A briefing paper prepared by Edward R. Roybal, Chairman, Select Committee on Aging, U.S. House of Representatives, February 3, 1984.

U.S. Public Law 93-383. *Housing and Community Development Act of 1974* (as Amended). Washington, DC: U.S. Government Printing Office, 1974.

U.S. Public Law 95-557. *Congregate Housing Services Act of 1978* (as Amended). Washington, DC: U.S. Government Printing Office, 1978.

U.S. Public Law 97-35. *Omnibus Budget Reconciliation Act (OBRA) of 1981.* Washington, DC: U.S. Government Printing Office, 1981.

U.S. Senate Special Committee on Aging. *Developments in Aging: 1981; 1982.* Washington, DC: U.S. Government Printing Office, 1982; 1983a.

————. Hearing: *Life Care Communities: Promises and Problems,* 1983. Washington, DC: U.S. Government Printing Office, 1983b.

————. *Nursing Home Care in the U.S.: Failure in Public Policy.* Introductory Report and Supporting papers, Nos. 1-7. Washington, DC: U.S. Government Printing Office, 1974–1976.

U.S. Social Security Administration (SSA), and A. L. Kahn. *Program and Demographic Characteristics of Supplemental Security Income Beneficiaries, December 1982.* SSA Pub. No. 13-11977. Washington, DC: U.S. Department of Health and Human Services, 1983.

Vladeck, B. C. "Equity, Access, and the Costs of Health Services." *Medical Care,* 19, No. 12, Suppl. (December 1981), 69-80.

————. *Unloving Care: The Nursing Home Tragedy.* New York: Basic, 1980.

Vogel, R. J., and H. C. Palmer, eds. *Long Term Care: Perspectives from Research and Demonstrations.* Baltimore: MD: U.S. Health Care Financing Administration, 1983.

Williamson, J. "Public Policy and Regulation of the Elderly Poor Prior to the Rise of the Welfare State." Paper presented to the Society for the Study of Social Problems, San Francisco, September 1982.

Wood, J. B., and C. L. Estes. "The Private Nonprofit Sector and Aging." In *Fiscal Austerity and Aging.* By C. L. Estes, R. J. Newcomer, and Associates. Beverly Hills, CA: Sage, 1983, pp. 227-247.

CHAPTER 2

HEALTH CARE NEEDS OF THE ELDERLY

Dorothy P. Rice

As more people live longer, chronic diseases, most commonly conditions of middle and old age, have emerged as major causes of disability and functional dependency. Services required by the chronically ill have an impact on many sectors of the U.S. economy: income security, health, housing, transportation, and recreation. Both private and public sectors, including all levels of government, are involved in the provision of the health and social services needed by the elderly. Improved standards of living and medical advances in the prevention and control of formerly fatal infectious diseases have made it possible for an increasing number of persons to reach an age at which they become vulnerable to heart disease, stroke, cancer, arthritis, mental disorders, and other chronic illnesses causing limited or total disability. The escalating costs of medical care for the elderly and the growing proportion of these costs paid by public funds have become major policy issues.

The changing structure of the population resulting from decline in mortality are first described in this chapter as a basis for understanding the magnitude of the aging problem. The health of the elderly is examined in terms of health status, use and costs of medical services, and future morbidity patterns. The final section addresses selected health care issues and challenges emerging from these demographic changes. Special attention is given to regional variations in population changes, use of medical services, and implications for future planning.

Author's Note: The research on which this chapter is based was supported by the Commonwealth Fund (Grant No. 6516).

The Changing Demographics

The shift in the distribution of the population in the United States has occurred with considerable rapidity. In recent years, we have experienced a significant increase in both the number and the proportion of the population aged 65 and over. At the turn of the century there were only 3.1 million elderly people, 4.0 percent of the total population (Table 2.1). Forty years later the number of elderly tripled to 9 million and the proportion increased to 6.8 percent. By 1980, the elderly population almost tripled again to 25.5 million persons, representing 11.3 percent of the total population.

Within the 65-and-over age group, the proportion of very old persons has also increased rapidly. In 1900, the proportion of the elderly population who were 75 years and over was 29 percent (1.2% of the general population); by 1980, it was 39 percent (4.4% of the general population). The impact of these changes is a startling rise in the demand for health services at the same time that the cost of medical care is increasing. The United States is spending almost 3 percent of its gross national product (GNP) on health services for the elderly. In 1983, health spending for the total population amounted to 10.8 percent of GNP, a proportion that many feel is about at its maximum without encroaching seriously on other needed services and resource allocations.

Mortality

The rapid increase in the elderly population has been due to declining mortality rates across the entire life span and to changing fertility rates. When mortality rates began to decline rapidly early in the century, the decline was greatest at younger ages so that the proportion of babies surviving to adulthood increased. Based on mortality experience in 1900, an individual born in that year could expect to live an average of 47.3 years (Table 2.2); by 1982 life expectancy reached 74.5 years (U.S. NCHS, 1983e).

Declining death rates among the elderly, especially in recent years, have also contributed to the growth in the elderly population. The leading causes of death for the elderly are heart disease, cancer, stroke, influenza and pneumonia, and arteriosclerosis. Death rates for all these causes except cancer have been declining. From 1950 to 1979,

TABLE 2.1 Number and Distribution of the U.S. Population,
All Ages and 65 Years and Over, 1900-2000

Year	Population All Ages	Population 65 Years and Over			
		Total	65 to 74 Years	75 to 84 Years	85 Years and Over
		Number (in thousands)			
1900	76,303	3,084	2,189	772	123
1910	91,972	3,950	2,793	989	167
1920	105,711	4,933	3,464	1,259	210
1930	122,775	6,634	4,721	1,641	272
1940	131,669	9,019	6,375	2,278	365
1950	150,697	12,270	8,415	3,278	577
1960	179,323	16,560	10,997	4,633	929
1970	203,302	19,980	12,447	6,124	1,409
1980	226,505	25,544	15,578	7,727	2,240
Projections:					
1990	249,731	31,799	18,054	10,284	3,461
2000	267,990	35,036	17,693	12,207	5,136
		Percentage Distribution			
1900	100.0	4.0	2.9	1.0	0.2
1910	100.0	4.3	3.0	1.1	0.2
1920	100.0	4.7	3.3	1.2	0.2
1930	100.0	5.4	3.8	1.3	0.2
1940	100.0	6.8	4.8	1.7	0.3
1950	100.0	8.1	5.6	2.2	0.4
1960	100.0	9.2	6.1	2.6	0.5
1970	100.0	9.8	6.1	3.0	0.7
1980	100.0	11.3	6.9	3.4	1.0
Projections:					
1990	100.0	12.7	7.2	4.1	1.4
2000	100.0	13.1	6.6	4.6	1.9

SOURCE: Adapted from U.S. Bureau of the Census (1983a).

the death rate for people 65 years and over decreased 17 percent. Since the population aged 85 years and over is growing more rapidly than that aged 65-84 years, a more accurate picture of mortality trends is provided by the age-adjusted death rate, which eliminates the distortions associated with changing age composition. The age-adjusted death rate for the population 65 years of age and over fell 27 percent from 1950 to 1979, and the decline for females was nearly twice as great as that for males.

According to the National Center for Health Statistics, heart disease, cancer, and stroke accounted for 75 percent of all deaths among

TABLE 2.2 Life Expectancy at Birth and at 65 Years of Age by Sex,
United States, Selected Years 1900-1982

| | Remaining Life Expectancy (in years) | | |
Specified Age and Year	Total	Males	Females
At birth:			
1900	47.3	46.3	48.3
1950	68.2	65.6	71.1
1960	69.7	66.6	73.1
1970	70.9	67.1	74.8
1980	73.7	70.0	77.5
1981*	74.1	70.3	77.9
1982*	74.5	70.8	78.2
At 65 years:			
1900	11.9	11.5	12.2
1950	13.9	12.8	15.0
1960	14.3	12.8	15.8
1970	15.2	13.1	17.0
1980	16.4	14.1	18.3
1981*	16.7	14.3	18.7
1982*	16.8	14.4	18.8

SOURCE: Adapted from NCHS (1983e).
*Provisional data.

the elderly population in 1979 as well as in 1950. About half of the overall decline in mortality among the elderly during the period 1950–1979 was a result of the decline in heart disease mortality, the leading cause of death; another quarter is associated with the fall in death rates for stroke, the third leading cause of death. Cancer, the second leading cause, is the only major cause of death to have increased (13%) U.S. NCHS, 1982c, p. 34). A variety of factors are responsible for the substantial declines in mortality from heart disease and stroke during the past three decades. Contributing factors include improved medical services, greater availability of coronary care units, advanced surgical and medical treatment of coronary heart disease, improved control of blood pressure, decreased smoking, modified eating habits, increased exercise, and more healthy life-styles in general.

Improvements in mortality have been shared by men and women throughout the three decades since 1950, but women have experienced more rapid improvements for most leading causes of death. In 1950, the age-adjusted rate for men 65 years and over was 34 percent higher than that for women; by 1979 the difference had increased to 69 percent (Rice, Hing, Kovar, Prager, 1984). Of the leading causes of death among the elderly in 1979, sex differences are most pronounced for cancer. Lung cancer exhibits the greatest disparity with male mortality nearly five times greater than female mortality.

Health Status

The incidence of chronic illness increases with age and is a major cause of illness and disability requiring medical care; the cost of care for those suffering from chronic illness accounts for a larger proportion of the nation's expenditures for health care. The elderly in the community report a high prevalence of chronic conditions: 44 percent have arthritis, 27 percent have heart conditions, 39 percent have hypertension, and 28 percent have a hearing impairment; many have more than one chronic condition (U.S. NCHS, 1981a).

As shown in Table 2.3, 30 percent of the noninstitutionalized elderly report that their health is fair or poor compared with people their age (U.S. NCHS, 1983a). Approximately 32 million persons of all ages—14 percent of the noninstitutionalized population—reported limitations of activity due to chronic disease in 1981. Not surprisingly, the number suffering limitation of activity increases with age, rising from 12 percent of the total under 45 years to 24 percent at ages 45-64 years, and 46 percent at age 65 and over. Almost 9 out of 10 aged persons with limitation of activity due to chronic conditions are limited in the amount or kind of major activity (e.g., keeping house or other work) they can perform. Among the elderly with restricted activity, 40 days per year were restricted-activity days, of which 14 days were confined to bed.

Although men and women differ little in the percent reporting fair or poor health, the proportions of each sex unable to carry out their major activity because of health differ substantially. Forty-five percent of elderly men, but only 35 percent of elderly women, report that they cannot carry on their major activity because of health problems. The men may actually be in poorer health—certainly death and hospital utilization rates are higher for men than for women—or their reports of poorer health may be a reaction to mandatory retirement because of age (Kovar, 1977).

Since the need for help increases sharply with age, the very old have more need for assistance than the younger-old. For instance, in 1979, of the noninstitutionalized population, 5 percent of those

TABLE 2.3 Health Status and Utilization Measures by Age, United States, 1981

Measure	All Ages	Under 17 Years	17-44 Years	45-64 Years	65 Years and Over
Percentage feeling fair or poor	11.8	4.0	8.3	22.0	30.1
Percentage limited in activity	14.4	3.8	8.4	23.9	45.7
Percentage unable to carry on major activity	3.6	0.2	1.2	6.8	17.5
Restricted-activity days	19.1	10.5	15.1	27.5	39.9
Bed-disability days	6.9	4.8	5.4	9.0	14.0
Physician visits per person	4.6	4.1	4.2	5.1	6.3
Discharges from short-stay hospitals per 1000 pop.	169.3	72.9*	148.7*	195.3	396.5
Days of care in short-stay hospitals per 1000 pop.	1217.7	337.1*	769.6*	1564.0	4155.3
Needs help in one or more basis physical activities per 1000 pop.	22.5**	–	5.1	20.6	90.2

SOURCE: Adapted from U.S. NCHS (1983b, 1983c); Feller (1983).
*The rates for the under 17 age group are for under 15 years and rates for 17-44 age group are for 15-44 years.
**Includes adults aged 18 and over.

65-74 years of age, compared with 35 percent of those 85 years and over, needed help in one or more basic physical activities such as walking, going outside, bathing, dressing, using the toilet, getting in and out of bed or chair, or eating. Similar patterns of need for other types of assistance are also reported (Feller, 1983).

Use of Medical Care Services

Older persons who suffer from chronic and disabling conditions are high utilizers of medical resources. The elderly with chronic activity limitation had 8.7 visits to physicians per year in contrast with 4.3 visits for persons with no activity limitation (U.S. NCHS, 1981c). They had 41.2 hospitalizations per 100 elderly persons per year in contrast with 14.8 for those with no limitation of activity. The 46 percent of elderly people who were limited in activity because of a chronic condition accounted for 63 percent of physician contacts with the elderly, 71 percent of hospitalizations, and 82 percent of all the days that older people spent in bed because of health conditions (U.S. NCHS, 1981a).

Elderly people make more frequent visits to physicians than younger people. In 1981, noninstitutionalized elderly people had a physician contact (other than visits to hospital inpatients) on an average of 6.3 times a year, in contrast to an average of 5.1 times for persons aged 45–64 (Table 2.3). About 80 percent had a physician contact within the preceding year and 70 percent within 6 months. Only about 5 percent had not seen a physician for 5 or more years (U.S. NCHS, 1982b). Nine out of ten elderly people had a regular source of care and eight out of ten saw a single doctor for their care. Three-fourths of the visits by elderly people living in the community were in physicians' offices in 1980. Another 10 percent were in hospital emergency rooms or outpatient departments, and 9 percent were telephone consultations. Visits to patients in their homes are rare, although more common for the elderly than for younger adults (Kovar, 1983a).

The number of physician visits per elderly person varies by race and income. In 1980, black elderly persons visited physicians slightly more often than whites—6.6 compared with 6.4 visits per person per year. The lowest rate of physician visits (6.1 visits) was reported by the elderly with family incomes of 5,000–9,000 dollars per year; the poorest elderly with annual incomes below 5,000 dollars report more physician visits (6.7 visits). The latter group is likely to be sicker and eligible for Medicaid benefits (U.S. NCHS, 1983g).

Elderly people are hospitalized more frequently and stay in the hospital longer than younger persons. There were more than 10 million aged discharges from nonfederal short stay hospitals in 1981 with a total of 109 million days of care (U.S. NCHS, 1983c). Although persons 65 years and over comprised 11.5 percent of the civilian noninstitutional population, more than one-quarter (27 percent) of all people discharged and almost two-fifths (39 percent) of all days spent in hospitals were by elderly people. Only 4 percent of the people were 75 years of age or older in 1981, yet they accounted for 13 percent of the discharges and 21 percent of all the days of care.

The major reasons for hospitalization are the conditions that are the leading causes of death. Heart disease, cancer, and stroke were the first-listed diagnoses for 10.4 million elderly hospitalizations, accounting for 34 percent of the total hospital discharges for this age group. About one-third of the hospitalizations of the elderly had at least one surgical procedure; prostatectomy was the most frequent for men and cataract surgery for women.

According to the 1977 National Nursing Home Survey, about 5 percent of the elderly—compared with 22 percent of the very old

(85 years and over)—are in nursing homes (U.S. NCHS, 1981b). Other chronically ill elderly persons are in psychiatric or other chronic disease hospitals, Veterans Administration hospitals, and other long term care facilities. The most common primary diagnoses for nursing home residents are hardening of the arteries, senility, stroke, and mental disorders—all diagnoses likely to give rise to functional impairments.

In general, elderly residents of nursing homes suffer from multiple chronic conditions and functional impairments. Almost two-thirds (63%) are senile, 36 percent have heart trouble, and 14 percent have diabetes. Orthopedic problems due to a variety of disease conditions are common. About a third are bedfast or chairfast and about a third are incontinent. Almost half of the elderly in nursing homes cannot see well enough to read an ordinary newspaper regardless of whether they wear glasses; one-third cannot hear a conversation on an ordinary telephone; and one-fourth have impaired speech (U.S. NCHS, 1981b).

Although life expectancy for women is higher than for men, women have more illnesses and disabilities, make more physician visits, and are hospitalized at higher rates than men. For the elderly, the picture is the same: relatively more elderly women are limited in activities of daily living, visit physicians more frequently, and also use more days of hospital care than men (Rice, 1983; U.S. NCHS, 1983d).

The use of medical care services is especially high during the last years of life. In 1978, the 1.3 million Medicare enrollees in their last year of life represented 5.2 percent of all enrollees, but they accounted for 28.2 percent of program expenditures (Lubitz and Prihoda, 1983). Medicare users who died in 1978 were reimbursed an average of 4,909 dollars for all covered services in their last year, about four times the amount reimbursed for services provided to survivors. Average reimbursement per decedent for hospital care was 7.3 times higher in the last year of life than for survivors; 3.9 times higher for physician and other medical services; and 12.7 times for nursing home care. Data from the 1980 National Medical Care Expenditure Survey confirm these conclusions. The elderly people approaching death or institutionalization have very high expenditures for medical care. They constitute a small proportion of the elderly population, but use a relatively large proportion of the medical care dollar (Kovar, 1983b).

Expenditures for Medical Care

The aged represented only 11 percent of the population in 1980, but since they experience higher use of health care services, they ac-

**TABLE 2.4 Total and Per Capita Personal Health Care Expenditures for
Leading Medical Conditions by Age and Sex, United States, 1980**

| Medical Condition | Total Amount (in $ millions) | All Ages | Per Capita Amount | | | |
| | | | Under 65 Years | | 65 Years and Over | |
			Males	Females	Males	Females
All conditions	219,400	947	627	791	2,278	2,667
Circulatory diseases	33,184	143	67	61	674	848
Digestive diseases	31,755	137	110	143	213	223
Mental disorders	20,301	88	73	69	181	246
Injury and poisoning	19,248	83	86	61	105	203
Nervous system and sense organ diseases	17,499	76	57	69	168	176
Respiratory diseases	17,305	75	60	68	192	137
Musculoskeletal system diseases	13,645	59	40	55	91	187
Neoplasms	13,623	59	30	50	244	178
Genitourinary system diseases	13,162	57	21	82	128	70
Endocrine, nutritional, metabolic diseases	7,656	33	15	31	82	138
All other diseases	32,022	138	67	104	200	261

SOURCE: Adapted from Hodgson and Kopstein (1983), p. 164.

counted for 29 percent of expenditures for personal health care. Per
capita spending was three and a half times greater for elderly persons
than for those under 65 years of age. Women used more medical
services and incurred higher expenditures than did men (Rice, 1983).
Women represented 59 percent of the aged population and incurred
63 percent of the expenditures.

The economic burden imposed by a disease category varies with
the age and sex of the population. Table 2.4 shows the expenditures
in 1980 for leading medical conditions according to age and sex (Hodgson
and Kopstein, 1983). For the elderly, diseases of the circulatory system
were the leading cause of health care expenditures, accounting for
about 30 percent of the total for older men and women and requiring
674 and 848 dollars per capita, respectively. Also among the five
most expensive conditions for both groups of elderly were diseases
of the digestive system and mental disorders. Injury and poisoning,
and diseases of the musculoskeletal system and connective tissue completed the top five most expensive conditions for older women but
ranked eighth and ninth for older men. Neoplasms were the second
expensive category among elderly men but ranked sixth for women
65 years of age and over. Similarly, diseases of the respiratory system
were relatively important for older men (ranking fourth) but ranked
ninth among women.

The level of per capita spending is directly related to the prevalence of disease, the number of services used by each patient, and the average cost of each service. The large differences in per capita spending between elderly and young persons are chiefly the result of the higher prevalence of heart disease among persons 65 years of age and over. In 1979, the prevalence of heart disease was 274 elderly persons per 1,000 population compared with 52 persons under 65 years of age per 1,000 population (U.S. NCHS, 1981a). In addition, older persons with heart disease used more health services on the average than the younger group, which also contributed to higher per capita expenditures.

Future Morbidity Patterns

There is considerable conjecture and controversy regarding future morbidity patterns. Fries and Crapo (1981) theorize that improvements in life style will result in a reduction in the prevalence of morbidity from chronic disease and a compression of morbidity at the older ages. They foresee a continuing decline in premature death and emergence of a pattern of natural death at the end of a natural life span. Fries states that the "rectangularization of the survival curve may be followed by rectangularization of the morbidity curve and by compression of morbidity" (Fries, 1980, p. 135).

Kramer and Gruenberg, on the other hand, believe that chronic disease prevalence and disability will increase as life expectancy is increased, leading to a "pandemic" of mental disorders and chronic diseases (Kramer, 1980; Gruenberg, 1977). Manton elucidates the disagreement between the opposing viewpoints and points out that stability of morbidity and health status levels has characterized the aged population during the past decade (Manton, 1982). He views human aging and mortality as complex phenomena and as dynamic multidimensional processes in which chronic degenerative diseases play an essential role. His concept of "dynamic equilibrium" implies that the severity and rate of progression of chronic disease are directly related to mortality changes, so that with mortality reductions there is a corresponding reduction in the rate of progressive aging of the vital body organ systems. He believes that the severity of chronic diseases will be reduced or the rate of progression slowed, resulting in reduced mortality rates and an increase in life expectancy.

Schneider and Brody review the evidence presented by Fries and conclude "that the number of very old people is increasing rapidly, that the average period of diminished vigor will probably increase, that chronic diseases will probably occupy a larger proportion of our life span, and that the needs for medical care in later life are likely to increase substantially" (Schneider and Brody, 1983, p. 854). It is, of course, quite possible that both phenomena will be taking place simultaneously: there may be an increasing number of individuals in quite good health nearly up to the point of death and an increasing number with prolonged severe functional limitation, with a decline in the duration of infirmity. The effect on the prevalence of morbidity would, of course, depend on the relative magnitude of the various changes.

National Projections

A decade-long trend in an accelerated downturn of the death rates from cardiovascular diseases became evident in 1978. Population projections and the resulting impact on health services utilization were first developed by Rice and others, based on the assumption of contained rapid reductions in mortality for the 25-year period of 1978–2003 (U.S. NCHS, 1983b). Rice and Feldman (1983), in a more recent estimate, based on the population projections made by the Social Security actuaries, show the impact of these demographic changes in the age structure of the population on health status, health services utilization, and expenditures for health care to the year 2040 (Table 2.5). The projections were based on current age-sex-specific rates of health status and utilization patterns, although it is expected that additional changes in levels of morbidity, therapies and technologies, availability, cost of care, and social and economic conditions also will contribute to altered patterns and levels of utilization of medical care services. Whatever else happens, however, the projected changes in the size and age distribution of the population would alone have a significant impact on utilization and consequently on expenditures. The implications of the aging of the population on the demand for long term care and on public policy are significant. The following summarizes the result of these projections for the 60-year period 1980–2040:

- The total population is projected to increase 41 percent, while the group aged 65 and over will increase 160 percent.

TABLE 2.5 Current and Projected Population, Limitations in Activities of Daily Living, Medical Care Utilization and Expenditures, United States, by Age, 1980-2040

Characteristic and Year	All Ages	Under 65	Total	Age 65 and Over 65-74	75 and Over
Population (thousands):					
1980	232,669	206,777	25,892	15,627	10,265
2000	273,949	237,697	36,252	18,334	17,918
2020	306,931	254,278	52,653	30,093	22,560
2040	328,503	261,247	67,256	29,425	37,831
Persons with limitation in activities of daily living (thousands):					
1980	3,142	1,362	1,780	648	1,132
2000	4,509	1,734	2,775	784	1,991
2020	5,952	1,998	3,954	1,309	2,645
2040	7,922	2,002	5,920	1,288	4,632
Physician visits (millions):					
1980	1,102	936	166	100	66
2000	1,314	1,083	231	116	115
2020	1,499	1,164	335	191	144
2040	1,621	1,193	428	187	241

Days of hospital care (millions):					
1980	274	169	105	49	56
2000	371	211	160	58	102
2020	459	234	225	95	130
2040	549	236	312	93	219
Nursing home residents (thousands):					
1980	1,511	196	1,315	227	1,088
2000	2,542	226	2,316	265	2,051
2020	3,371	242	3,129	434	2,695
2040	5,227	248	4,979	425	4,554
Personal health expenditures (in constant 1980 $ billions)					
1980	219.4	154.9	64.5	n.a	n.a.
2000	273.4	183.1	90.3	n.a.	n.a.
2020	328.3	197.1	131.2	n.a.	n.a.
2040	369.0	201.5	167.5	n.a.	n.a.

SOURCE: Rice and Feldman (1983).
n. a. = not available.

- The total number of persons limited in activities of daily living is projected to more than double; the elderly with limitations will more than triple.

- Only 6 percent of the 47 percent increase in physician visits will result from the aging of the population.

- Total short-stay hospital days will double with more than half this increase due to the aging of the population. Forty percent of the days of care in 2040 are projected for those aged 75 and over, compared with 20 percent in 1980.

- The number of nursing home residents is projected to increase from 1.5 million to 5.2 million in 2040—a three-and-one-half-fold increase. A five-fold increase is projected in the number of nursing home residents aged 85 and older from 37 percent in 1980 to 56 percent in 2040.

- Total personal health expenditures are projected in increase 68 percent; for the elderly an increase of 159 percent is projected. In 1980, 11 percent of the population aged 65 and over consumed 29 percent of total health expenditures; by 2040 the elderly are projected to comprise 21 percent of the population, and almost half of the expenditures would be made in their behalf.

Regional Projections

The decline in mortality and changes in fertility have occurred throughout the United States, although the rates of change differ for various population groups. The Bureau of the Census recently published a set of projections to the year 2000 of the population of states (U.S. Bureau of the Census, 1983). Table 2.6 shows these projections of the population by region and by age. For the United States, the population is projected to increase 10 percent in the 1980–1990 decade and 7 percent in the last decade of the century. The projected increase in the total population during the next two decades is 18 percent. There are, however, important regional variations in these population projections:

- The West will be the fastest growing region in the country, increasing 44.8 percent from 1980–2000, more than twice the rate of increase for the nation.

- The South is projected to be the second fastest growing region, increasing 31 percent from 1980 to 2000.

TABLE 2.6 Population Projections by Region and Age, United States, 1980-2000

Census	Census April 1, 1980	Projections 1990	Projections 2000	% Change 1980-1990	% Change 1990-2000	% Change 1980-2000	% Distribution 1980	% Distribution 1990	% Distribution 2000
Total all ages	226,505	249,203	267,462	10.0	7.3	18.1	100.0	100.0	100.0
Under 15	51,282	54,576	55,900	6.4	2.4	9.0	22.6	21.9	20.9
15-44	105,181	116,355	115,660	10.6	-0.6	10.0	46.4	46.7	43.2
45-64	44,497	46,474	60,866	4.4	31.0	36.8	19.6	18.6	22.8
65 and over	25,544	31,799	35,036	24.5	10.2	37.2	11.3	12.8	13.1
Northeast, all ages	49,137	48,423	46,401	-1.5	-4.2	-5.6	100.0	100.0	100.0
Under 15	10,383	9,441	8,677	-8.2	-8.1	-16.4	21.1	19.3	18.7
15-44	22,151	22,293	19,626	0.6	-12.0	-11.4	45.1	46.0	42.3
45-64	10,531	9,778	11,271	-7.2	15.3	7.0	21.4	20.2	24.3
65 and over	6,072	6,912	6,828	13.8	-1.2	12.4	12.4	14.3	14.7
North Central, all ages	58,854	60,265	59,714	2.4	-0.9	1.5	100.0	100.0	100.0
Under 15	13,610	13,629	12,856	0.1	-5.7	-5.5	23.1	22.6	21.5
15-44	27,072	27,791	25,590	2.7	-7.9	-5.5	46.0	46.1	42.9
45-64	11,481	11,190	13,506	-2.5	20.7	17.6	19.5	18.6	22.6
65 and over	6,691	7,656	7,763	14.4	1.4	16.0	11.4	12.7	13.0

(continued)

TABLE 2.6 Continued

	Population (in thousands)			% Change			% Distribution		
	Census April 1, 1980	Projections 1990	2000	1980-1990	1990-2000	1980-2000	1980	1990	2000
South, all ages	75,349	87,594	98,828	16.3	12.8	31.2	100.0	100.0	100.0
Under 15	17,452	19,256	20,544	10.3	6.7	17.7	23.2	22.0	20.8
15-44	34,978	40,635	42,272	16.2	4.0	20.9	46.4	46.4	42.8
45-64	14,436	16,301	22,430	12.9	37.6	55.4	19.2	18.6	22.7
65 and over	8,484	11,403	13,582	34.4	19.1	60.1	11.3	13.0	13.7
West, all ages	43,165	52,920	62,519	22.6	18.1	44.8	100.0	100.0	100.0
Under 15	9,838	12,250	13,823	24.5	12.8	40.5	22.8	23.2	22.1
15-44	20,980	25,636	28,172	22.2	9.9	34.3	48.6	48.4	45.1
45-64	8,049	9,205	13,660	14.4	48.4	69.7	18.6	17.4	21.8
65 and over	4,298	5,829	6,864	35.6	17.7	59.7	10.0	11.0	11.0

SOURCE: Adapted from U.S. Bureau of the Census (1983b).
NOTE: Numbers may not add due to rounding.

- The rate of growth in the North Central region will slow to only 2.4 percent from 1980 to 1990 and then become negative for the 1990s.

- The Northeast is projected to lose population in both decades.

The population groups aged 45-64 and 65 and over are projected to be the fastest growing segments of the population, each rising 37 percent in the two decades from 1980 to 2000. For the United States, the percentage aged 65 and over will increase from 11.3 percent in 1980 to 13.1 percent in 2000. The differential rates of changes of the population will have a significant impact on planning for health and social services in the various regions of the country. Declining population may result in a surplus of resources; increasing population, especially of the elderly who require more services, may mean a shortage of resources, especially long term care services.

Changing demographics will have differential impacts by region on the use of medical care services. The Northeast will continue to have the oldest age distribution with almost 15 percent of its population aged 65 and over. In 2000, the West will have the youngest age distribution of the four regions, with over 22 percent of its population below age 15, 45 percent between the ages of 15 and 44, 22 percent between ages 45 and 64, and 11 percent aged 65 and over. Table 2.7 shows the impact of the aging of the population from 1980 to 2000 for the health care systems of the United States and the four regions as summarized below:

- The days of hospital care are projected to increase 28 percent (U.S. NCHS, 1982a). The projected increases vary significantly by region, from only 6 percent in the Northeast to 57 percent in the West, reflecting regional population shifts as well as the aging of the population.

- The total number of physician visits is projected to increase 19 percent, with significant regional variations. A 5 percent decrease in physician visits is indicated for the Northeast. The West and South, however, with their large projected population growth, will see increases in physician visits of 46 and 33 percent, respectively.

- The aging effect is much greater for nursing home care. The number of residents is projected to increase 69 percent, almost 4 times the growth in the population (U.S. NCHS, 1983f). In the Northeast and North Central regions, the number of nursing home residents will need to

TABLE 2.7 Projected Population and Medical Care Utilization by Region and Age, 1980-2000 (in thousands)

Region and Age	Population			Hospital Days			Physician Visits			Nursing Home Residents		
	1980	2000	% Change	1980	2000*	% Change	1980	2000*	% Change	1980	2000*	% Change
United States, total	226.505	267.462	18.1	274.509	350.806	27.8	1,036.097	1,232.787	19.0	1,396	2,354	68.6
Under 65	200.956	232.426	15.7	169.152	200.478	18.5	882.743	1,022.581	15.8	185	212	14.6
65 and over	25.549	35.036	37.1	105.357	150.328	42.7	153.354	210.206	37.1	1,211	2,142	76.9
65-74	15.581	17.693	13.6	48.789	54.057	10.8	97.055	110.722	14.1	219	245	11.9
75 and over	9.968	17.343	74.0	56.568	96.271	70.2	56.299	99.484	76.7	992	1,897	91.2
Northeast, total	49.137	46.401	-5.6	67.237	71.480	6.3	229.491	218.512	-4.8	300	432	44.0
Under 65	43.065	39.573	-8.1	38.572	37.294	-3.3	194.983	179.595	-7.9	36	33	-8.3
65 and over	6.072	6.828	12.5	28.665	34.186	19.3	34.508	38.917	12.8	264	399	51.1
65-74	3.663	3.353	-8.5	12.918	11.832	-8.4	20.543	18.769	-8.6	48	43	-10.4
75 and over	2.409	3.475	44.3	15.747	22.354	42.0	13.965	20.148	44.3	216	356	64.8
North Central, total	58.854	59.714	1.5	82.000	90.625	10.5	274.569	278.797	1.5	468	674	44.0
Under 65	52.162	51.951	-0.4	51.442	53.488	4.0	236.307	235.809	-0.2	59	59	0.0
65 and over	6.692	7.763	16.0	30.558	37.137	21.5	38.262	42.988	12.4	409	615	50.4
65-74	3.957	3.825	-3.3	14.365	13.897	-3.3	25.470	24.605	-3.4	69	67	-2.9
75 and over	2.735	3.938	44.0	16.193	23.240	43.5	12.792	18.383	43.7	340	548	61.2
South, total	75.349	98.828	31.2	88.217	130.711	48.2	328.940	438.122	33.2	380	752	97.9
Under 65	66.861	85.247	27.5	55.552	74.569	34.2	279.951	360.036	28.6	53	68	28.3
65 and over	8.488	13.581	60.0	32.665	56.142	71.9	48.989	78.086	59.4	327	684	109.2
65-74	5.313	7.032	32.4	15.233	20.179	32.5	31.095	41.124	32.3	64	85	32.8
75 and over	3.175	6.549	106.3	17.432	35.963	106.3	17.894	36.962	106.6	263	599	127.8
West, total	43.165	62.519	44.8	37.055	57.990	56.5	203.097	297.356	46.4	248	496	100.0
Under 65	38.867	55.655	43.2	23.586	35.127	48.9	171.502	247.141	44.1	37	52	40.5
65 and over	4.298	6.864	59.7	13.469	22.863	69.7	31.595	50.215	58.9	211	444	110.4
65-74	2.649	3.483	31.5	6.273	8.149	29.9	19.947	26.224	31.5	38	50	31.6
75 and over	1.649	3.381	105.0	7.196	14.714	104.5	11.648	23.991	106.0	173	394	127.7

SOURCE: Population (1980 and 2000)—see Table 6; Hospital days (1980)—adapted from U.S. NCHS (1982a); Physician visits (1980)—adapted from U.S. NCHS (1983g); Nursing homes (1980)—adapted from U.S. NCHS (1983f).
*Estimated by applying 1980 age-sex-specific regional utilization rates to the projected population.

increase 44 percent. In the South and West, where the elderly will increase around 60 percent, the number of nursing home residents will have to more than double to meet the needs of the projected elderly population.

Issues and Challenges for the Future

The aging of the population raises a variety of issues and challenges for the nation's economic, social, and health institutions. For example, the costs and financing of Social Security programs will be affected, including Medicare benefits and cash benefits for retired workers and disabled persons. Since the future financing of Social Security depends on the number of retirees in relation to workers, the burden on the working population to support the rapidly growing aged population is a major concern (Rice and Feldman, 1983). A significant policy issue is whether the supply of medical personnel and facilities in the future will be sufficient to care for the elderly population and whether alternatives to institutionalization will assist in meeting their needs.

MEDICAL PERSONNEL

In 1980, there were 439,301 non-federal physicians in the United States, a ratio of 194 physicians per 100,000 population, with the highest concentration of physicians in the Northeast (American Medical Association, 1983). The Bureau of Health Manpower estimated the physician requirements by 1990 and concluded that physician supply is expected to be somewhat greater than requirements (U.S. Bureau of Health Manpower, 1980). The number of physician visits will increase 12.5 percent nationwide and 46 percent in the West by the year 2000. The estimated supply of physicians both in the nation as a while and in each of the regions should be adequate to handle the projected number of visits resulting from the aging of the population.

Due to the special medical care needs of the elderly, however, an important consideration is whether the United States will have adequate numbers of physicians specially trained in geriatric medicine. Kane and his colleagues estimate that the United States will require about 8,000 geriatricians by the year 1990, assuming that geriatricians will provide improved consultant and primary care to people aged 75 and older. In addition, they assume that geriatricians will delegate a moderate amount of responsibility to nurse practitioners, physician assistants, and social workers (Kane, Solomon, Beck, Keeler, and Kane, 1980). Although no absolute increase in the number of physicians is implied in these estimates, there is a clear need to broaden medical education programs to provide more and improved coverage of geriatrics and gerontology (U.S. IOM, 1978).

Owing to the fact that age-sex specific rates of physician visits are not projected to increase significantly for the elderly, it appears that the aging of the population by the year 2000 will not require an increased supply of physicians in the United States beyond the total number expected to be trained. However, there will clearly be a need for physicians trained in geriatrics.

In addition to physician services, the long term care needs of the elderly require the services of a wide range of personnel: dentists, nurses (registered, licensed practical, aides); therapists' (physical, rehabilitation), nutritionists, social workers, recreation workers, and others. A recent Institute of Medicine study addressed various aspects of nursing and nursing education, including supply projections and nursing education for care of the elderly (U.S. IOM, 1983). The study concluded that there was not a significant national shortage of generalist registered nurses (RNs) or of licensed practical nurses (LPNs). However, shortages were identified in different geographic areas, in different health care settings, and in specialty nursing. The elderly population was identified as the largest single population group that suffers from a lack of adequate nursing services. It was noted that nursing homes were grossly understaffed in 1980 and that future demand for RNs employed in nursing homes will substantially exceed supply. Registered nurses are not attracted to work in nursing homes because working conditions are poor, salaries are low, and fringe benefits are rarely offered. The study concluded that programs should be supported to upgrade the knowledge and skills of aides, LPNs, and RNs who work with elderly patients and recommended that nursing education programs should provide more formal instruction and clinical experience in geriatric nursing.

Detailed studies of the education and supply of other health and social service workers are not available. It is likely, however, that there are similar shortages and training needs for other types of personnel involved in long term care. The growing number of elderly persons undoubtedly will exacerbate current shortages.

HEALTH FACILITIES

Hospital days projected for the year 2000 to meet the needs of the nation's aging population are estimated at 351 million days, a 28 percent increase during the twenty-year period 1980–2000. In 1980, the United States had 959,979 beds in non-federal short-term general and other special hospitals operating at a 75.6 percent occupancy rate, representing 4.25 beds per 1,000 population (American Hospital Association, 1981). Under assumption of increased occupancy rates to 80 percent, as recommended by the Institute of Medicine, the number of hospital beds required to meet the needs of an aging population would have to increase by 282,163, or 28.5 percent, in the nation as a whole by the year 2000 (U.S. IOM, 1976). This represents an average of 4.64 beds per 1,000 total population.

Many factors interact to determine supply and demand, including the possibility that supply creates demand (Ginsberg and Koretz, 1983). Although there are some trends toward lower per capita use of hospitals, such as declining average lengths of stay and tightening of hospital admissions, the effect of these and other factors on utilization rates over the long run is uncertain. Changes in hospital reimbursement may also impact on hospital use. As of October 1, 1983, Medicare's new DRG-based (diagnosis-related groups) reimbursement went into effect, in which hospitals are paid a flat amount for each diagnosis regardless of length of stay and severity of illness. The states are also currently placing limits on hospital reimbursement under Medicaid (reimbursement policies in eight states are described in detail in Chapter 3). Private insurance companies are negotiating preferred rates with providers. The future impact of these reimbursement changes on hospital utilization, however, is difficult to forecast. A careful watch should be kept on this fluctuating climate and on the need for and supply of hospital beds to meet the needs of the elderly in the future.

As already indicated, the aging effect will have the greatest impact on the need for nursing home beds. According to the National Master Facility Inventory, there were 1.5 million nursing and related care homes in 1980, or 60 beds per 1,000 aged persons (U.S. NCHS, 1983f; for details on nursing home bed supply, see Chapter 7). If average lengths of stay do not change, 2.6 million nursing home beds, or 74 beds per 1,000 population 65 years and over, will be required in the United States to accommodate the number of residents projected for the year 2000. Regionally, the number of nursing home beds for 1,000 elderly will range from 61 in the South to 97 in the North Central. Other studies indicate the projected shortage of nursing home beds. For example, a recent report of the General Accounting Office reviewed the characteristics leading to nursing home use and concluded that the future at-risk population will grow:

> Overall, unless major break-throughs in the treatment of chronic diseases occur, extended life expectancies, with greater likelihood of chronic

disabling diseases and a reduced number of family members able to provide informal care, will lead to a net increase in the population most likely to need intensive nursing home services. (U.S. GAO, 1983, p. 36)

ALTERNATIVES TO INSTITUTIONALIZATION

With the growing numbers of chronically ill elderly and the rising costs of hospital and nursing home care, increased consideration is being given to alternatives for providing long term care services and to preventing the need for institutionalization. These alternatives are aimed at maintaining the independence of the aged or disabled person at home to avoid institutional placement, often viewed as a measure of last resort. Many states are attempting to reduce utilization of nursing home beds in favor of community-based alternatives to institutionalization. Community services include a wide range of health and social services: day health care programs and sheltered workshops offer a range of services such as nursing, occupational therapy, physical therapy, recreational services, and other rehabilitative services in a supervised community setting on less than a 24-hour basis. Also included are home-health care, "meals on wheels," homemaker services, as well as counseling and guidance, and care and protection with respect to carrying out the tasks of daily living. Hospice services are designed for the care of the terminally ill and may be offered in the hospital, a free-standing facility, or the home. Respite care usually is provided on a short-term basis to relieve caretakers for a period of time.

Several studies indicate that some nursing home patients do not need the level of care provided in an institution and could remain in their homes if community-based services were available. At the same time, a significant number of the noninstitutionalized population need, but do not receive, long term care (U.S. CBO, 1977). The General Accounting Office recently studied this issue and found that when expanded home health care services were made available to the chronically ill elderly, longevity and client-reported satisfaction are improved. These services, however, do not necessarily reduce nursing home or hospital use or total service costs (U.S. GAO, 1982).

The growing public support for a wide variety of alternatives to institutionalization indicates that the initial policy issue is not whether home health services are less costly, but how these services should be organized and financed for maximum efficiency and effectiveness. Whether a shift in medical care utilization patterns can be accomplished, thus reducing the projected need for nursing home beds, remains to be seen.

Because of the difficulty of counting the alternative service programs for long term care, an accurate picture of the number of services cannot be presented. A rapid increase in the development of such programs has been reported across the country (see Chapter 9). Some programs are being promoted as more humane approaches to care of the aged and disabled, others are being developed as lower-cost alternatives. The expansion of home health programs in particular is anticipated because of less stringent federal restrictions under the Medicare program. The use of DRGs for hospital reimbursement also will encourage the growth of home care to speed hospital discharge. Projections of the growth of alternative community-based long term care services cannot be made at this time. It is clearly possible that public policies can be used to expand the use of alternatives such as ambulatory care and surgi-centers in place of hospital care and community-based long term care instead of nursing home care. These alternatives to costly institutionalization are possible approaches to meeting the long term care needs of the growing elderly population while reducing requirements for capital investments in health facilities.

Conclusion

The longer the period of projection, the more difficult is an accurate forecast of changes and the effect of changes in patterns of medical treatment, government regulations and legislation, inflation, insurance coverage, education, income, and other important parameters of health and health care. This discussion has purposely focused on the health status of the elderly and changes in the size and age of the population, although other forces will have an impact on health care use and expenditures.

It is not known whether the momentum of sharp reductions in mortality levels experienced during the recent past will continue. However, because there is so much uncertainty over factors associated with trends in major causes of death, no other effective substitute exists for projecting the future health care needs and demands of the U.S. population. Continuing rapid growth in the number and proportion of aged in the population seems assured. Assuming that current utilization patterns will continue, the number of hospital days, nursing home residents, physician visits, and corresponding health expenditures will need to increase to meet the needs of the elderly. These projections indicate a need to provide alternatives to costly institutionalization and to maintain the independence of the elderly. The implications of the aging of the population will have a major impact on policy planning in the years ahead for U.S. social institutions, including the health care delivery system.

References

American Hospital Association (AHA). *Hospital Statistics.* 1981 ed. Chicago: AHA, 1981.

American Medical Association (AMA), and M. A. Eiler. *Physician Characteristics and Distribution in the U.S.* 1982 ed. Chicago: AMA, 1983.

Feller, B. A. "Americans Needing Help to Function at Home." In *National Center for Health Statistics: Advanced Data,* 92, DHHS Pub. No. (PHS) 83-1250. Hyattsville, MD: U.S. National Center for Health Statistics, 1983.

Fries, J. F. "Aging, Natural Death, and the Compression of Morbidity." *New England Journal of Medicine,* 303, No. 3 (July 17, 1980), 130-135.

Fries, J. F., and C. M. Crapo. *Vitality and Aging: Implications of the Rectangular Curve.* San Francisco, CA: Freeman, 1981.

Ginsburg, P. B., and D. M. Koretz. "Bed Availability and Hospital Utilization: Estimates of the 'Roemer Effect'." *Health Care Financing Review,* 3, No. 1 (Fall 1983), 87-92.

Gruenberg, E. M. "The Failures of Success." *Milbank Memorial Fund Quarterly/Health and Society,* 55, No. 1 (Winter 1977), 3-24.

Hodgson, T. A., and A. N. Kopstein. "Health Care Expenditures for Major Diseases." In *Health: United States, 1983.* National Center for Health Statistics. DHHS Pub. No. (PHS) 84-1232. Washington, DC: U.S. Government Printing Office, 1983, 157-163.

Kane, R., D. Solomon, J. Beck, E. Keeler, and R. Kane. "The Future Need for Geriatric Manpower in the United States." *New England Journal of Medicine,* 302, No. 24 (June 12, 1980), 1327-1332.

Kovar, M. G. "Elderly People and Their Medical Care in the United States: Data, Data Sources and Comments." Working Paper Series, Number 17. Hyattsville, MD: U.S. National Center for Health Statistics, 1983a.

———. "Expenditures for the Medical Care of Elderly People Living in the Community Throughout 1980." *National Medical Care Utilization and Expenditure Survey, Data Report No. 4.* DHHS Pub. No. (PHS) 84-2000. Washington, DC: U.S. Government Printing Office, 1983b.

———. "Health of the Elderly and Use of Health Services." *Public Health Reports,* 42, No. 1 (January-February 1977), 9-19.

Kramer, M. "The Rising Pandemic of Mental Disorders and Associated Chronic Diseases and Disorders." *Acta Psychiatrica Scandinavica,* Supplement 285, Vol. 62 (1980), 382-396.

Lubitz, J., and R. Prihoda. "Use and Costs of Medicare Services in the Last Years of Life." In *Health: United States, 1983.* National Center for Health Statistics. DHHS Pub. No. (PHS) 94-1232. Washington, DC: U.S. Government Printing Office, 1983, 141-149.

Manton, K. C. "Changing Concepts of Morbidity and Mortality in the Elderly Population." *Milbank Memorial Fund Quarterly/Health and Society,* 60, No. 2 (Spring 1982), 183-244.

Rice, D. P. "Sex Differences in Mortality and Morbidity: Some Aspects of the Economic Burden." In *Sex Differentials in Mortality: Trends, Determinants and Consequences.* Ed. A. D. Lopez and L. T. Ruzicka. Miscellaneous Series No. 4. Canberra: Department of Demography, Australian National University, 1983.

Rice, D. P., and J. J. Feldman. "Living Longer in the United States: Demographic Changes and Health Needs of the Elderly." *Milbank Fund Memorial Quarterly/Health and Society,* 61, No. 3 (Summer 1983), 362-396.

Rice, D. P., E. Hing, M. G. Kovar, and K. Prager. "Sex Differences in Disease Risk." In *The Changing Risk of Disease in Women: An Epidemiologic Approach.* Ed. E. B. Gold. Lexington, MA: Heath, 1984.

Schneider, E. L., and J. A. Brody, "Aging, Natural Death, and the Compression of Morbidity: Another View." *New England Journal of Medicine,* 309, No. 14 (October 6, 1983), 854-856.

U.S. Bureau of Health Manpower. *A Report to the President and Congress on the Status of Health Professions Personnel in the United States.* DHEW Publication No. (HRA) 80-53. Washington, DC: U.S. Government Printing Office, 1980.

U.S. Bureau of the Census. "America in Transition: An Aging Society." *Current Population Reports,* Series P-23, No. 128. Washington, DC: U.S. Government Printing Office, 1983a.

U.S. Bureau of the Census. *Provisional Projections of the Population of States, by Age and Sex: 1980 to 2000.* Series P-25, No. 937. Washington, DC: U.S. Government Printing Office, Current Population Reports 1983.

U.S. Congressional Budget Office (CBO). *Long Term Care for the Elderly and the Disabled.* Washington, DC: U.S. CBO, 1977.

U.S. General Accounting Office (GAO). *The Elderly Should Benefit From Expanded Home Health Care But Increasing These Services Will Not Insure Cost Reductions.* GAO/IDE-83-1. Washington, DC: U.S. GAO 1982.

———. *Medicaid and Nursing Home Care: Cost Increases and the Need for Services are Creating Problems for the States and the Elderly.* Report to the Chairman of the Subcommittee on Health and the Environment, Committee on Energy and Commerce, House of Representatives. GAO/IPE-84-1. Washington, DC: U.S. GAO, 1983.

U.S. Institute of Medicine (IOM). *Aging and Medical Education.* Washington, DC: National Academy of Sciences, 1978.

———. *Controlling The Supply of Hospital Beds.* Washington, DC: National Academy of Sciences, 1976.

———. *Nursing and Nursing Education: Public Policies and Private Actions.* Washington, DC: National Academy of Sciences, 1983.

U.S. National Center for Health Statistics (NCHS), and S. S. Jack. "Current Estimates from the National Health Interview Survey: United States, 1979." *Vital and Health Statistics,* Series 10, No. 136. DHHS Pub. No. (PHS) 81-1564. Washington, DC: U.S. Government Printing Office, 1981a.

U.S. National Center for Health Statistics (NCHS). "Characteristics of Nursing Home Residents, Health Status, and Care Received: National Nursing Home Survey, United States, May-December 1977." *Vital and Health Statistics,* Series 13, No. 51. DHHS Pub. No. (PHS) 81-1712. Washington, DC: U.S. Government Printing Office, 1981b.

U.S. National Center for Health Statistics (NCHS), and B. A. Feller. "Health Characteristics of Persons with Chronic Activity Limitations, 1979." *Vital and Health Statistics,* Series 10, No. 137. DHHS Pub. No. (PHS) 81-1565. Washington, DC: U.S. Government Printing Office, 1981c.

U.S. National Center for Health Statistics (NCHS), and B. J. Haupt. "Utilizing Short-Stay Hospitals: Annual Summary for the United States: 1980." *Vital and Health Statistics,* Series 13, No. 64. DHHS Publication No. (PHS) 82-1725. Washington, DC: U.S. Government Printing Office, 1982a.

U.S. National Center for Health Statistics (NCHS), and B. Bloom. "Current Estimates from the National Health Interview Survey, United States, 1981." *Vital and Health Statistics,* Series 10, No. 141. DHHS Pub. No. (PHS) 83-1569. Washington, DC: U.S. Government Printing Office, October 1982b.

U.S. National Center for Health Statistics (NCHS). *Health: United States, 1982.* DHHS Pub. No. (PHS) 83-1232. Washington, DC: U.S. Government Printing Office, 1982c.

U.S. National Center for Health Statistics (NCHS), and P. W. Ries. "Americans Assess Their Health: 1978." *Vital and Health Statistics,* Series 10, No. 142. DHHS Pub. No. (PHS) 83-1570. Washington, DC: U.S. Government Printing Office, 1983a.

U.S. National Center for Health Statistics (NCHS), D. P. Rice, H. M. Rosenberg, L. R. Curtin, and T. A. Hodgson. "Changing Mortality Patterns, Health Services Utilization, and Health Care Expenditures: United States, 1978–2003." *Vital and Health Statistics,* Series 3, No. 23. DHHS Pub. No. (PHS) 83-1407. Washington, DC: U.S. Government Printing Office, 1983b.

U.S. National Center for Health Statistics (NCHS), E. Graves, and B. O. Haupt. "Utilization of Short-Stay Hospitals; United States, 1981, Annual Summary." *Vital and Health Statistics,* Series 13, No. 72. DHHS Pub. No. (PHS) 83-1733. Washington, DC: U.S. Government Printing Office, 1983c.

U.S. National Center for Health Statistics (NCHS), D. P. Rice, H. M. Rosenberg, L. R. Curtin, and T. A. Hodgson. "Changing Mortality Patterns, Health Services Utilization, and Health Care Expenditures. United States, 1978–2003." *Vital and Health Statistics,* Series 3, No. 23. DHHS Pub. No. (PHS) 83-1407. Washington, DC: U.S. Government Printing Office, 1983d.

U.S. National Center for Health Statistics (NCHS). *Health: United States, 1983.* DHHS Pub. No. (PHS) 84-1232. Washington, DC: U.S. Government Printing Office, 1983e.

U.S. National Center for Health Statistics (NCHS), and A. Sirrocco. "Nursing and Related Care Homes as Reported from the 1980 NMFI Survey." *Vital and Health Statistics,* Series 14, No. 29. DHHS Pub. No. (PHS) 84-1824. Washington, DC: U.S. Government Printing Office, 1983f.

U.S. National Center for Health Statistics (NCHS), and J. G. Collins. "Physician Visits, Volume and Interval Since Last Visit, United States, 1980." *Vital and Health Statistics,* Series 10, No. 144. DHHS Pub. No. (PHS) 83-1572. Washington, DC: U.S. Government Printing Office, 1983g.

CHAPTER 3

STATE POLICIES ON LONG TERM CARE

Charlene Harrington
Carroll L. Estes
Philip R. Lee
Robert J. Newcomer

The effects of state policies on long term care may be traced through the major state programs that finance long term care: Medicaid, Social Services (Title XX), and Supplemental Security Income (SSI). States have significant discretion in setting policies for these programs that affect access, utilization, and expenditures for long term care. New initiatives by the President and Congress in 1981 and 1982 made dramatic changes by giving states greater policy discretion at the same time that federal funds were reduced for Medicaid and Social Services (U.S. PL 97-35; U.S. PL 97-248). This chapter discusses state policy trends in long term care, particularly state responses subsequent to the 1981 and 1982 federal policy changes.

Medicaid has been a particular focus of concern for federal, state, and local policymakers as expenditures have increased nationally from 17.9 billion dollars in 1978 to 29.3 billion dollars in 1982. This represents an increase of 64 percent, while the consumer price index for the same five-year period increased by 48 percent (U.S. HCFA, 1984; U.S. DOL, 1983a). The rapid increase in Medicaid expenditures relates primarily to the fact that over 70 percent of Medicaid expenditures are for nursing homes and hospital care, the two segments of the health care system where costs have been rising most rapidly. Medicaid, in effect, bought into a health care system that, since its enactment in 1965, has provided few incentives to hospitals, physicians, nursing homes, or consumers to reduce utilization or to constrain price increases.

Authors' Note: The research on which this chapter is based was funded by the Health Care Financing Administration (Grant No. 18-P9762019) and the National Center for Health Services Research (Grant No. HS04042).

In 1981, provisions in the Omnibus Budget Reconciliation Act (U.S. PL 97-35) reduced the federal Medicaid budget from levels expected by the states, but the states were given greater flexibility to operate their programs. States were permitted to reduce eligibility for specific subgroups and services, and were no longer required to use the Medicare cost-based hospital reimbursement formula in the Medicaid program. Thus, a costly, inflationary system that paid hospitals for services (that had already been provided) could be replaced by a prospectively determined payment system. The Tax Equity and Fiscal Responsibility Act (TEFRA) of 1982 (U.S. PL 97-248) was designed to give states even greater policy discretion and to encourage states to control costs in the Medicaid program. These changes dramatically affected programs providing for long term care.

The growth of Social Service (Title XX) programs nationally was held at a relatively constant level between 1973 and 1980 under a federal program ceiling of 2.9 billion dollars. As described in Chapter 1, substantial federal reductions were made in the program in 1981 and 1982, amounting to a loss of approximately 20 percent in the social service program budgets of the states. These federal funding cuts in social services were important to many local agencies providing social services for the elderly. In addition, the federal Title XX program was converted into a block grant for social services in 1982, with the Omnibus Budget Reconciliation Act of 1981. This change virtually eliminated all prior restrictions, including federal reporting requirements.

The federal Supplementary Security Income (SSI) program, as briefly described in Chapter 1, provides a minimum federal income maintenance level for the aged, blind, and disabled whose incomes are below the poverty level. Established in 1972, the federal SSI payment levels have been indexed to inflation since the early 1970s. States have the option of providing state supplementary payments (SSP) in addition to the federal SSI payment, and to change their state program as long as the benefits remain above the minimum standards set in 1974. The combined SSI/SSP payment is particularly important to the very poor elderly because it is likely to be their primary source of income, and an individual who is eligible for SSI/SSP is automatically eligible for Medicaid.

This chapter reports on the findings of a comparative study of the trends in Medicaid, SSI/SSP, and Title XX during the period for 1978 through 1982. The study addressed several questions regarding: the impact of state fiscal crisis and federal reductions on state program expenditures and the move toward cost containment; trends in eligibility and what policies, if any, states are adopting to control the number of eligibles in Medicaid, Title XX, and SSI/SSP; state trends in Medicaid eligibles, recipients (users), utilization patterns, and policy changes that states are making in the scope of benefit and utilization controls to contain costs; and state provider reimbursement rate increases and policies that states are adopting to reduce the growth in reimbursement rates.

This comparative analysis is based on data from in-depth descriptive case studies in eight states: California, Florida, Massachusetts, Missouri, Pennsylvania, Texas, Washington, and Wisconsin. These states, with about one-third of the nation's elderly, have varying human service policies and programs. These eight sample states rank among the top 20 urban states and represent regional geographic variability on two major dimensions believed to affect resource and policy commitments in human services for the aging: (1) state-level centralization and decentralization of taxing and revenue sources and (2) state-level historical commitment to aging. Both of these sampling criteria were utilized in order to account for factors that might contribute for significant state variations. We have presented data analyzed from primary data using the eight sample states along with trends from the fifty states using secondary data sources. The findings presented here are important not only in pointing to trends that may continue into the future but also in terms of the outcomes on long term care for specific population groups, particularly the aged.[1]

Program Expenditures

MEDICAID EXPENDITURES

While national Medicaid expenditures increased by 64 percent between 1978 and 1982, there was wide variation in increases among the states. For example, Florida had an increase of 126 percent between 1978 and 1982, while Pennsylvania's Medicaid costs only increased by 42 percent. There are also marked differences among the states in some of the following expenditure increases: hospital, nursing home, physician, and home health services. For example, between 1978 and 1982, national Medicaid expenditures (federal, state and local) for hospitals increased by 54 percent and for skilled nursing facilities (SNFs) and intermediate care facilities (ICFs) by 51 percent (Table

3.1). Physician services increased by 36 percent, well below the rate of consumer price index overall. Home health expenditures showed the largest increase (136%) between 1978 and 1982.

Although home health service expenditures increased rapidly, total home health expenditures nationwide are dwarfed by total nursing home (SNF/ICF) and hospital expenditures. The home health growth rate was not a major concern to state officials since total expenditures for this service are small and states are attempting to reduce hospital lengths of stay, which would be expected to shift some costs to home health services. The wide variation among states in expenditures per recipient is a reflection of the differences in public policies among the states and in the state costs of providing services.

State officials interviewed in 1982 and 1983 considered the increase in Medicaid expenditures to be a problem. Most states adopted cost containment policies of one sort or another in 1982 and 1983, after enactment of the Omnibus Budget Reconciliation Act of 1981 and when the 1981–82 recession began to affect state revenues. The attention of legislators and state officials was focused on policy changes that would control costs and program growth. Concern about increases in the Medicaid program were caused, in part, by the size and growth of state Medicaid expenditures in proportion to total state budgets. For example, Medicaid is 15.3 percent of the Pennsylvania state budget (Benjamin, Pardini, Kreger, Bogaert, and Peguillan-Shea, 1983) while it is 13.4 percent of the Wisconsin budget (Pardini, Benjamin, Peguillan-Shea and Lindeman, 1983). Overall, Medicaid expenditures represented about 10 percent of total state expenditures for the eight states.

SOCIAL SERVICE (TITLE XX) EXPENDITURES

In contrast to Medicaid, Social Service (Title XX) program expenditures are small. Nationally the total federal expenditure was only 2.9 billion dollars in 1981 and 2.5 billion dollars in 1982. States have had severely limited federal social service funds since a ceiling on federal Title XX expenditures was established in 1973. The most difficult problem for the states was adjusting to the substantial federal budget reduction in the social service programs initiated after enactment of the Omnibus Budget Reconciliation Act of 1981. Some states increased their state contribution to social services to offset the federal reductions (e.g., Massachusetts and Wisconsin), while others decreased their state contribution at the same time federal cuts were made. Other state strategies were to call for increased local support, develop

TABLE 3.1 Percentage Change in Medicaid Expenditures, Fiscal Years 1978-1982

State	Service Category	Expenditures (in $ thousands)		% Change FY 1978-FY 1982	Expenditures Per Recipient		% Change FY 1978-FY 1982
		FY 1978	FY 1982		FY 1978	FY 1982	
CA	Inpatient hospital	829,361	1,255,367	51.4	1,632	2,462	50.9
	SNF/ICF facilities	551,289	678,074	23.0	4,062	5,042	24.1
	Physician	345,875	515,178	49.0	138	198	43.5
	Home health	2,435	4,586	88.4	217	284	30.9
	All services	2,356,813	3,536,548	50.1	686	944	37.6
FL	Inpatient hospital	76,576	177,845	132.2	951	1,790	88.2
	SNF/ICF facilities	94,213	181,700	92.9	3,265	4,988	52.8
	Physician	26,292	40,994	55.9	89	108	21.4
	Home health	219	3,053	1,294.1	100	86	−14.0
	All services	244,931	553,441	126.0	567	1,064	87.7
MA	Inpatient hospital	263,494	416,889	58.2	1,305	2,455	88.1
	SNF/ICF facilities	209,179	374,304	78.9	3,732	9,221	147.1
	Physician	40,103	44,567	11.1	89	96	7.9
	Home health	7,188	14,642	103.7	382	744	94.8
	All services	724,081	1,207,454	66.8	900	1,803	100.3
MO	Inpatient hospital	63,027	97,216	54.2	829	1,522	83.6
	SNF/ICF facilities	59,226	150,242	153.7	3,676	6,380	73.6
	Physician	20,385	20,873	2.4	74	106	43.2
	Home health	357	730	104.5	270	491	81.9
	All services	200,301	384,367	91.9	537	1,137	111.7
PA*	Inpatient hospital	396,223	396,627	0.10	1,040	3,111	199.1
	SNF/ICF facilities	296,124	548,502	85.2	3,985	11,088	178.2
	Physician	51,205	33,406	−34.8	47	70	48.9
	Home health	2,317	2,583	11.5	48	331	589.6
	All services	1,160,208	1,651,772	42.4	734	1,504	104.9

TABLE 3.1 Continued

State	Service Category	Expenditures (in $ thousands)		% Change	Expenditures Per Recipient		% Change
		FY 1978	FY 1982	FY 1978-FY 1982	FY 1978	FY 1982	FY 1978-FY 1982
TX	Inpatient hospital	136,567	221,178	62.0	824	1,298	57.5
	SNF/ICF facilities	351,963	405,027	15.1	3,831	4,750	24.0
	Physician	71,929	118,477	64.7	126	214	69.8
	Home health	845	1,310	55.0	300	633	111.0
	All services	730,142	1,157,522	58.5	1,093	1,712	56.6
WA	Inpatient hospital	65,784	85,661	30.2	1,303	1,798	38.0
	SNF/ICF facilities	84,079	152,143	81.0	3,063	6,986	128.1
	Physician	29,440	32,215	9.4	128	158	23.4
	Home health	971	2,639	171.8	415	999	140.7
	All services	245,802	425,884	73.3	876	1,683	92.1
WI	Inpatient hospital	90,340	128,003	41.7	1,001	2,461	145.9
	SNF/ICF facilities	276,928	426,456	54.0	5,813	6,335	9.0
	Physician	20,627	31,657	53.5	62	145	133.9
	Home health	2,662	4,909	84.4	464	859	85.1
	All services	501,369	820,891	63.7	1,189	1,785	50.1
U.S. Total Medicaid Expenditures (in $ thousands)**							
	Inpatient hospital	4,944,286	7,636,140	54.4	1,197	2,051	71.3
	SNF/ICF facilities	6,229,416	9,405,703	51.0	4,492	7,149	59.2
	Physician	1,532,155	2,085,465	36.1	109	157	44.0
	Home health	209,991	495,523	136.0	368	780	111.9
	All services	17,892,538	29,280,256	63.6	881	1,514	71.9

SOURCE: Adapted from U.S. HFCA (1984).
*These data from Pennsylvania were reported to HCFA on Form 2082. One state data report was significantly different. State data showed inpatient hospital expenditures of $412,856 in FY 1978 and $703,534 in FY 1982. Nursing home expenditures were reported at $470,113 in FY 1978 and $898,587 in FY 1982. The source was: Pennsylvania Department of Public Welfare, Office of Medical Assitance. *The Pennsylvania Medical Program: Past and Present.* Harrisburg, PA, August 1981.
**Includes District of Columbia and 49 states (excludes Arizona).

Medicaid waivers for social service programs, or shift funds from other programs to social services (Pardini and Lindeman, 1983).

Programmatic changes included expanding programs, holding programs at the pre-1981 level, and making significant program cuts. Reductions in social service programs were effected by reducing the number of services, increasing client fees, or reducing the number of eligibles. Unfortunately, states are not required to report which clients are receiving what services. In 1982 and 1983 interviews, some state officials reported reductions in services to the elderly proportionate to overall program reductions. A few reported more reductions for the aged than for children and other groups, but in a sample of states studied (Wood and Estes, 1983), the aged appeared to be faring somewhat better, at least initially, than other social service recipient groups in obtaining service benefits (see also Chapter 10). Further study is needed in this area, especially at the state level, along with better data reporting systems.

SUPPLEMENTAL SECURITY INCOME (SSI) EXPENDITURES

For those aged, blind, and disabled who are determined to be eligible for the Supplemental Security Income (SSI) program, states have the option of providing them with State Supplemental Payments (SSP) in addition to the basic federal Supplemental Security Income (SSI). Among all 50 states, 28 provide SSP payments for living independently (see Chapter 4). Between 1978 and 1982 only two of the eight states studied (e.g., Florida and Missouri [Lindeman, Peguillan-Shea, and Newcomer, 1983; Harrington, Wallace, Schneider, and Swan, 1983c] showed increases in SSI/SSP expenditures to maintain the federally mandated minimum standards set in 1974. Three of the eight states (e.g., Massachusetts, Pennsylvania, and Washington) actually reduced their state SSP expenditures. Even with some of these changes, most of the sample states, however, did not maintain SSP rates of increase at the level of the counsumer price index. This was true nationally as well, as the U.S. total state supplementary payments increased by only 24 percent for the period, compared to a 48 percent rate for the consumer price index (U.S. SSA, 1979; 1983).

The Impact of State Fiscal Crisis

Fiscal crisis played a critical role in the development of cost containment strategies in the study states between 1978 and 1982. Fiscal

TABLE 3.2   Change in Total State Supplemental Payments (SSP)
            for the Aged, Blind, and Disabled Between 1978 and 1982
            (in $ thousands)

State	1978	1982	% Change
California	897,625	1,205,885	34.3
Florida*	1,502	3,408	126.9
Massachusetts	126,149	114,428	−9.3
Missouri*	14,826	37,050	149.9
Pennsylvania	60,742	55,626	−8.4
Texas	−	−	−
Washington	17,490	16,011	−8.4
Wisconsin	53,276	60,965	14.4
U.S. Total**	$1,670,991	$2,074,265	24.1

SOURCE: Adapted from U.S. SSA (1979; 1983).
*State administered programs. Other states have federally administered state supplementary income programs. Texas has no state supplementary payment program.
**Includes District of Columbia and 49 states (excludes Arizona).

crises are the actual fiscal problems determined by projected revenue shortfalls or deficits, low state budget reserves, and unemployment rates. Fiscal crisis also involves the perception by state officials of fiscal problems. The many states that have constitutional limitations on the amount of indebtedness that can be incurred must correct projected imbalances before the end of each fiscal year. Therefore, projected deficits indicate the extent of pressure placed on states to reduce spending or increase revenues (NGA, 1979; 1982b). The state balance of 5 percent has generally been considered a reasonable level to serve as a hedge against economic uncertainty, misjudgments in forecasting, or emergencies (NGA, 1979; 1982b).

Since states vary in economic condition, the responses of states to economic conditions also vary. The national average of the fifty-state budget balances has gradually decreased from 8.6 percent of actual operating expenditures in 1978 to 1.4 percent projected for 1982. These state decreases reflect the impact of federal policies and the general economic recession of 1981–82. State tax revenues have been reduced as a result of federal policies, and the recession has meant higher costs of borrowing, higher expenditure rates, and lower overall revenues (NGA 1979; 1982b).

The effects of fiscal crises have been experienced by states in a variety of ways. Most states experienced serious financial problems due to the impact on state revenues of general economic recession and high unemployment rates. The financial problems of these states were exacerbated by other factors such as large state tax reductions. For example, California used up its multibillion dollar state surplus between 1978 and 1981, when the state began projecting no reserves. California's condition worsened, with a major projected budget deficit in 1982 averted by program cuts. A 1983 deficit of minus 7.4 percent or over 1.4 billion dollars was incurred and carried over into 1984. Financial problems in states such as Massachusetts resulted from passage of local property tax reductions with the state government making up for a portion of the local losses to make possible continued operation of public schools and local governments.

Washington state, for example, probably experienced one of the greatest state fiscal crises with projected deficits as high as 11.8 percent for the 1981-1983 biennium. This crisis was, in part, a reflection of the severe impact of the recession on the timber and other industries in the state. Washington began a series of major budget cuts in April of 1981, reducing Medicaid and other human service programs by 430 million dollars. By October of 1983, the state had held five additional sessions to reduce the budget, making the most drastic program reductions in the state's history. Washington raised 20 million dollars in revenues from a state lottery and imposed a food tax. By making these changes the state was able to lower its projected deficits to 4.8 percent for 1982 with a slight reserve projected for 1983.

Only two of the eight states studied did not report having state fiscal crises (i.e., Florida and Texas [Lindeman et al., 1983; Harrington, Wood, LaLonde-Berg, and Bogaert, 1983d]). High unemployment rates continued to be a problem for all of the eight states, although there was substantial variation among the states. Nationwide, unemployment increased from an average of 6.5 percent in 1978 to 10.2 percent in June of 1982, and 10.0 percent in June of 1983 (U.S. DOL, 1983b; 1983c).

The fiscal crises experienced by the states were further exacerbated by federal budget reductions. Many budget cuts and new cost containment policies in the Medicaid program followed directly from the extent of fiscal crisis experienced by the states. Those states with their own financial crises were not able to cover the losses of federal funds with state dollars in order to provide Medicaid and social service program funds to keep pace with either inflation or demand for services.

States with the greatest fiscal crises, as might be predicted, made the greatest budget cuts in their Medicaid programs. In direct response to the fiscal crisis, states made policy changes such as program reductions, benefit and eligibility limitations, and other austerity measures related to expenditures and personnel. For example, more than 60 policy changes were made in California's Medicaid program for 1983, more than in any other state. Washington and Missouri also made more substantial changes in 1981 and 1982 than in any year since the program started in 1966. In contrast, Pennsylvania, which had experienced high unemployment and serious budget problems since 1978, had already made substantial program reductions in Medicaid before 1981 and 1982, necessitating fewer policy changes during that time than in other states.

Medicaid Eligibility Trends and State Policies

The number of eligibles for a program determines the potential number of recipients (users) of services, and is thus a key variable influencing program expenditures. As described in more detail in Chapter 4, there are four types of eligibility for medical assistance under Medicaid. The first and predominant form is known as "categorically needy." This refers to persons who meet income, resources, and other standards that qualify for Supplemental Security Income (SSI), State Supplemental Payments (SSP), or Aid to Families with Dependent Children (AFDC). All the individuals who qualify for SSI, SSP, and AFDC are automatically eligible for Medicaid in the state where they live.

States may choose whether or not to cover certain optional categorically linked needy groups (AFDC, SSI) and whether to include the medically needy, defined as those who do not qualify for public assistance (AFDC or SSI) because of their income or resource levels, but who have medical bills greater than their ability to pay and thus may qualify. States also may cover individuals (called medically indigent adults) who do not meet the federal guidelines for AFDC or SSI because they are between the ages of 21 and 64 and are not blind or disabled, but services for these individuals must be financed entirely from state funds. State policies thus affect the number of eligibles for the Medicaid program and the level of state Medicaid expenditure.

TRENDS IN NUMBER OF ELIGIBLES

Although national data are not available on all categories of Medicaid eligibles for all states, a national trend in reduction of recipients (1.3% between 1978 and 1982) is clear. The number of aged Medicaid recipients also declined by 4 percent nationally during the same period (U.S. HCFA, 1984).

Most vulnerable to state eligibility reductions, as was expected, were the programs funded entirely by state funds, including general relief and the medically indigent adult program. Programs in which state participation was optional, such as the medically needy program, were also vulnerable. Reductions in the numbers eligible for the medically needy program were dramatic in three of the eight states studied. Washington, for example, reduced its medically needy total by 47 percent. Two of the eight states increased medically needy programs, while other states had no programs. Because the medically needy program primarily pays for SNF/ICF care, it is particularly important for the elderly and their families.

TRENDS IN ELIGIBILITY POLICIES

State eligibility policies for Aid to Families with Dependent Children (AFDC), and for those aged, blind, and disabled who are eligible for Supplemental Security Income (SSI) programs and State Supplemental Payments (SSP) programs must follow federal standards. Within those Federal standards, states have discretion to include in the Medicaid Program AFDC and SSI eligibility groups in the optional categorically needy and the medically needy groups and to set income levels for each eligibility category. States have generally chosen cost-control options that attempt to reduce the number of specific types of Medicaid eligibles rather than to abolish whole eligibility categories, such as the medically needy. In other words, there have been few policy changes in whether or not a state had a medically needy or a state supplemental income program (both are optional). Rather, states with these programs have kept them, but attempted to limit eligibles within them. States without medically needy or supplemental income programs continued not to offer these Medicaid options.

Enactment of the Omnibus Budget Reconciliation Act of 1981 (OBRA; U.S. PL 97-35) caused changes in AFDC policies, eliminating large numbers of AFDC eligibles (especially the working poor) from eligibility in the Medicaid program between 1982 and 1983. Other eligibility policy changes tended to reduce the number of eligibles after the Omnibus Budget Reconciliation Act and in response to state fiscal crisis. For example, California eliminated its special income deductions and reduced the maximum allowable income for the medically needy (including SSI) from 115 percent of the AFDC cash grant level down to 100 percent of the AFDC grant level, for a projected savings of 42 million dollars in 1983 (Harrington, Pardini, Peguillan-Shea, Wallace, LaLonde-Berg, and Newcomer, 1983b).

In many states, projected reductions in eligibles expected as a result of policy changes initiated in 1982 were not accomplished in 1983. The projected reductions were offset by the effects of the recession as an increased number of unemployed poor became eligible for AFDC or SSI. Thus, newly qualified unemployed and low-income applicants for the Medicaid programs increased, maintaining the number of eligibles for the program despite policy reductions of formerly eligible groups.

Significantly, most states reduced their Medicaid eligibles on AFDC and SSI/SSP (described above) by failing to raise income levels in one or both programs to keep pace with inflation. Even though SSP cost-of-living increases generally fared better than AFDC payments, few states matched inflation for the SSP program (see Table 3.3). Among the eight states studied, the increases in SSP maximum benefits ranged from 31 percent in California to 16 percent in Wisconsin between 1978 and 1982. In a few states such as Washington, the SSP average monthly grants for the aged actually decreased by 6 percent between 1978 and 1982. The average aged individual payment rate increases made by states generally were well below inflation, with the U.S. average individual payment showing a 31 percent increase between 1978 and 1982 (U.S. SSA, 1978b; 1982b). When SSP increases are adjusted for inflation (48% between 1978 and 1982), most states show declines in the real payment level during the last five years. There was an 18 percent reduction in the number of aged receiving SSP in the United States between 1978 and 1982 (U.S. SSA, 1978b; 1982b). Overall reductions in eligibles seem primarily tied to state policies that fail to make cost-of-living adjustments in AFDC or SSI/SSP.

The full effect of 1982 eligibility policy changes in these income and health programs cannot be measured until 1983 data are available. Interviews of state officials, however, indicated that some states expected the total number of Medicaid eligibles to drop during 1984 as a result of federal budget reductions to the Medicaid program and resulting policy restrictions on eligibility adopted by many states.

Trends in Medicaid Utilization Patterns and Policies

UTILIZATION PATTERNS

Changes in AFDC and SSI eligibility had a direct effect on both the number of Medicaid eligibles and the number of Medicaid recipients (users). Recipients are those who were not only eligible for services, but also who actually used some type of Medicaid service.

TABLE 3.3 Change in State Supplemental Income Payments: Total Number of Aged and Average Payments for the Aged, 1978 to 1982

State	Total Number of Aged Persons			Maximum Optional Monthly Payment for Aged Individuals			Average Aged Individual Payment		
	1978	1982	% Change	1978	1982	% Change	1978	1982	% Change
California	313,910	271,074	−13.6	$168.60	$221.30	31.3	$99.38	$139.00	39.9
Florida*	1,519	3,949	160.0	0	0	0	41.72	64.17	53.8
Massachusetts	72,628	53,274	−26.6	126.40	137.22	8.5	86.84	90.33	4.0
Missouri*	28,107	15,435	−45.1	0	0	0	29.84	30.33	1.6
Pennsylvania	59,676	44,093	−26.1	32.40	32.40	0	31.46	31.29	−0.5
Texas	–	–	–	–	–	–	–	–	–
Washington	16,161	11,898	−26.4	40.85	38.30	−6.2	31.50	30.77	−2.5
Wisconsin	31,047	22,589	−27.2	86.20	99.70	15.7	71.49	79.44	11.1
U.S. Total**	882,745	723,928	−18.0	NA	NA	–	71.20	93.41	31.2

SOURCES: Adapted from U.S. SSA (1978a, 1982a, 1978b, 1982b).
*State administered program. The other states have federally administered state supplementation programs, except Texas which has no program.
**Includes District of Columbia and 49 states (excludes Arizona).

A comparison of total Medicaid eligibles with total Medicaid recipients, by state, shows a wide variation among states. These different patterns suggest that some states had a policy of increasing eligibles and recipients, but most states were attempting to restrict both eligibility and utilization. Nationally, the decline in numbers of recipients already described is even more dramatic when utilization for specific services is examined in comparison to total utilization. For example, the number of recipients using hospital services declined by six percent, nationally between 1978 and 1982, and skilled nursing (SNF) and intermediate care (ICF) recipients declined by four percent, although utilization of intermediate care facilities for the mentally retarded (ICF/MR) increased when this program was implemented by states. Physician service utilization and home health service recipients declined slightly (U.S. HCFA, 1984).

Another approach to examining utilization is to compare the length of stay or number of services received in a given time period. Unfortunately, there is some concern that the average days per user are not consistently reported accurately by states; and methods of reporting across states sometimes vary. The available data from the eight study states indicates that most states have been successful in reducing the average number of hospital days by substantial amounts. Some have reduced the total skilled nursing facility/intermediate care facility (SNF/ICF) days, while others have experienced increases. A few have reduced the average number of physician visits. Some states attempted to decrease the number of inpatient days and to shift to greater use of physician and outpatient services.

Patterns of utilization varied greatly among states for each service category. Benefit coverage and limitations on benefits affect the utilization patterns observed. Changes in days of care in institutions and use of other services are also related to utilization control mechanisms. But other factors, such as reductions in the number of eligibles, and regional patterns, such as the shorter lengths of stay (on the West Coast), appear to be factors influencing the decline in the average number of services used.

SCOPE OF MEDICAID BENEFITS

States offer two types of benefits in the Medicaid program: mandatory and optional. The mandatory services are those required by the federal government: hospital, physician, skilled nursing care, hospital outpatient, rural health clinic, home health, family planning, and laboratory and x-ray services. Optional services are those selected by states such as drug, intermediate care, dental care and many others (see Chapter 5).

A review of benefit changes since 1978 across all 50 states shows that most states either maintained their benefit packages or expanded benefits until 1982 (Muse and Sawyer, 1982; IHPP and NGA, 1982; NGA, 1982a; La Jolla Management Corporation 1982). After the adoption of OBRA and TEFRA by the federal government in 1981 and 1982, some states made few changes in their benefit packages, while others made major reductions. All of the states that made reduction in their benefit packages were experiencing serious state budget deficits.

States have discretion to specify the scope and duration of services provided under the Medicaid program. Since 1981 states have tended to restrict rather than eliminate benefits. For example, some states introduced benefit restrictions for dentures for adults, and hearing aid battery and eyeglass replacements. Nonemergency transportation services were eliminated in some states. Other optional benefits were severely limited to emergency situations. Some states that had made cost cuts in benefits in 1980 and 1981 adopted even more several limitations after OBRA in 1982 and in 1983. Only a few states restricted benefits to the medically needy while continuing full benefits to the categorically needy, but even fewer developed different benefits for different groups within the medically needy category during 1982 or 1983 as allowed by OBRA.

UTILIZATION CONTROLS

Most of the 50 states have adopted utilization controls on some service categories such as limits on the number or frequency of services than can be obtained, or prior authorization requirements by which a provider must obtain approval before providing services. Utilization control procedures have been fairly stable within states since 1978, although substantial variation exists among states (La Jolla Management Corporation, 1982).

The legislatures of most of the eight states studied chose in 1982 to strengthen utilization controls rather than eliminate benefits. This decision reflected the impact on program recipients as well as the political unpopularity of such policies. For example, in California, a state which already had extensive utilization controls, the state legislature cut an estimated 28.5 million dollars for 1983 by (1) limiting benefits to only those necessary to protect life or prevent significant disability (rather than covering those considered "medically necessary" by a physician), and (2) imposing prior authorization requirements on outpatient and physician services for the first time. A Superior Court Judge ruled that these utilization controls were unlawful, but the case is currently under appeal (Harrington et al., 1983b). Other states used strategies such as tightening hospital review standards for length of stay or attempting to strenghten controls with the implementation of the new Medicaid Management Information System (MMIS).

In 1983, 35 states requested and received the new home and community-based waiver programs (Section 2176 of OBRA) designed as alternatives to nursing home care. These programs are not expected to increase Medicaid costs above those currently incurred. These alternative projects were generally small and limited to selected population groups and/or geographic areas. Most states are attempting to strengthen their prior authorization approvals for nursing home care and to divert patients into less costly, more appropriate care settings. Measurable benefits from these programs have not yet been documented, but state officials considered them to be having some impact on controlling utilization and costs.

Another major change in utilization policies was the increase in copayments adopted by states. Six of the eight states adopted copayments in 1982 or 1983. Most copayments were attached to drugs and optional services such as dentures, hearing aids, optometry, podiatry, and other such services. States such as California and Washington did not consider copayments to be revenue generating, but rather to be barriers to utilization and symbolic political statements about efforts to control the use of services. Even though the copayments were generally small ($.50 to $5.00), there may be an adverse impact on the aged, primary users of such services. It is too early to measure the effect. Other copayments were attached to emergency room, outpatient, and hospital services.

Other Medicaid control activities being considered by states are requirements for second opinions for surgery and limitation of preoperative days and weekend admissions to hospitals. These types of cost containment efforts are expected to be expanded in the future.

Trends in Medicaid Provider
Reimbursement Rates and Policies

Since price for units of service is one of the key components of Medicaid program expenditure, changes in Medicaid reimbursement rates for selected services are significant. As shown in Chapter 1, growth in hospital, nursing home, and home health expenditures have been high, while most states have controlled physicians costs. Home health growth rates appear extremely high, but even small dollar expenditures may represent high percentage increases since home health expenditures were extremely low to begin with. Home health expenditures are also of less concern to policymakers because home health still represents less than five percent of total Medicaid expenditures, and because states are attempting to use home health services as a substitute for more expensive institutional care. Reimbursement policy restriction is a primary method used by states to control expenditure growth.

Reimbursement policies were more dramatically changed between 1982 and 1983 than other state Medicaid policy, accounting for most of the cost savings in the Medicaid program in the states. States made changes both by adopting new reimbursement methods and by controlling cost-of-living increases on reimbursement rates.

HOSPITALS

In the past, state Medicaid reimbursement policies for hospitals generally followed federal guidelines for the Medicare program. In 1980, only 10 out of 50 states had alternative reimbursement methodologies for hospitals (NGA, 1982a; AHPC, 1983). These alternatives required a federal waiver. Medicare hospital reimbursement at that time was determined on the basis of actual costs determined after services were rendered (retrospective reimbursement). The alternatives included a variety of approaches such as the regulation of all payers (Medicaid, Medicare, and private payers) through establishment of rates prior to delivery of services (prospectively determined payment system). It should be noted that after TEFRA and the Social Security Amendments of 1983 (U.S. PL 98-21), Medicare changed its reimbursement method to a prospectively determined payment system.

By 1982, there were 18 states (up from 10 in 1980) that had modified Medicaid hospital reimbursement methods. The 1981 federal policy changes had given states greater flexibility in developing approved alternatives. Even more states are expected to develop alternatives in the future. Some states adopted alternatives because of high growth in hospital charges and costs, while others were prompted by budgetary constraints to prevent future increases.

One approach to controlling hospital expenditures was adopted in California, which had a 51 percent increase in Medicaid hospital expenditures between 1978 and 1982. In 1982, the state adopted a ceiling on hospital rate increases, which was later disallowed by the courts. California then adopted a new contracting system with hospitals that wished to care for Medicaid recipients. The contract was based on a prospectively negotiated all-inclusion rate for Medicaid patients. This policy change was expected to save about 200 million dollars the first year. It is a dramatic departure from the retrospectively determined cost-based system used in California prior to 1983. Massachusetts, in spite of its Rate Setting Commission, also experienced high growth rates for hospitals. In contrast to California, Massachusetts adopted a prospective rate-setting system for all payers in 1983 with phase-in periods (Harrington, Pardini, Peguillan-Shea, LaLonde-Berg, and Bogaert, 1983a).

States such as Washington, with a prospective rate-setting system for all hospitals since 1973, were considered to be more effective in controlling costs. Washington kept the total hospital expenditure growth well below inflation (30% between 1978 and 1982) and its hospital expenditures per recipient low (Peguillan-Shea, Wood, and Newcomer, 1983).

Some states have made major changes recently through independent cost containment committees or commissions composed of senior citizens and leaders in business, labor, and insurance appointed by either the governor or the legislatures, or jointly. This approach has been successful in generating political support for legislative reforms to counter opposition efforts by hospital associations.

The new interest by states in preferred provider organizations, primary care network contracts, and prepaid health care programs has changed the character of hospital reimbursement in most of the states. Most states have targeted hospital rates as the primary focus for future cost containment efforts and are expected to develop more complex alternatives.

NURSING HOMES

Most states have nursing home reimbursement policies that vary from Medicare policies. Medicare reimbursement for nursing homes is based on costs incurred as determined after services are rendered (retrospective reimbursement). By 1982, 26 states reported prospective facility-specific systems. In these systems rates are set in advance, usually on a per diem basis, for each facility. Five states reported prospective class-based systems, in which per diem rates are set in advance for groups of facilities; twelve states reported retrospective systems, with reimbursement determined after services are rendered; and six states reported a combination of these systems (La Jolla Management Corporation, 1982; NGA, 1982a).

States have moved to nursing home prospective reimbursement as a means of controlling costs (Spitz and Atkinson, 1982; Harrington and Swan, 1984). An analysis of the relationship between rates and reimbursement methods found that states with class-based prospectively determined payment systems have the lowest per diem rates, while prospective facility-specific rates are also significantly lower than retrospective reimbursement systems (Harrington and Swan, 1984).

States are focusing substantial efforts on refining and strengthening their methods for Medicaid payment for nursing home care. While subject to controversy, these alternative methods are expected by state officials in most of the states studied to control both per diem and overall expenditure rates.

Conclusion

No one Medicaid policy explains the wide range in expenditure patterns among states. Price increases by providers, as well as Medicaid reimbursement rates and methods, are of critical importance. Eligibility, the scope of benefits, and utilization control policies all play a part in determining expenditure patterns. State demographic factors, including poverty levels and the number of aged in the population, also affect policies and expenditure patterns.

State policymakers will continue their efforts to contain costs in the Medicaid program. If some states do not share in the current economic recovery and continue to experience fiscal crises; if federal program revenues continue to shrink (e.g., program cuts in an attempt to reduce the federal deficit); and if the provider price increases continue to be considerably higher than the general consumer price index, states will have to make some hard policy choices. Most states either already had stringent limits on their benefits, eligibility, and utilization policies, or have made substantial reductions in the last two-year time period. If additional cuts are required, they will have to be directed toward providers, recipients, or both. As an alternative, some states may raise taxes and others may advocate the federalization of portions (e.g., hospital and physicians) of the Medicaid program.

The effects of recent state cuts on particular population groups are not yet fully known. Clearly, increases in copayments, reductions in eligibility, failure to raise the cost-of-living for both AFDC and SSP to keep pace with inflation, and restrictions on benefits and utilization have had some direct effects. While these may adversely affect the aged, the evidence is not yet available on this issue.

In states such as California, Missouri, and Washington, which have made multiple policy changes at the same time, it is difficult to determine which policy changes have produced the greatest impact on expenditures, utilization, or eligibility. The number of changes make it difficult to separate the effects of any given policy, or to determine actual cost implications.

Although states should be studying the effects of policy changes on recipient groups and on providers, little systematic research is being conducted by states on the dramatic changes made in the last two years. Legislators are asked to reply heavily on anecdotal evidence of the impact, or on state forecasts, because states have not designed systematic studies to assess the impacts of policy changes. Nor do they seem willing at this time to make the necessary investment in health services and policy research to better determine the consequences of their policy decisions.

The central question is whether Medicaid costs can be controlled, a necessity unless hospital costs are controlled across the board. Is the best approach an all-payer system at the state level? As states develop rate regulation for all hospital payers, increases in hospital costs may be brought down. State officials are focusing on hospital costs as the primary target for controlling growth in the Medicaid expenditure pattern. Policy controls on the number of Medicaid eligibles and utilization rates has already been a major target for control by state programs. The real test will be whether states can bring hospital costs into line to keep program expenditures in balance with inflation trends.

The availability of long term care resources clearly depends on the ability of federal and state policymakers to constrain these hospital and other acute care costs, *and* to shift these savings to finance in-home and community-based alternatives, including income and housing alternatives.

Note

1. Data for the research reported in this chapter were collected from four sources: state documents, federal documents, personal interviews, and telephone interviews with policymakers, providers, and program managers.

References

Aging Health Policy Center (AHPC). "State Medicaid Program Data." Unpublished Data. San Francisco, CA: AHPC, University of California, 1983.

Benjamin, A. E., A. Pardini, M. C. Kreger, M. P. Bogaert, and V. Peguillan-Shea. *Pennsylvania: State Discretionary Policies and Services in the Medicaid Social Services, and Supplemental Security Income Programs.* San Francisco, CA: Aging Health Policy Center, University of California, 1983.

Harrington, C., A. Pardini, V. Peguillan-Shea, G. R. LaLonde-Berg, and M. P. Bogaert. *Massachusetts: State Discretionary Policies and Services in the Medicaid, Social Services, and Supplemental Security Income Programs.* San Francisco, CA: Aging Health Policy Center, University of California, 1983a.

Harrington, C., A. Pardini, V. Peguillan-Shea, S. P. Wallace, G. R. LaLonde-Berg, and R. J. Newcomer. *California: State Discretionary Policies and Services in the Medicaid, Social Services, and Supplemental Security Income Programs.* San Francisco, CA: Aging Health Policy Center, University of California, 1983b.

Harrington, C., and J. Swan. *Medicaid Nursing Home Reimbursement Policies and Rates.* Working Paper. San Francisco, CA: Aging Health Policy Center, University of California, 1984.

Harrington, C., S. P. Wallace, J. A. Schneider, and J. H. Swan. *Missouri: State Discretionary Policies and Services in the Medicaid, Social Services, and Supplemental Security Income Programs.* San Francisco, CA: Aging Health Policy Center, University of California, 1983c.

Harrington, C., J. B. Wood, G. R. LaLonde-Berg, and M. P. Bogaert. *Texas: State Discretionary Policies and Services in the Medicaid, Social Services, and Supplemental Security Income Programs.* San Francisco, CA: Aging Health Policy Center, University of California, 1983d.

Intergovernmental Health Policy Project (IHPP), and National Governors' Association (NGA) State Medicaid Information Center. *Recent and Proposed Changes in State Medicaid Programs: A Fifty State Survey.* Washington, DC: Intergovernmental Health Policy Project, 1982.

La Jolla Management Corporation. *Medicaid Program Characteristics: Summary Tables.* Volume 1. Washington, DC: U.S. Health Care Financing Administration, Office of Research and Demonstrations, 1982.

Lindeman, D. A., V. Peguillan-Shea, and R. J. Newcomer. *Florida: State Discretionary Policies and Services in the Medicaid, Social Services, and Supplemental Security Income Programs.* San Francisco, CA: Aging Health Policy Center, University of California, 1983.

Muse, D. N., and D. Sawyer. *The Medicare and Medicaid Data Book, 1981.* Washington, DC: U.S. Health Care Financing Administration, Office of Research and Demonstrations, 1982.

National Governors' Association (NGA). The State Medicaid Program Information Center. *A Catalogue of State Medicaid Program Changes.* Washington, DC: NGA, 1982a.

———. *Fiscal Survey of the States, 1978-1979.* Washington, DC: NGA, 1979.

———. *Fiscal Survey of the States, December 1982 Update.* Washington, DC: NGA, 1982b.

Pardini, A., A. E. Benjamin, V. Peguillan-Shea, and D. A. Lindeman. *Wisconsin: State Discretionary Policies and Services in the Medicaid, Social Services, and Supplemental Security Income Programs.* San Francisco, CA: Aging Health Policy Center, University of California, 1983.

Pardini, A., and D. A. Lindeman. "Social Services: The Impact of Fiscal Austerity." In *Fiscal Austerity and Aging*. By C. L. Estes, R. J. Newcomer, and Associates. Beverly Hills, CA: Sage, 1983, pp. 133-155.

Peguillan-Shea, V., J. B. Wood, and R. J. Newcomer. *Washington: State Discretionary Policies and Services in the Medicaid, Social Services, and Supplemental Security Income Programs*. San Francisco, CA: Aging Health Policy Center, University of California, 1983.

Spitz, B., and G. Atkinson. *Nursing Homes, Hospitals and Medicaid: Reimbursement Policy Adjustments 1981-82*. Washington, DC: National Governors' Association, 1982.

U.S. Department of Labor (DOL), Bureau of Labor Statistics. *Consumer Price Index, Detailed Report*. Washington, DC: U.S. DOL, 1983a.

———. *Employment and Earnings,* 30, No. 9, September 1983b.

———. *Geographic Profile of Employment and Unemployment, Annual*. Washington, DC: U.S. Department of Labor, 1983c.

U.S. Health Care Financing Administration (HCFA). *National Medicaid Statistics: Fiscal Years 1975 to 1982*. State 2082 Tables data tape. Baltimore, MD: U.S. Department of Health and Human Services, 1984.

U.S. Public Law 97-35. *Omnibus Budget Reconciliation Act (OBRA) of 1981*. Washington, DC: U.S. Government Printing Office, 1981.

U.S. Public Law 97-248. *Tax Equity and Fiscal Responsibility Act (TEFRA) of 1982*. Washington, DC: U.S. Government Printing Office, 1982.

U.S. Public Law 98-21. *Social Security Amendments of 1983*. Washington, DC: U.S. Government Printing Office, 1983.

U.S. Social Security Administration (SSA). *Program and Demographic Characteristics of Supplemental Security Beneficiaries, December 1978; December 1982*. Washington, DC: U.S. Government Printing Office, 1979; 1983.

U.S. Social Security Administration (SSA). *Social Security Bulletin* (June). Washington, DC: Social Security Administration, 1978a; 1982a.

U.S. Social Security Administration (SSA), Office of Program Operations. *Supplemental Security Income for the Aged, Blind, and Disabled: Summary of State Payment Levels, State Supplementation and Medicaid Decisions. Unpublished Data, (October)*. Washington, DC: Social Security Administration, 1978b.; 1982b.

Wood, J. B., and C. L. Estes. "The Private Nonprofit Sector and Aging." In *Fiscal Austerity and Aging*. By C. L. Estes, R. J. Newcomer, and Associates. Beverly Hills, CA: Sage, 1983, pp. 227-247.

CHAPTER 4

EQUITY AND INCENTIVES IN MEDICAID PROGRAM ELIGIBILITY

Robert J. Newcomer
A. E. Benjamin, Jr.
Carol E. Sattler

The 1965 Amendments to the Social Security Act included provisions that transformed and expanded medical assistance for the poor. Widespread support for the notion of health care as a right and growing concern about market barriers to access of medical care for the poor and elderly helped shape the goals of this legislation that created the Medicaid program. In the ensuing years, the utilization of health care services and their costs have grown rapidly. As early as 1975 concerns about improved access had been supplanted by alarm over growing expenditures. Initially, evidence suggested that growth in program enrollment outweighed other factors in explaining the rate of Medicaid cost increases (Rymer, Oksman, Bailes, and Ellwood, 1979). While more recent evidence pinpoints price inflation as the primary problem in cost increases (Gibson, Waldo, and Levit, 1983), federal and state policy has continued to give attention to constraining, rather than expanding, access to Medicaid eligibility in an effort to stem the rising cost of the program. The consequences of these shifts in program eligibility policy are the subject of this chapter.

This chapter examines the extent to which particular groups are targeted for Medicaid coverage, the relative equity of benefits across these groups, and how this has changed over time. In addition, the chapter discusses the various incentives inherent in state Medicaid

Authors' Note: The compilation of the data and the writing of this chapter were financed under Grant No. HS04042 from the U.S. National Center for Health Services Research. We want to acknowledge Marjorie Bogaert-Tullis and Patricia Saliba for their assistance in this work.

programs and how they may shape the behavior of Medicaid recipients.

Most governmental programs fail to achieve full equity in their eligibility criteria because resources are limited and because there are often competing priorities inherent in the programs. One such conflict is that between the "deserving poor" (e.g., aged, blind, and disabled) and those poor sometimes stigmatized as "less deserving" (e.g., poverty-level households of women and children). A second conflict involves those who may eventually become self-supporting if they receive help (e.g., low-income families) and those who can never be expected to be self-supporting (e.g., the severely disabled).

Since 1976, there have been a variety of changes in state and federal Medicaid and income maintenance policies, as well as in the U.S. economy. How these conditions have affected the equitability of the Medicaid eligibility system and the resulting consequences are explored in this chapter. Because Medicaid is the major source of funding for long term care services, it is important in the context of this book to consider fundamental issues regarding who may receive services and who may not.

Definitions of Equity and Incentives[1]

Equity may be divided into two types: horizontal equity and vertical equity. Horizontal equity refers to the concept that persons in similar circumstances should be treated similarly. For instance, are all low-income aged, blind, and disabled persons and low-income families with children determined to be eligible for Medicaid by similar income standards? Vertical equity, as applied here, refers to the principle that, within a given target group classification, individuals and families with greater needs should receive more assistance than those with fewer needs (i.e., that program response should be adjusted to levels of recipient need).

Incentives refer to the notion of rewarding or penalizing certain behaviors. The following sections discuss the extent to which Medicaid eligibility policy provides incentives for behavior that society generally views as desirable: work, family stability, and deinstitutionalization.

Medicaid Financial Eligibility

In general, there are three types of eligibility for medical assistance under Medicaid. The primary way to qualify is to be "categorically needy." This refers to most people who meet income, resources, and other standards for any one of several income maintenance programs. These include the federal Supplemental Security Income (SSI) program, state supplemental payments (SSP; i.e., state payments to supplement SSI), and Aid to Families with Dependent Children (AFDC). (See Chapter 1 for a discussion of the SSI program.) Typically, low-income aged, blind, and disabled persons are eligible under SSI and/or SSP; while low-income families with children, deprived of the support of at least one parent, are eligible under AFDC.

In addition to the coverage of categorically needy individuals under Medicaid (which is mandated by federal law), each state has the option of providing coverage for a variety of other groups. Two of the major optional coverage groups are medically needy individuals and individuals who could qualify for public assistance (i.e., they would be income eligible) if they applied. Those who are medically needy do not qualify for public assistance because of their income or resource levels, but they have medical bills that are large enough to reduce their income below a medically needy maximum. States can choose to offer this "spend down" eligibility to all persons with high medical expenses or only to those who are institutionalized.

Medicaid assistance to any of these mandatory or optional eligibility groups is jointly financed through federal and state funds.[2] Each state determines benefits and eligibility for the Medicaid program within federal guidelines. Because of these areas of state discretion, there are differences among the states in terms of who is eligible, as well as the level of benefits that is offered under Medicaid.

Both vertical and horizontal inequities can occur in the Medicaid program as a result of the different eligibility standards utilized in the various income maintenance programs. The most important of these standards is the maximum income levels used by the states to determine eligibility (persons with incomes above these levels do not qualify as categorically needy). Four types of income levels are considered here: (1) AFDC, (2) medically needy, (3) the special need standard for the institutionalized, and (4) SSI/SSP. There is considerable variation between states in these income standards, as well as variability across the different eligibility coverage groups within a given state. Both of these types of variation indicate horizontal inequities in the Medicaid eligibility system.

INCOME NEEDS STANDARD INEQUITY

Table 4.1 provides one indicator of income inequity by showing the average income standard for each of several income maintenance

TABLE 4.1   State Average of Maximum Monthly Income Standards for
Selected Income Maintenance Programs, Fiscal Years 1978-1982

	1978	1980	1982
AFDC			
1 child	$165	$153	$175
2 person household	245	257	282
4 person household	359	377	408
Medically needy			
1 person household	205	234	261
2 person household	272	313	351
Special need standard for the institutionalized	474	570	742
SSI/SSP living independently			
1 person household	201	235	296
2 person household	304	358	448
SSI/SSP living in supportive housing			
1 person household	249	303	365
2 person household	416	496	594

SOURCE: Adapted from AHPC (1983); and SSA (1978; 1980; 1982).

programs between 1978 and 1982 (AHPC, 1983; U.S. SSA, 1978; 1980; 1982). Within federal guidelines, states determine the standard for AFDC, medically needy and the special need standard for the institutionalized. They also elect whether or not to supplement the federal SSI payment. In terms of these standards, states have generally been more responsive to the aged, blind, and disabled populations than to children or families living in poverty. This is reflected in income standards that are higher for one- and two-person households under the SSI/SSP program than they are under AFDC.

The differences between AFDC and the other income standards have widened between 1978 and 1982. For example, the average AFDC standard for a two-person household was 80 percent of the average SSI/SSP two-person living independently standard in 1978. By 1982, this percentage had decreased to 62 percent. The disparity is even more clear when one compares AFDC households with SSI/SSP eligibles in supportive housing. Most striking of all is the fact that the average income standard for an AFDC family of four in 1982 was lower than the income standard for the SSI/SSP two-person household living independently.

A major factor contributing to the widening disparity across age groups is that states have tended to hold AFDC income standards constant over this time period, or to increase them only at a slow rate. Twenty-one states made no increase in the AFDC standards for either two- or four-person households between 1979 and 1982, whereas the basic federal SSI payment increased annually with the cost of living. Between fiscal years 1978 and 1982, the basic federal SSI payment increased 60 percent for both individuals and couples. During the same time period, the average increase in SSP was 14 percent for individuals living independently and 51 percent for these in supportive housing, while the actual cost of living increased an average of 48 percent.

RECIPIENT INEQUITIES

One explanation for these differential financial eligibility standards is suggested by the number of persons receiving Medicaid. Table 4.2 shows the number of recipients in various categories between 1976 and 1982. The number of recipients, rather than eligibles, has been used because Medicaid program statistics are compiled on the basis of those receiving care—the number of persons annually eligible for care is usually not reported by the states. In general, the number of Medicaid recipients peaked in 1976 and has slowly declined since then. Only the disabled and adult AFDC recipients are greater in number in 1982 than in 1976 (U.S. HCFA, 1984). In view of the constancy of the AFDC income eligibility standards, the relative stability in the number of AFDC recipients suggests that states may have held AFDC levels constant in order to avoid even sharper increases in eligibles. SSI/SSP recipients, on the other hand, generally declined in number in spite of cost of living increases allowed in the federal SSI income eligibility standards.

While these trends suggest a rational response by state governments to their own budget constraints (i.e., to constrain standards where numbers are growing) another issue requires attention: How well are these programs serving the income disadvantaged? Table 4.3 presents the proportion of total Medicaid recipients to the total low-income population for each year for 1976 to 1982 (U.S. BOC 1979; 1980 and 1982a; 1982b; U.S. HCFA 1984). As shown in Table 4.3, the proportion of Medicaid recipients to all persons in poverty has declined

TABLE 4.2   Number of Medicaid Recipients, 1976 to 1982

	1976	1978	1980	1982	% Change 1976-1982
SSI/SSP recipients					
Aged	3,587,310	3,362,445	3,438,726	3,238,298	−9.7
Blind	96,634	79,959	91,399	83,531	−13.6
Disabled	2,546,664	2,595,938	2,783,048	2,754,378	8.2
AFDC recipients					
Children	9,468,330	8,954,113	8,920,944	9,167,934	−3.2
Adult	4,567,117	4,369,699	4,584,672	5,023,424	10.0
Other recipients	1,081,178	1,093,217	841,288	762,719	−29.5
Total recipients	21,298,515	20,408,754	20,205,184	20,149,771	−5.4

SOURCE: Adapted from U.S. HCFA (1984, which includes the District of Columbia and 49 states, excluding Arizona).

22 percent from 85 percent in 1976 to 63 percent in 1982. The proportion of aged Medicaid recipients to the aged in poverty has also declined from 108 percent in 1976 to 86 percent in 1982—a decline of about 25 percent. Per capita Medicaid expenditures between 1976 and 1982 are also shown in Table 4.3. In contrast to recipient patterns, costs per population and per recipient in poverty show marked increases. This table suggests that states may have elected generally to reduce access of the poor to Medicaid programs in an effort to help compensate for rising costs.

Issues of inequity are evident from the trends shown in Tables 4.2 and 4.3. All low-income groups have suffered as a result of these shifts in federal and state policy, but low-income families with children seem to have borne a higher proportion of the burden of program cutbacks than have the elderly. This is supported by evidence that income standards for AFDC have not grown at the same rate as those for SSI/SSP and that benefit levels for the elderly are at a higher level than those AFDC recipients.

Medicaid Coverage Groups

As previously noted, there are three major eligibility groups under the Medicaid program: the categorically needy, the medically needy, and those who would be eligible if they applied for AFDC or SSI. These groups may be further differentiated into children, low-income

TABLE 4.3 Proportion of Medicaid Recipients to Selected Low-Income Population, 1976 to 1982*

	Medicaid Recipients per 100 Persons in Poverty**	Number of Aged Medicaid Recipients per 100 Aged in Poverty**	Medicaid Expenditures per Population	Medicaid Expenditures per Poverty Population
1976	85	108	65	560
1977	85	114	75	653
1978	83	104	82	730
1979	73	95	93	741
1980	69	89	102	793
1981	70	87	118	852
1982	63	86	126	851

SOURCES: Adapted from U.S. BOC (1979; 1980; 1982a; 1982b) and U.S. HCFA (1984, which includes the District of Columbia and 49 states, excluding Arizona).
*These data were calculated from the above sources by the Aging Health Policy Center, University of California, San Francisco.
**Poverty data for years other than 1975 and 1979 are from estimates made by the Aging Health Policy Center, University of California, San Francisco.

parents of dependent children, the aged, the blind, and the disabled. An examination of the population groups targeted for benefits under the state Medicaid programs illustrates the range of incentives and disincentives that may influence the behavior of program recipients.

EMPLOYMENT AND FAMILY STABILITY INCENTIVES

To what extent do state Medicaid eligibility policies operate to encourage or reward employment among low-income populations? And to what extent do they encourage family stability? In order to answer these questions it is necessary to analyze some of the policy choices made by the states with respect to Medicaid eligibility. The major policy decisions for the states involve their determination of which groups to include in the AFDC program and which other groups to declare eligible for Medicaid even though they may not be eligible for AFDC. Each state has the option of including or excluding three specific groups: families with unemployed parents, pregnant women with no other eligible children, and children age 18 regularly in school (42 CFR 435.110). If a state decides to extend AFDC coverage to any of these groups, it must extend Medicaid coverage as well.

Coverage of these categories is designed to assist unemployed two-parent families and, more important, to offer a safety-net program for children. In effect, children are covered under all three approaches, low-income adults under only one. There is also a federally required positive work incentive in place in all states in that the states continue to provide Medicaid eligibility for four months to all members of the AFDC program if they lose AFDC eligibility solely because of an increased income from employment or increased hours of employment (42 CFR 435.112 and 435.116). Because there are important differences among the states in the breadth of group coverage, coverage of adults and children is examined separately.

The Coverage of Adults

The presence or absence of coverage for non-elderly, -blind, or -disabled low-income adults has been the most volatile of all Medicaid eligibility issues. As seen in Table 4.4, twenty-two states included unemployed parents within their AFDC programs in 1982 (La Jolla Management Corporation, 1982). Another two states have allowed such families to be eligible for Medicaid benefits even though they were not eligible for AFDC cash benefits. Since 1978, four states have stopped offering Medicaid coverage to this group. States that do not cover families with unemployed parents under AFDC and Medicaid programs encourage family dissolution, since the only other applicable AFDC and Medicaid eligibility categories are for single parents with children.

Pregnant women with no other eligible children were covered by AFDC—and therefore by Medicaid—in 31 states in 1982. Under this option, AFDC covers pregnant women only during the last four months of pregnancy. However, all states have the option of extending Medicaid benefits to eligible women throughout their pregnancy. Twenty-one of the original 31 states, plus an additional eight states, have chosen this option. Furthermore, of the eleven states which do not cover pregnant women under the AFDC program, nine have medically needy programs that require them to provide Medicaid benefits to eligible pregnant women. Table 4.4 shows that pregnant women are, to some degree, covered by Medicaid in a total of 48 states.

Work incentives for single-parent households are also affected by state eligibility policies. States may elect to cover individuals within their Medicaid programs who would be eligible for AFDC if their work-related child care expenses were paid from earnings rather than

TABLE 4.4   Coverage of Specific Groups in State Medicaid Plans, 1982

	Number of States Providing Coverage
Families with unemployed parents	22
Pregnant women*	48
Children under age 18 attending school*	43
Nondependent children**	49

SOURCE: Adapted from La Jolla Management Corporation (1982).
*Includes coverage under medically needy programs.
**Children living in publicly supported foster homes or private institutions.

by a public agency (42 CFR 435.220). Only 15 states include this option in their program. And as was seen in the data presented in Table 4.1, few states have an income standard for AFDC eligibility that is high enough to provide child care costs.

In short, within the AFDC program there is only one major work incentive applicable in all states: the ability to remain Medicaid-eligible for a four-month period of time if one's income increases due to employment. Fewer than half the states encourage family stability by offering Medicaid coverage to low-income families with unemployed parents. In contrast, virtually all states have a safety-net program in place to provide Medicaid coverage for pregnant women and single-parent households with dependent children. For this latter group, there are few examples of positive work incentives among the state policies.

The Coverage of Children

The coverage of children is rather extensive within both the state AFDC and SSI programs. State variation in this coverage occurs largely in terms of the eligible age ranges and living situations for children. Children under age 18 regularly attending school are a mandatory coverage group under the Medicaid program if the state AFDC program includes this category. Moreover, if a state offers a medically needy program, it must provide Medicaid eligibility (42 CFR 435.301) to all pregnant women who, except for income and resources, would be categorically needy; and to all individuals or reasonable classifications of individuals under age 21 (or under age 20, 19, or 18 depending on the state) who meet the income and resource standards defined for the medically needy. Seven states do not cover at least some classifications of children under Medicaid as a result of their eligibility in either AFDC or medically needy programs or both.

INSTITUTIONALIZATION

Through their income maintenance programs and the linking of eligibility to specific residential locations, states can provide important incentives for recipients either to seek or to maintain specific living arrangements. This issue is most salient for states in relation to the SSI and medically needy population, although there are also implications for AFDC-eligible groups.

The Coverage of Adults

The most germane indicator of state incentives for independent versus institutional living among its low-income adults is the SSI/SSP program. Benefit levels within this program vary according to living arrangements and household size. Table 4.5 lists the number of states that offer a supplement to the SSI program for persons and couples living independently, and for those in some form of supportive housing (e.g., residential care facilities, board and care, or adult foster care; see U.S. SSA 1978; 1980; 1982).

By virtue of the federal SSI program, there is a minimum monthly benefit available to the SSI population in all states; this was set at 264 dollars for an individual and 397 dollars for a couple in fiscal year 1982. At that time, twenty-eight states elected to supplement this benefit level—through State Supplemental Payments (SSP)—for aged, blind, and disabled people living independently. Thirty-six states offered supplementation to those in supportive housing during the same period. The presence or absence of a state supplemental payment for these groups reflects the degree of horizontal equity across states. The difference in supplemental payment levels within those states offering this benefit also reflects the degree of horizontal equity across states and groups. The disparity among recipient groups within a state is much less than the disparity among the states. In other words, each state has largely treated the aged, blind, and disabled quite similarly with respect to its SSP benefit levels. Whether this apparent horizontal equity fully reflects the needs of these groups is not determined through this analysis.

TABLE 4.5   State Average of Maximum Monthly State Supplemental Payments for
Living Independently and Living in Supportive Housing,
Fiscal Years 1978-1982

	1978	1980	1982
Basic federal SSI payment			
Individual	$178	$208	$264
Couple	267	312	397
Living independently			
Number of states with supplemental payment (SSP)	27	30	28
Average state supplement for individuals*			
Aged	49	52	60
Blind	52	57	63
Disabled	48	50	58
Average state supplement for couples*			
Aged	78	86	95
Blind	97	106	115
Disabled	76	87	90
Living in supportive housing			
Number of states with supplement payment	35	39	36
Average state supplement for individuals*			
Aged	117	141	160
Blind	117	142	158
Disabled	116	153	157
Average state supplement for couples*			
Aged	298	333	401
Blind	296	335	397
Disabled	293	362	393

SOURCES: Adapted from U.S. SSA (1978; 1980; 1982).
*These averages are calculated from only those states offering a supplemental
payment.

Table 4.5 also indicates at least some dimensions of vertical equity.
Persons in supportive or semi-dependent housing might be logically
thought to be in greater need of care and to have higher self-maintenance
costs than those living independently. Without considering the ade-
quacy of the supplements involved, it seems as if a higher SSP benefit
level for those living in semi-dependent housing, compared to these
living independently, would address this need to varying degrees. While
on the average, states provide more for the former group, data on
individual states indicates that this is not true for one-fourth of the states.

In addition to SSP levels, states can also influence the effect of
income maintenance policy on the use of institutional care through
"spend down" procedures. All states allow for spend down through

either medically needy, special institutional standards, or 209(b) procedures. (The 209[b] option allows states to have more restrictive standards for Medicaid eligibility than those used under the federal SSI program.)[2] In reality, all of these approaches are most applicable to individuals residing in institutions, since such people on average have incurred the highest cumulative out-of-pocket medical expenses. Nevertheless, the presence of a medically needy program indicates a state's expressed willingness to extend noninstitutional service coverage of its population. Consequently, it might be expected that there are fewer incentives for institutionalization in states with medically needy programs that in states that expressly tie their spend down eligibility to institutional status.

The Coverage of Children

As noted in a preceding section, Medicaid coverage for children is available in varying forms through the AFDC or medically needy program. Most states also cover one or more forms of institutional care. Children eligible as dependents under AFDC are automatically covered for such care. Another group of optional recipients are those individuals under age 21 who would be eligible for AFDC but do not qualify as dependent children (42 CFR 435.222). Twenty-eight states cover all such children regardless of their living situation under the AFDC program. All states with a medically needy program also automatically cover these groups (42 CFR 435.301). An additional 17 states provide coverage to nondependent children living in publicly supported foster homes or private institutions. Twelve of these same states also extend coverage to children in settings such as Intermediate Care Facilities (ICFs), ICF-MRs (Mentally Retarded), or other psychiatric facilities. Only two states limit this coverage to children in psychiatric facilities. Five of these 17 states and all states with medically needy programs also provide Medicaid coverage to children whose adoption was subsidized by a public agency (La Jolla Management Corporation, 1982).

The essential feature evident from this analysis is that either through the AFDC optional eligibility or medically needy programs, there are public programs in place to extend Medicaid coverage to persons aged 21 or under, whether or not they are dependent. About one-third of the states have tied this eligibility to institutional settings of one type or another. In this sense there is vertical equity in this coverage, but horizontal inequity among states.

Conclusion

The analysis of Medicaid eligibility policy represents a complex and challenging task for the policy scholar and activist alike for at least three reasons: first, altering eligibility policy is likely to be more politically controversial than changing less visible benefit or reimbursement policies. As a result, where alterations are made, they often are accomplished in minimally visible ways; for example, states do not often directly reduce income standards, they simply do not increase these income standards despite inflation. As a consequence, less people become eligible as inflation continuously reduces the level of real income (i.e., income corrected for inflation) allowed for Medicaid eligibility. Second, Medicaid eligibility policy is highly interactive with state-level income maintenance policy, namely that for AFDC and for SSI/SSP. Medicaid policy can thus be altered through policy shifts in these other income programs, without paying the explicit political price associated with depriving the poor of health care. Third, Medicaid eligibility policy is blurred by a multiplicity of categories and population definitions that complicate connections to the two income programs. This permits each state to pursue various policy paths to similar goals, and defy the analyst to follow the trail.

This chapter has attempted to cut through this policy thicket in order to highlight several salient patterns in recent Medicaid eligibility policy. We have noted that inequities in the income standards for AFDC eligibility, when compared to those for SSI/SSP, have increased between 1978 and 1982. We have presented evidence that the number of Medicaid recipients declined somewhat but appears to have remained fairly constant in terms of absolute numbers of recipients between 1976 and 1982, while the ratio of recipients to the total low-income population declined markedly. Expenditures—expressed both in terms of the total and poverty populations—on the other hand, have clearly increased.

Further analysis of what has been termed the incentive structure of Medicaid eligibility suggests several additional conclusions. Since fewer than half of the states cover families with unemployed parents, incentives for family stability tend to be primarily negative. With respect to employment behavior, state Medicaid policy provides conflicting incentives. On one hand, most states do not cover single parents who would be eligible for AFDC if their work-related child care were paid from earnings rather than by a public agency, but all states permit recipients to remain Medicaid eligible for a brief period after their income increases due to employment. Finally, incentives to provide and expand alternatives to institutional care are influenced by state SSP policy and by eligibility for Medicaid that may accompany it. To the extent that states cover persons living independently under SSP (about half do) and persons living in supportive housing (about three-fourths do), these incentive-effects are positive.

Both Medicaid and income maintenance policies are important in understanding broader patterns of availability and utilization of health care services. The issues involved are not merely technical ones and interest in them is not confined to those few policymakers and scholars who can claim to understand the eligibility provision of human service programs. Rather, these issues touch upon basic ethical and political questions regarding to whom public resources are allocated and how these choices are to be made. Because the poor, frail, and vulnerable include several populations—the young, the old, and the disabled among others—it is important to analyze patterns of policy allocations and their outcomes for the various groups as well as to examine the value basis for allocating resources.

The task of analysis becomes more significant in periods when resources are highly constrained—as they presently are for both political and economic reasons. Pressures increase on policymakers to cut back public expenditures, and the intensity of competition among representatives of various vulnerable groups grows notably. This process is most apparent at the state level, because recent new federalism policies have shifted many of the important choices to the state level. This is especially so in long term care, where federal policy is most notable for its absence. Intergenerational issues (i.e., the young and old) are intensified at the state level because the two largest human service items in most state budgets benefit these respective groups, namely, education and health care. Those who are appalled at the prospect of a political struggle between advocates for the young and for the old are pursuing at least three strategies to address this threat: First, to challenge the argument that fiscal crisis represents a solely economic event, and propose instead that important political decisions limit the resources available to government (Estes, Newcomer, and Associates, 1983); second, to argue for enhancing the role of the federal government in the human services, with the expectation that clear federal policy will reduce the likelihood that intergenerational conflicts will be aired in fifty state policy arenas (Estes, 1979); and third, to improve existing knowledge about current policy patterns and their consequences for particular population groups (Benjamin, Estes, Swan, and Newcomer, 1980).

Notes

1. This section was adapted from Barth, Carcagno, and Palmer (1974) and Rymer et al. (1979).

2. At their option, states can offer a medically needy **program or special income** standards for the institutionalized. States can also elect to have eligibility standards that are more restrictive for their Medicaid programs than those for the federal SSI program. Such states are termed 209(b) states in reference to the Social Security Act provision giving them this authority. While they can set more restrictive standards under this provision, states must also deduct health care expenditures from a client's income before determining eligibility. The net result is that the 209(b) states also have a spend down provision in their programs. When all three of these possible spend down approaches are considered, all states (with the exception of Arizona) offer some form of spend down under Medicaid.

References

Aging Health Policy Center (AHPC). Unpublished telephone survey. San Francisco, CA: AHPC, University of California, 1983.

Barth, Carcagno, and Palmer. *Towards an Effective Income Support System.* Madison, WI: Institute for Research on Poverty, 1974.

Benjamin, A. E., C. L. Estes, J. H. Swan, and R. J. Newcomer. "Elders and Children: Patterns of Public Policy in the 50 States." *Journal of Gerontology,* 35, No. 6 (November 1980), 928-934.

Estes, C. L. *The Aging Enterprise.* San Francisco, CA: Jossey-Bass, 1979.

Estes, C. L., R. J. Newcomer, and Associates. *Fiscal Austerity and Aging: Shifting Governmental Responsibility for the Elderly.* Beverly Hills, CA: Sage, 1983.

Gibson, R. M., D. R. Waldo, and K. R. Levit. "National Health Expenditures, 1982." *Health Care Financing Review,* 5, No. 1 (Fall 1983), 1-31.

La Jolla Management Corporation. *Medicaid Program Characteristics: Summary Tables.* Volume 1. Washington, DC: U.S. Health Care Financing Administration, Office of Research and Demonstrations, 1982.

Rymer, M., C . Oksman, L. Bailes, and D. Ellwood. *Medicaid Eligibility: Problems and Solutions.* Boulder, CO: Westview, 1979.

U.S. Bureau of the Census (BOC). Current Population Reports, Series P-25, #875 and #913. Washington, DC: U.S. Department of Commerce, 1980 and 1982a.

U.S. Bureau of the Census (BOC). *1980 Census of Population and Housing— Supplementary Report: Provisional Estimates of Social, Economic and Housing Characteristics.* Washington, DC: U.S. Department of Commerce, 1982b.

U.S. Bureau of the Census (BOC). *State and Metropolitan Area Data Book 1979.* Washington, DC: U.S. Department of Commerce, 1979.

U.S. Code of Federal Regulation (CFR). Washington, DC: U.S. Government Printing Office, 1984.

U.S. Health Care Financing Administration (HCFA). Medicaid Program Data Branch. *National Medicaid Statistics: Fiscal Years 1975 to 1982.* State 2082 Tables data tape. Baltimore, MD: U.S. Department of Health and Human Services, 1984.

U.S. Social Security Administration (SSA). *The Supplemental Security Income Program for the Aged, Blind, and Disabled: Selected Characteristics of State Supplementation Programs as of October 1977.* Washington, DC: U.S. Department of Health, Education, and Welfare, 1978.

U.S. Social Security Administration (SSA). *The Supplemental Security Income Program for the Aged, Blind, and Disabled: Selected Characteristics of State Supplementation Programs as of October 1979.* Washington, DC: U.S. Department of Health and Human Services, 1980.

U.S. Social Security Administration (SSA). *The Supplemental Security Income Program for the Aged, Blind, and Disabled: Selected Characteristics of State Supplementation Programs as of January 1982.* Washington, DC: U.S. Department of Health and Human Services, 1982.

CHAPTER 5

MEDICAID COST CONTAINMENT TRIALS AND INNOVATIONS

Robert J. Newcomer
Marjorie P. Bogaert-Tullis

When the Medicaid program was enacted in 1965, it provided federal matching funds for state medical assistance programs to low-income individuals and families and shifted a major proportion of the financial responsibility for this care to federal and state government. This shift provided relief to local governments and those hospitals and physicians who had been providing free care to the poor. During the early years of implementation, most states sought to expand their medical assistance programs and benefits. Since the late 1970s, however, attention had switched to improving program efficiency, cost effectiveness in services, and cost containment. This chapter examines recent state trends in the benefits offered, the controls placed on these benefits, and some of the innovations that have begun to emerge.

The Medicaid Program Structure

A perspective on the scope of the Medicaid program and the structure of the delivery system is useful in understanding the context in which changes are occurring. Generally, Medicaid operates as a third-party insurance coverage program. The state pays bills for ser-

Authors' Note: The preparation of this chapter, including the compilation of data sources was supported by the National Center for Health Services Research under Grant No. HS04042. An earlier version of this chapter was presented at a National Conference of State Legislatures meeting on "Human Services Financing: State Issues and Options," 1984. We wish to acknowledge Carol Sattler for her assistance in compiling the data reported here.

vices rendered to individuals eligible for the program. The services received are determined by the provider rather than by Medicaid staff. States assert fiscal control over the program mainly by changing program policies such as eligibility standards (discussed in Chapter 4), scope or duration of services covered, utilization controls, and reimbursement rates.

The benefits or services covered by a state Medicaid program fall into two general categories—mandatory and optional. Federal regulations require or mandate that certain basic services be offered (42 CFR 440). Among these are physician, inpatient and outpatient hospital, laboratory, and x-ray services; skilled nursing facilities for those aged 21 or older, and home health care.[1] States can also provide any number of thirty-two optional services.

Each service must be sufficient in amount, duration, and scope to reasonably achieve its purpose. States receive Federal Financial Participation (FFP) for both mandatory and optional services. Table 5.1 lists the total Medicaid expenditures and expenditures on the aged for a selected list of services in 1978 and 1982.

From this list it can be seen that inpatient hospitals, skilled nursing facilities (SNFs), intermediate care facilities (ICFs), intermediate care facilities for the mentally retarded (ICF-MRs), physicians, and prescription drugs have been the major service expenditures. Together they account for about 82 percent of all expenditures in 1982; in 1978 they accounted for almost 84 percent of all expenditures. Among the aged, these same services have been uniformly dominant, accounting for about 90 percent of all expenditures in both years. SNFs and ICFs alone have accounted for about two-thirds of Medicaid spending on the aged. The tendency for these selected services to decline as a proportion of total expenditures since 1978 reflects a changing patient population, and the consequence of state policy. For example, mental hospitals, outpatient hospital services, clinics, and home health care have all experienced substantial growth rates.

Under federal regulations, states have from the outset of the Medicaid program been able to regulate the amount and duration of the services offered under their programs. In 1981, under the Omnibus Budget Reconciliation Act (OBRA; U.S. PL 97-35), states were given more flexibility in service coverage, utilization control, and reimbursement. For example, a state could selectively limit services. While all covered services have to be available to those eligible as categorically

TABLE 5.1 Medicaid Expenditures for Health Services and Other Costs, 1978 and 1982, in Fifty States

	All Groups[a] (in billions)		Aged[b] (in billions)	
	1978	1982	1978	1982
Inpatient hospital	$ 4.94	$ 7.64	$ .38	$ 1.01
Physicians	1.53	2.09	.17	.25
Dental	.39	.49	.03	.04
Skilled nursing facilities	3.13	4.43	2.43	3.68
Intermediate care facilities	3.10	4.98	2.33	3.99
Intermediate care facilities for the mentally retarded	1.19	3.47	.03	.09
Mental hospitals	.67	.97	.28	.37
Outpatient hsopitals	.83	1.35	.04	.09
Clinic services	.20	.41	.006	.02
Home health	.21	.50	.08	.31
Prescribed drugs	1.06	1.60	.41	.63
Laboratory and radiological services	.18	.16	.03	.02
Other practitioners' services	.14	.23	.03	.04
Other care (family planning, early periodic screening, and rural health clinic)	.32	.99	.06	.20
Total federal, state, and local expenditures[c]	17.89	29.31	6.31	10.74

SOURCE: Adapted from U.S. HCFA (1984, which includes the District of Columbia and 49 states, excluding Arizona).

a. Includes all Medicaid-eligible persons (e.g., aged, blind, disabled, and low-income families).

b. Includes only Medicaid-eligible persons classified as aged 65 or over. Does not usually include persons of this age who were blind or disabled prior to reaching age 65, as they may be counted within these other categorically eligible groups.

c. These figures represent only the service expenditures for fifty states. They do not include administrative costs in these states or any expenditures in the territories. Columns may not equal total due to rounding.

needy, not all services had to be available to the medically needy. States were also allowed for the first time to enter into competitive bidding arrangements for buying services, and for limiting the freedom of choice for services. These changes in Medicaid regulation gave states more discretion in the exercise of their regulatory controls and permitted them to expand the role of market competition in the health care sector.

The Regulatory Approach

Typically states have imposed a variety of utilization controls on mandatory Medicaid services. These include limits on days or other units of treatment, prior authorization of services, and restrictions on specific procedures (e.g., weekend hospital admissions, elective surgery). In addition to these specific controls, mandatory services are also subject to a number of federally established limitations. Among inpatient hospitals, for example, these limitations include the requirement that there be a utilization review applicable to all Medicaid patients (42 CFR 440.10); in skilled nursing homes it is necessary that all patients be certified and periodically recertified as needing inpatient care (42 CFR 440.40).

Table 5.2 lists the proportion of states electing a variety of selected utilization controls for their mandatory services. In general, states have shown an increasing willingness to impose some form of limitation or utilization controls beyond federal minimums. This was true in 1978 through 1982. Among hospital, outpatient, and physician services, the predominant controls have been on specific procedures. In 1982, slightly over one-third of the states placed limits on the hospital days per year; only about half had limits on physician visits. Prior authorization of care, even among skilled nursing facilities, has not been particularly common.[2] The absence among the states of uniform controls for high-cost services reflects several conditions—perhaps the most important is that many states until 1982 were tying their Medicaid programs into the Medicare reimbursement and utilization controls system.[3] In other words, states relied on federal Medicare standards in these areas to control costs and monitor service quality and appropriateness in hospitals. This was also true in the area of skilled nursing services where the role of the federal government is focused on certification and recertification of patient service needs.

Reliance on federal regulatory approaches has not proven to be particularly successful. Two such approaches—certificate of need (CON) and the professional standards review organization (PSRO)—are discussed here, as is the emerging state regulatory strategy of rate setting.[4] These approaches, though largely targeted to the hospital sector, have implications for other service sectors as well, especially physician reimbursement. A fourth strategy just getting underway is the diagnosis-related group (DRG) prospective reimbursement approach being na-

TABLE 5.2   Selected Utilization Controls on Selected Mandatory Services in 1978-1982*

Services	% States with Controls			
	1978	1979	1981	1982
General hospital inpatient services				
Any limits on hospital services	80	80	78	90
Limits on days per year	46	50	46	38
Prior authorization	14	34	38	30
Weekend or pre-op limitations	2	2	4	22
Other limits	16	16	36	66
Outpatient services**				
Any limits on services	–	–	58	74
Limits on number of visits	–	–	18	22
Prior authorization	–	–	34	32
Other limits	–	–	28	52
Skilled nursing facility services				
Any limits on services	50	58	56	72
Prior authorization (or pre-authorization)	38	46	42	46
Other limits	12	14	28	30
Physician services				
Any limits on services	72	74	76	86
Limits on number or frequency of limits	44	42	48	56
Prior or pre-authorization	32	36	42	58
Other limits (including limits on specific procedures)	24	58	52	72
Home Health Services				
Part-time nursing**				
Any limits on services	–	–	72	74
Prior authorization	–	–	28	22
Other limits (including services limited)	–	–	58	60
Aide services**				
Any limits on services	–	–	70	76
Prior authorization	–	–	32	26
Other limits	–	–	48	62
Medical supplies equipment**				
Any limits on services	–	–	90	92
Prior authorization	–	–	56	56
Other limits	–	–	48	64

SOURCES: Adapted from La Jolla Management Corporation (1982); U.S. HCFA (1979); and U.S. HCFA (1982).
*1980 policy information was not available.
**Policy information not available when not shown.

tionally implemented by Medicare. It is too early to report on the outcome of the DRG program or the Medicaid adaptation of it. The issue of state optional benefits will also be discussed.

CERTIFICATE OF NEED (CON)

Certificate of need (CON) legislation seeks to control the number and distribution of hospital beds, as well as major capital equipment purchases, in a community. Federal support for CON was provided with the passage of the National Health Planning and Resources Development Act of 1974 (U.S. PL 93-641), which created a national network of health systems agencies (HSAs) to administer the program at the local level. By February 1980, all but three states had enacted CON laws.[5]

Empirical research on the effectiveness of capital expansion regulation has generated surprisingly consistent results. Whether measured on a per capita, per case, or per diem basis, CON programs have not been successful in holding down hospital costs (Salkever and Bice, 1976; Steinwald and Sloan, 1981; Coelen and Sullivan, 1980).

UTILIZATION AND QUALITY REVIEW (PSROs)

In contrast to CON and rate-setting efforts, PSROs directly involve physicians. As a self-policing mechanism designed to ascertain the necessity of prescribed care, utilization review has been pursued by numerous hospitals for many years. In the mid-1960s, utilization review was made mandatory for hospitals seeking Medicare and medicaid reimbursement, and in 1972 this policy was supplemented by the establishment of PSROs under Social Security Amendments (U.S. PL 92-603). It was the responsibility of PSROs, which ranged in size from small local groups to large statewide organizations, to provide for local review of the quality and appropriateness of hospital care (Freund and Jellinek, 1983).

Much of the research on PSROs and traditional utilization review programs has taken the form of case studies, which tend to preclude straightforward generalization of the results. Nevertheless, the findings suggest that the program had no impact on hospital days, admissions, or length of stay (Brook, Williams, and Rolfe, 1978; Gertman, Monheit, Anderson, Engle, and Levenson, 1979; Coelen and Sullivan, 1980).

RATE-SETTING

Rate setting is a generic designation for an array of rate-setting and revenue negotiation programs imposed on hospitals by all levels of government. A common feature is the use of prospective reimbursement. Instead of billing third-party payers after the services have been provided—the hospital (or other provider) receives a fixed payment in advance, or knows in advance what its per diem or per patient reimbursement will be.

The essence of this approach is that it shifts the responsibility for absorbing costs from the third-party payer to the hospital or other corporate entity responsible for the program. In principle, providers that overrun their reimbursement rate must sustain the loss, while those underspending their reimbursement are permitted to keep some fraction of the cost saving. Actual reimbursement levels may be established by formula, by negotiation, or, as is increasingly the case, by a combination of the two. Prospective reimbursement rate setting is used commonly by state governments, although a number of individual insurers such as Blue Cross have adopted it as well. Consequently, there is variation across programs regarding which reimbursements are involved (Freund and Jellinek, 1983).

Since 1981, more and more state Medicaid programs have adopted some form of prospective payment structure for hospitals and physicians. This is seen in Table 5.3, which lists the number of states having alternatives to Medicare payment systems in 1978-1982. Most states have had such systems in place for nursing homes for some time (see Chapter 6).

Mandatory hospital rate-setting programs were established in New York in 1970; Colorado, New Jersey, and Rhode Island in 1971; Connecticut, Maryland, Massachusetts, and Wisconsin in 1974; and Washington in 1975. Of these states, Maryland, Massachusetts, New Jersey, and New York operate under an "all-payer" system. Under these all-payer systems, Medicare, Medicaid, and private insurance (both Blue Cross and commercial carriers) all operate under the same rate setting levels.

As a group, mandatory rate-setting programs have generally constrained hospital expenditures per diem and per admission. This effect of these mandatory programs is a reduction of approximately two to four percentage points in the annual rate of cost increase over that which would have otherwise been expected (Steinwald and Sloan, 1981; Biles, Schramm, and Atkinson, 1980; Coelen and Sullivan, 1980; and U.S. CBO, 1979). Even programs showing this effect have had negligible impact during their first two years. However, it appears that the cumulative impact of these programs continues to grow for

TABLE 5.3   Changes in State Medicaid Reimbursement Policy, 1978-1982*

	1978	1979	1981	1982
Inpatient hospitals				
Reimbursement method– Medicare principle	80% (40)	80% (40)	64% (32)	66% (33)
Average payment per patient day (national average)	$163.94	$184.64	$276.78	$320.85
Outpatient hospitals				
Reimbursement method– Medicare principle	32% (16)	31% (15)	37% (18)	71% (34)
Physician services				
Reimbursement method– Medicare principle	26% (13)	28% (14)	20% (10)	50% (25)
Percentage of Medicare– less than 75%	–	–	–	48% (12)
Percentage of Medicare– 75%	–	–	–	52% (13)
Fixed fee or Relative Value Scale (RVS)	12% (6)	16% (8)	18% (9)	48% (24)
Maximum allowable fee-payment level GPT-4-90040-GP (national average)	$11.92 (21)	$11.99 (25)	$12.99 (31)	$13.65 (37)

SOURCES: Adapted from AHPC (1983); AHA (1983); La Jolla Management Corporation (1982); U.S. HCFA (1979); and U.S. HCFA (1982).
*1980 data were not available.

a period longer than any existing, mature program has been in effect (Vladeck, 1982). Rate-setting systems that are not fixed in some way to total patient costs (as opposed to unit costs such as per diem rate) have been much less effective (Morone, 1983).

The experience of states like Massachusetts and New Jersey was that, in the absence of all-payer rate setting, there are major cost shifts to Medicare and private payers. This, in turn, had an adverse effect on private insurance rates, employers costs, and the solvency of hospitals serving high proportions of Medicaid or indigent patients (Morone, 1983; Crosier, 1983). Such problems stimulated these states to adopt all-payer systems.

Physician payments under Medicare are expected to be 24 billion dollars in 1984—as large as Medicaid payments and growing at over

20 percent a year. One reason for the high cost of this program is the cost incentives within it. Medicare pays surgeons five times as much per hour as physicians who provide care on an outpatient basis, and internists twice as much per hour for services in the hospital as for services in the office (Etheredge, 1983).

Furthermore, Medicare and many insurance plans pay physicians retrospectively, with rates based on their charges. States have chosen to deal with this practice through a variety of utilization controls (such as restrictions on number of patient visits or procedures), or more structurally through the setting of prospective reimbursement rates. In a prospective reimbursement strategy, fees are typically set below "usual and customary" reimbursement rates. The usual and customary rates are the rates received from private patients and charged to Medicare. As seen in Table 5.3, about half the state Medicaid programs have established physician fee structures tied to specific procedures.

The tradeoffs between these strategies have presented distinct problems for states. In programs tied to Medicare methods, costs are high. Low fees, on the other hand, discourage private physician participation in Medicaid, while encouraging the consequent substitution of higher-priced hospital outpatient departments, emergency rooms, and clinics. Ideally, fees should be high enough to prevent these more costly substitutions. There have been few attempts to integrate physician and hospital charges in order to generate incentives for physician efficiency. The most successful efforts have been in health maintenance organizations (HMOs).

OPTIONAL BENEFITS

In addition to the federally mandated benefits, states have the option of providing an array of other services. These include: intermediate care facilities, private duty nursing, clinic services, prescribed drugs, and physical therapy and related services. Since the Omnibus Budget Reconciliation Act of 1981, states have had the option of not providing any of these services to the medically needy, or to certain groups within the medically needy category.

Thirty-two states have medically needy programs and 24 of the 32 have the same coverage for mandatory services for all medically needy groups as for the categorically needy (see Chapter 4). Twenty-one of the 24 states have the same coverage for optional services for all medically needy groups as for the categorically needy.

Table 5.4 briefly lists the proportion of states offering each of a variety of selected optional benefits. For the period 1978 to 1982, a higher percentage of medically needy states offered the optional benefits than the non-medically needy states. Personal care, private duty nursing, and care for the aged in tuberculosis institutions (TB) have been among the more restricted benefits, with less than half of the states offering these benefits. Intermediate care facilities (ICFs) and prescription drugs, on the other hand, have been almost universally available. The other services are available in at least three-quarters of the states. Since 1978 only chiropractic and TB institutional services have become available in fewer states. In 1982, 7 percent of the medically needy states had copayments for dental services and/or dentures, 17 percent had copayments for eyeglasses and optometry, and 33 percent had copayments for prescription drugs.

The current health care delivery structure is fragmented in terms of location of service provision and source of payment. Hospitals and physicians are largely paid from private insurance and Medicare; nursing homes, from private pay and Medicaid; home care, from mostly private pay.

Federal policy changes in the Medicare program, particularly the diagnosis-related group (DRG) program, may prove to be effective catalysts for more concerted state efforts to control utilization.[6] The DRG strategy has a direct impact on hospital utilization in an attempt to reduce Medicare costs. By so doing, the change is likely to produce an effect on nursing homes and home health care as well. Cost shifts and service substitutions will result.

The Competitive Approach

Advocates of competition contend that solutions to cost containment must meet certain market criteria, two of which are that: consumers must be induced to make cost-effective choices of health insurance plans and services; and providers must be induced to deliver care more efficiently.

Two major orientations have emerged from this strategy. To meet the first criterion, Enthoven (1980) suggested that consumers be pro-

TABLE 5.4 Selected Optional State Medicaid Benefits in 1978, 1981, and 1982

	Percentage of States with Benefits								
	All States (n = 50)			Medically Needy States (n = 32)			Non-Medically Needy States (n = 18)		
Services	1978	1981	1982	1978	1981	1982	1978	1981	1982
Chiropractic	56	52	52	59	54	50	50	56	50
Clinic	78	88	88	88	100	100	61	67	67
Dental	62	68	68	69	72	72	50	62	62
Copayments for medically needy— Dental services and/or dentures	–	–	–	–	–	7	–	–	–
Emergency Hospital	82	86	88	84	82	85	78	89	89
Eyeglasses	66	68	68	75	72	72	50	62	62
Copayments for medically needy	–	–	–	–	–	17	–	–	–
Institutional services in intermediate care facilities (ICFs)	100	100	100	100	100	100	100	100	100
Optometry	74	82	82	81	82	82	61	84	84
Copayments for medically needy	–	–	–	–	17	–	–	–	–
Other diagnostic screening, preventive and rehabilitative	38	64	60	50	66	66	17	62	45
Personal care	–	38	38	–	41	41	–	23	23
Physical therapy and related services	60	88	76	69	97	75	44	73	78
Podiatry	72	80	60	78	85	56	61	67	67
Prescription drugs	96	96	96	100	100	100	89	89	89
Copayments for medically needy	–	–	–	–	–	33	–	–	–
Private duty nursing	36	34	34	44	44	57	22	17	17
Prosthetic devices	82	92	92	91	94	94	67	89	89
SNF services for patients under 21	86	94	90	88	94	91	83	90	89
Care for patients 65 or older in institutions for mental disease	82	88	86	97	94	94	56	78	73
Care for patients 65 or older in institutions for tuberculosis	52	46	44	59	50	50	39	39	34
Care for patients under 21 in psychiatric hospitals	64	72	76	72	79	85	50	56	56

SOURCES: Adapted from La Jolla Management Corporation (1982); and U.S. HCFA (1979).

vided with fixed dollar employer or government contributions to their insurance and at the same time offered options from which to choose. This approach has begun to emerge in the form of alternative insurance coverage and price packages. To meet the second criterion, Enthoven proposed that reorganized systems of care be formed that would not be dependent on the traditional fee-for-service mode of payment—in other words, that alternative delivery systems (ADSs) be widely adopted as a central feature of the medical care market. While ADSs are not inconsistent with the regulatory approach, they are absolutely critical to competitive approaches. Several states, particularly in the West, and Southwest, appear to be eager to move forward with competitive approaches to health care reform. In addition, health maintenance organization (HMO) Medicare competition projects are underway in sixteen states. Seven of these same states are also experimenting with alternative models for prepaid Medicare capitation of health care services. Medicaid competition projects are being conducted in nine states (Luce, Dobson, and Cooper, 1983).

TYPES OF ALTERNATIVE DELIVERY SYSTEMS (ADSs)

An alternative delivery system (ADS), to a greater or lesser extent, consolidates the financing and provision of care within the same organizational entity. The most common type of ADS is the federally qualified closed panel prepaid group practice—or as it has come to be called, the health maintenance organization (HMO). Others include the primary care network (PCN), individual practice association (IPA), health care alliance (HCA), and preferred provider organization (PPO). Enrollments in all forms of these systems doubled between 1974 and 1981 with over 10.3 million enrolled persons in 1981 (Freund and Jellinek, 1983).

The Health Maintenance Organization (HMO)

Health maintenance organizations fully integrate the provision and financing of services. Services generally are provided by a large multispecialty fixed group of physicians and may be available either at a single location or at multiple sites.[7] This is more commonly referred to as a closed panel of physicians, meaning that the patient selects from among the physicians affiliated with the HMO. While the specifics of financing arrangements vary from one HMO to another, in general the physician group is at risk—the higher the expenditures out of the overall group revenue pool, the lower the physicians' incomes.

The Individual Practice Association (IPA)

Individual practice associations blend prepayment with traditional fee-for-service payment. Enrollees prepay a fixed premium in exchange for "free" care from IPA physicians. These doctors are reimbursed on a fee-for-service basis and most frequently also retain fee-for-service practices. If costs outrun revenues, the physician ultimately must take a reduction in reimbursement. In an IPA, physicians retain responsibility for the organization and delivery of care, members conduct peer review to ensure appropriate utilization, and enrollees maintain freedom of choice of physician (Egdahl, Taff, Friedland, and Linde, 1977).

The Primary Care Network (PCN)

Primary care network enrollees designate a participating primary care physician to serve as coordinator of all their services. The physician directly provides all needed primary care and refers the enrollee to specialists or a hospital as necessary. The physician serves as the enrollees' primary provider and financial manager.

Typically, a PCN physician's account consists of two parts. Direct physician services are paid on a fee-for-service basis until the physician reaches some threshold number of enrollees (e.g., under the SAFECO-United Health Care plan, the threshold is 200), at which point the method of payment converts to negotiated capitation. The other part is for referral and hospital care. Bills for these services must be authorized by the primary care physician, with actual payment handled by the insurance company. PCN physicians share in both the surpluses and deficits of the part two accounts, so they have an incentive for cost-consciousness (Moore, 1979).

The Health Care Alliance (HCA)

Health care alliances are structurally simpler than the other ADSs. HCA enrollees agree to obtain all of their medical care from a given panel of physicians, who may be organized as a large multispecialty group or perhaps simply as an association of individual doctors in private practice. As in an IPA, participating physicians may continue to have fee-for-service patients along with HCA enrollees. In addition, physicians face no financial risk in the HCA. HCA premiums simply reflect the cost of the benefits package offered. Responsibility for establishing premium levels, collecting payments, and marketing the plan is delegated to an insurance company (Freund and Jellinek, 1983).

The Preferred Provider Organization (PPO)

Preferred provider organizations are the newest type of ADS. PPOs are groups of hospitals and physicians that contract on a fee-for-service basis with employers, insurance companies, or third-party administrators to provide comprehensive medical services to subscribers (*Federation of American Hospitals Review*, 1982, p. 12). In return for using a preferred provider, subscribers receive economic rewards such as reduced coinsurance and copayments. General features of PPOs include the use of a closed provider panel, a negotiated fee that reflects a discount, utilization review, and more rapid payment by insurance carriers. Unlike HMOs, capitation payment is not used and subscribers are not "locked in" to the plan for any given period of time.

COST TRENDS UNDER ALTERNATIVE SYSTEMS

On the face of it, the evidence on whether or not ADSs contain costs is unambiguous: they do, particularly those that follow the pure prepaid group model, such as HMOs. Based on an extensive analysis of the empirical literature, Luft (1981) concluded that total per capita costs were some 10 to 40 percent lower for prepaid group enrollees than for patients of traditional fee-for-service practices.

Four areas have been extensively explored in an attempt to answer the question of how these savings have been generated: economies of scale, hospital utilization, ambulatory care, and enrollee self-selection. The cost savings are not attributable to lower per-unit costs (Luft, 1981), but hospital utilization (both in terms of average length of stay and number of admissions) was reduced among HMOs. IPAs were also found to reduce hospital utilization under some circumstances (Gaus, Cooper, and Hirschman, 1976; Luft, 1981).

Findings with regard to ambulatory care and self-selection are ambiguous. Luft (1978) found that in 18 of 26 cases, ambulatory care utilization was lower under an ADS than under fee-for-service plans, with eight cases (including the five IPAs in the sample) pointing the other way. With regard to self-selection, some believe that an ADS might actively seek to enroll healthier populations in order to keep costs low and maintain a competitive edge. On the other hand, sicker individuals might be attracted to the ADS by the more comprehensive coverage offered. Findings to date are mixed. Some studies have concluded that there is no evidence of adverse selection while others (Eggers, 1980) have found that there is.

Conclusion

One temptation in reviewing the accomplishments and shortcomings of state Medicaid benefit and utilization controls is to lay out a panoply of specific programmatic options or criticisms. To do so would be misleading, for the central point to be made about state Medicaid programs is as much philosophical as technical. States have been accustomed to following the federal lead in the application of reimbursement and utilization control policies for some of their major services (i.e., hospitals and physicians). As a result, they have been paying more for these services than they absolutely had to. Partly as a consequence of this practice, states have pursued a policy of tight constraint on many of their other Medicaid services. With the advent of prospective payment in the Medicare program (in the form of DRGs), expansion of alternative delivery systems, and greater state flexibility in the operation of their programs, states now have the option of reassessing and reprioritizing their Medicaid program approaches. There are no clearly identifiable or universal solutions to the problems facing state Medicaid programs or the health care industry itself. But many innovations have been begun, and many of these have produced positive effects.

The adoption of prospective reimbursement for hospitals, physicians, and nursing homes appears to be particularly desirable and reproducible. In such cases, however, it seems essential that rates be tied to patients or admissions rather than to patient days or other variable service units. Fixed budget risk-sharing approaches and mandatory all-payer rate setting both seem to produce desirable cost savings.

Complementing this regulatory approach is the expansion of alternative delivery systems. There has been too little experience with IPAs, PCNs, HCAs, and PPOs to know whether these forms should be encouraged over the more established HMOs, but federal and state demonstrations in these areas will eventually help clarify this issue. The willingness to experiment in these areas in particularly encouraging.

In pointing toward these positive directions, it is important to note that most state innovations or other program changes (with the exception of ADSs) are oriented to specific services. The health care system is more comprehensive and dynamic than the Medicaid program itself. Each element whether it be hospital care, nursing homes, physicians, or other services is interactive across the range of financial resources with each element attempting to maximize its revenue and patient volume. State policies must be formulated for appropriateness in this larger context. As state and federal program officials begin to recognize the interactions dramatized by innovative experiments and policy changes, the dynamic interrelationships between the acute and the chronic care systems and among Medicare, Medicaid, and private pay financing will finally be apparent. Financing and delivery systems that appropriately cut across these dimensions will be needed. Particularly needed is a mechanism for transferring acute care cost savings into expanded community care programs.

For too long, state regulatory policy has, with different policy approaches, gripped only one element or another of the health system that is generating costs. As a consequence, there have been many cost shifts and service substitutions, but few cost reductions overall. Yet in spite of these shortcomings, states have demonstrated a capacity to administer extensive health care programs. This experience may now be directed toward reasoned systematic innovation to fill gaps in the current system and to reach those in need of the care available. Continued program cutbacks and eligibility tightening need not be the only alternatives open to states in fulfilling their health care responsibility to the public of all ages and their long term care responsibility to the elderly.

Notes

1. Other mandatory services included rural health clinic services, EPSDT, family planning services and supplies, and nurse-midwife services.

2. Six states (Arkansas, Oklahoma, Pennsylvania, Rhode Island, Tennessee, Washington) have more restrictive limitations on the medically needy for at least one mandatory service. Tennessee has more restrictive limitations on inpatient hospital services; outpatient hospital services are more restrictive in Rhode Island and are not provided in Tennessee; SNF services are more restrictive in Rhode Island and are not provided in Arkansas; EPSDT services are not provided in Washington; physician services are more restrictive in Pennsylvania and Washington, and not provided in Oklahoma; and nurse-midwife services are not provided in Arkansas, Oklahoma, Pennsylvania, Rhode Island, or Tennessee (La Jolla Management Corporation, 1982).

3. Other explanations include the political power and opposition of hospitals and physician groups in influencing state legislation; and the ability of states, at least among physicians and home health agencies, to control utilization by setting low reimbursement rates.

4. For a fuller discussion of the success of regulatory strategies in controlling costs see Schwartz, 1981.

5. Additional measures to regulate hospital capital expansion include Section 221 of the Social Security Amendments of 1972 (U.S. PL 92-603) which gave regulators the authority to withhold federal reimbursement (such as Medicare and Medicaid funds) from hospitals violating established capital expansion limits. Various Blue Cross and Blue Shield programs also have sought to exercise the same kind of leverage with their powers of reimbursement.

6. The essence of the DRG or any prospective rate approach is that it shifts the responsibility for absorbing costs from the third party payer to the hospital or other corporate entity responsible for the program.

7. This brief discussion of the various types of alternative delivery systems has been adapted from Freund and Jellinek, 1983.

References

Aging Health Policy Center (AHPC). Unpublished telephone survey of states, reimbursement data. San Francisco, CA: AHPC, University of California, 1983.

American Hospital Association (AHA). *Hospital Statistics, 1982 AHA Survey Data.* Chicago, IL: AHA, 1983.

Biles, B., C. J. Schramm, and J. G. Atkinson. "Hospital Cost Inflation Under State Role-Setting Programs." *The New England Journal of Medicine,* 303, No. 12 (September 1980), 664-668.

Brook, R. H., K. N. Williams, and J. E. Rolfe. "Controlling the Use and Cost of Medical Services: The New Mexico Experimental Medical Care Review Organization—A Four-Year Case Study." *Medical Care,* 16, No. 9, Supplement (September 1978), 1-76.

Coelen, C., and D. Sullivan. "An Analysis of Prospective Reimbursement Programs on Hospital Cost." Unpublished paper. Cambridge, MA: Abt, 1980.

Crosier, J. Testimony before the U.S. Senate, Special Committee on Aging. In Hearing: *Controlling Health Care Costs: State, Local and Private Sector Initiatives,* October 26, 1983. Washington, DC: U.S. Government Printing Office, 1983.

Egdahl, R. H., C. H. Taff, J. Friedland, and K. Linde. "The Potential of Organization of Fee-For-Service Physicians for Achieving Significant Decreases in Hospitalization." *Annals of Surgery,* 186, No. 3 (September 1977), 388-399.

Eggers, P. "Risk Differential Between Medicare Beneficiaries Enrolled and Not Enrolled in an HMO." *Health Care Financing Review,* 1, No. 3 (Winter 1980), 91-99.

Enthoven, A. C. *Health Plan: The Only Practical Solution to the Soaring Cost of Medical Care.* Reading, MA: Addison-Wesley, 1980.

Etheredge, L. Testimony before the U.S. Senate Special Committee on Aging. In Hearing: *Controlling Health Care Costs: State, Local and Private Sector Initiatives,* October 26, 1983. Washington, DC: U.S. Government Printing Office, 1983.

Federation of American Hospitals Review, 15, No. 6 (July–August 1982), 12.

Freund, D. A., and P. S. Jellinek. "Financing and Cost Containment for Personal Health Services in the 1980s." In *Policy Issues in Personal Health Services: Current Perspectives.* Ed. S. C. Jain and J. E. Paul. Rockville, MD: Aspen Publications, 1983.

Gaus, C., B. Cooper, and F. Hirschman. "Contrasts in HMO and Fee-For-Service Performance." *Social Security Bulletin,* 39, No. 5 (May 1976), 3-14.

Gertman, P. M., A. C. Monheit, J. J. Anderson, J. B. Engle, and D. K. Levenson. "Utilization Review in the United States: Results from a 1976–77 National Survey of Hospitals." *Medical Care,* 17, No. 8, supplement (August 1979), i-iii, 1-148.

La Jolla Management Corporation. *Medicaid Program Characteristics: Summary Tables.* Washington, DC: U.S. Department of Health and Human Services, Health Care Financing Administration, 1982.

Luce, B., A. Dobson, and B. Cooper. *Health Care Financing Status Report: Research and Demonstrations in Health Care Financing.* Baltimore, MD: U.S. Department of Health and Human Services, Health Care Financing Administration, 1983.

Luft, H. "How Do Health Maintenance Organizations Achieve Their Savings? Rhetoric and Evidence." *The New England Journal of Medicine,* 298, No. 24 (June 15, 1978), 1336-1343.

———. *Health Maintenance Organizations: Dimensions of Performance.* New York: John Wiley, 1981.

Moore, S. "Cost Containment Through Risk Sharing by Primary-Care Physicians." *The New England Journal of Medicine,* 300, No. 24 (June 14, 1979), 1359-1362.

Morone, J. Testimony before the U.S. Senate, Special Committee on Aging. In Hearing: *Controlling Health Care Costs: State, Local and Private Sector Initiatives,* October 26, 1983. Washington, DC: U.S. Government Printing Office, 1983.

Salkever, D. S., and T. Bice. "The Impact of Certificate of Need Controls on Hospital Investment." *Milbank Memorial Fund Quarterly/Health and Society,* 54, No. 1 (Spring 1976), 185-214.

Schwartz, W. "The Regulation Strategy for Controlling Hospital Costs: Problems and Prospects." *The New England Journal of Medicine,* 305, No. 21 (1981), 1249-1255.

Steinwald, B., and F. A. Sloan. "Regulatory Approaces to Hospital Cost Containment: A Synthesis of the Empirical Evidence." In *A New Approach to the Economics of Health Care.* Ed. M. Olson. Washington, DC: American Enterprise Institute, 1981, pp. 273-307.

U.S. Code of Federal Regulations (CFR). Washington, DC: U.S. Government Printing Office, 1984.

U.S. Congressional Budget Office (CBO). *Controlling Rising Hospital Costs.* Washington, DC: U.S. Government Printing Office, 1979.

U.S. Health Care Financing Administration (HCFA). *Data on the Medicaid Program: Eligibility, Services, Expenditures,* 1979 ed. rev. Baltimore, MD: U.S. Department of Health, Education, and Welfare, 1979.

U.S. Health Care Financing Administration (HCFA). Medicaid Program Data Branch. *National Medicaid Statistics: Fiscal Year 1975 to 1982.* State 2082 Tables data tape. Baltimore, MD: U.S. Department of Health and Human Services, 1984.

U.S. Health Care Financing Administration (HCFA). Office of Research and Demonstrations. *Health Care Financing Program Statistics. The Medicare and Medicaid Book, 1981.* Baltimore: MD: U.S. Department of Health and Human Services, 1982.

U.S. Public Law 92-603. *Social Security Amendments of 1972.* Washington, DC: U.S. Government Printing Office, 1972.

U.S. Public Law 93-641. *National Health Planning and Development Act of 1974.* Washington, DC: U.S. Government Printing Office, 1974.

U.S. Public Law 97-35. *Omnibus Budget Reconciliation Act (OBRA) of 1981.* Washington, DC: U.S. Government Printing Office, 1981.

Vladeck, B. "Paying Hospitals." In *New Approaches to the Medicaid Crisis.* Ed. R. Blendon and T. Maloney. New York, NY: F&S Press, 1982.

CHAPTER 6

MEDICAID NURSING HOME
REIMBURSEMENT POLICIES

James H. Swan
Charlene Harrington

Nursing home expenditures, along with those for hospitals, have been a target of public cost containment efforts because of their growing share of overall health expenditures. As described in Chapter 1, of the total 287 billion dollars spent in 1982 for personal health care services, 27 billion dollars (9.5%) was spent on nursing home care (Gibson, Waldo, and Levit, 1983). Nursing home care expenditures increased at a rate of 17.4 percent between 1980 and 1981 and 12.9 percent between 1981 and 1982.

These expenditures are a particular concern to public policymakers because public programs paid over half (55%) of total health care expenditures in 1982 (Gibson et al., 1983). While nursing home care accounted for only one percent of Medicare dollars, 39 percent of Medicaid dollars were spent on nursing home services in 1982 (Gibson et al., 1983). Of all Medicaid expenditures for the elderly, nursing home care represented 75 percent in 1978 and 71 percent of the total in 1982 (U.S. HCFA, 1984).

The primary payers for nursing home services are Medicaid and private individuals (see Chapter 1). Although Medicare covers nursing home services, its benefits are restricted only to individuals who meet stringent requirements. As a result, Medicare and other programs combined pay for only for a very small (about 5%) percent of total nursing home costs.

Authors' Note: The research on which this chapter is based was funded by the National Center for Health Services Research (Grant No. HS04042) and the Health Care Financing Administration (Grant No. 18-P9762019).

125

As outlined in previous chapters, states have discretion in the setting of policies that determine state expenditures for Medicaid programs. These policies are of vital concern to those individuals and their families who receive public payments for nursing home services, to providers who deliver services, to taxpayers who contribute and policymakers who allocate public dollars to the program.

Medicaid nursing home expenditures are computed (see Figure 6.1) by multiplying the number of users (recipients) by the number of units of service provided per user (utilization) by the cost of each service. Research indicates that the number of users and the number of services provided to each are influenced by state Medicaid policies, as well as by overall characteristics of the state. Scanlon (1980b) found that patterns of nursing home utilization in the states were influenced by factors such as the age of the population, the social and economic resources of individuals and families, geographic area, climate, and the price of care (Scanlon, 1980b; also see Chapter 7). In addition to these influences, state Medicaid eligibility policies are expected to affect the number of users and utilization control policies to affect the number of services per user (Scanlon, 1980b).

Medicaid expenditures for nursing home services, usually described on a cost per diem basis, are determined in part by state reimbursement policies. States develop Medicaid reimbursement policies to control state rates for nursing home services and are actively using such policies to control overall expenditures on nursing homes. States may take into account the structure of the supply (number and type of nursing beds and providers) and the demand (number of individuals desiring services) for nursing home care (Feder and Scanlon, 1980; Scanlon, 1980a and 1980b). Historical delivery patterns, inflation rates, prices for services, political pressures, and many other factors may also be taken into account by policymakers in setting Medicaid reimbursement policies.

Even though the rates may be changed, policymakers must keep in mind the effects of rate changes on supply and demand for services, and on factors that affect overall quality and access. The dilemma is how to ensure quality and access while controlling costs. Fee-for-service reimbursement models have inherent inflationary incentives because providers are paid a fee for each unit of service provided. Nursing homes can increase their revenues and profits under a fee-for-service system by providing more units of service and by increasing

Medicaid expenditures for nursing homes	=	Number of users (recipients)	X	Number of units of service per user	X	Cost of each service

Figure 6.1:   Medicaid Expenditures for Nursing Homes

their charges for each unit of service provided. This type of payment system thus builds in incentives for expansion of both the number of services (patient days) and the charges for each service (rates per day). Nursing home providers seek higher rates to maximize profits (81 percent of the homes are proprietary or profit-making) and/or to expand services (both proprietary and nonprofit facilities; U.S. NCHS, 1983). Nursing homes are, however, in direct competition with other providers for the limited resources of the Medicaid program.

The purpose of this chapter is to examine state Medicaid reimbursement policies for nursing homes and their effects on nursing home expenditures. Reimbursement is important because it is related not only to expenditures (public and private) but to profits as well. It influences supply and demand and provides incentives for facility behavior. Background information needed for an understanding of the issues includes a description of the types of facilities, a history of changes in federal guidelines for reimbursement, a compendium of state policy options for controlling reimbursement of nursing homes, and a description of variations in reimbursement policy components. Classification and trends in state reimbursement methods; empirical data on relationships between reimbursement rates and methods; and state nursing home expenditure patterns between 1978 and 1982 to help to explain why and how state policymakers are dealing with nursing home reimbursement issues and the mechanisms available to control costs and shape the nursing home market.

Types of Facilities and Patterns of Use

Nursing home services are provided by three distinct categories of facilities: skilled nursing (SNF), intermediate care (ICF), and intermediate care for the mentally retarded (ICF-MR). Medicare pays for skilled nursing care only when such services are considered to lead to rehabilitation. As a result, Medicare covers neither custodial care in skilled nursing facilities nor intermediate care in any facility. These are the predominant types of care provided in nursing homes. In contrast, Medicaid covers care in all three types of nursing home facility, and is the primary payer for custodial services. Because the aged are the primary recipients of SNF and ICF services[1] and Medicaid pays for a significant portion of these services, Medicaid reimbursement issues for these types of nursing homes are central to an understanding of long term care policy (see Chapter 7 for details on levels of care).

Methods of Nursing Home Reimbursement

The federal Medicaid statute designated two levels of nursing home care in order to allow for different types of services. Skilled nursing care was required; intermediate care was optional. Intermediate care, as a less intensive level of care, has fewer requirements for nursing services and a lower reimbursement rate. States may establish their own standards for care, and the rates that states pay nursing homes are based on these different standards and levels of care. Some states have established rate differences in what the Medicaid program will pay for SNF or ICF level of care based upon the type of facility (SNF or ICF) in which the care is provided. Other states take level of care into account with reimbursement rates based upon the proportion of patients in the facility classified as either SNF or ICF patients (U.S. GAO, 1983). Wisconsin and Rhode Island, for example, categorize their SNF and ICF facilities into five subcategories representing different levels of care (U.S. GAO, 1983).

CURRENT AND HISTORICAL VARIATIONS

Nursing homes charges are not the same for all payers (individual, Medicare, or Medicaid patients). Traditionally, private patient pay rates are based upon charges determined by the nursing homes themselves. Medicare reimbursement for nursing home services is based upon "reasonable cost" as specified in the federal legislation and regulations. Because of differences in the methods of defining reimbursable costs, Medicare rates are usually higher than state Medicaid rates (Grimaldi, 1982). The Medicare reasonable cost formula for nursing homes is designed to cover all those costs associated with providing services with limited exclusions for unrelated expenses (e.g., administrative travel). The basic Medicare methodology covers actual costs of providing care—that is, whatever nursing home owners spend, regardless of wide cost variations among providers (U.S. DHHS, 1982). This type of reimbursement encourages facilities to increase spending in order to increase their revenues from Medicare, since payment is based on the amount of facility costs determined after care is provided.

Medicaid statutes have traditionally given states discretion in setting nursing home rates within the federal guidelines. When Medicaid was established, states were given considerable latitude in setting their rates for nursing home services. Social Security Amendments of 1972 (U.S. PL 92-603) required states to implement "reasonable cost-related" reimbursement plans for nursing homes although this term was not clearly defined. These changes were enacted, in part, because providers complained that states were too restrictive in their policies. Each state was required to explain its cost-reporting requirements (information and reporting periods). Submission of facility cost reports were required at least annually, and no less than one-third of the facilities were to receive an on-site audit to determine the accuracy and reasonableness of costs (Grimaldi, 1982). Some states met Medicaid criteria by using the Medicare reimbursement formula. This requirement still allowed considerable state discretion because states were able to defend their methods as reasonable to gain federal approval.

In 1980, the Omnibus Reconciliation Act again changed Medicaid reimbursement requirements for nursing homes to give states greater flexibility. The law was changed to allow rate methods and standards that are

> reasonable and adequate to meet the costs which must be incurred by efficiently and economically operated facilities in order to provide care and services in conformity with applicable state and federal laws, regulations, and quality and safety standards. (U.S. PL 96-499, sec. 962)

States were required to continue uniform cost reports and periodic audits of such reports. These statutory changes were made because states asked for greater flexibility in the law to reduce reliance on Medicare reimbursement methods. The Senate Finance Committee recommended the change because it found the reasonable cost-related requirements to be inflationary and without incentives for efficient operation by providers (see CCH (H.R. 934), 1979). With the current federal regulations, states have greater discretion in setting rates. States have generally used their discretion by setting their Medicaid rates below those of Medicare and private payers.

REIMBURSEMENT POLICY COMPONENTS

An important component of state Medicaid program nursing home reimbursement policy is established through payment rates. Rates are generally set on a per diem basis and made dependent upon a number of components. "Allowable costs," as defined by Medicare or Medicaid, are major determinants of public payment. Medicare and Medicaid will only allow payment for certain expenses related to patient care, and prohibit payments for bad debts, courtesy allowances, and charity care. Physician services are generally excluded from per diem rates and are paid for separately. Medicare and Medicaid pay physicians on a fee-for-service basis. Some states have disallowed management fees, travel outside the state, political contributions, legal fees for unnecessary suits, and association dues (Spitz, Engquist-Seidenberg, Teitelbaum, and Curtis 1980; Spitz, 1981b; U.S. HCFA, 1981a). Each state has discretion in determining which costs are "allowable" for Medicaid. In 1978, only six states used the allowable cost rules of the Medicare program, the remaining states having developed their own definitions, in some instances incorporating Medicare rules (AHCA, 1978).

States individually determine the extent of ancillary services included in the per diem rate. The type of ancillary services covered may include: physical and occupational therapy, nonprescription drugs, prescription drugs, medical supplies, durable medical equipment, and other ancillaries. Most states include nonprescription drugs and medical supplies, but the extent of coverage for therapies varies.

In addition to determining which costs may be allowable, states may also place certain restrictions on the maximum level that will be reimbursed for selected items under Medicaid. These restrictions are sometimes made by distinguishing between fixed and variable costs. Variable costs, determined to a greater extent by the facility itself, include the following: wages and salaries, payroll taxes and benefits, food and other dietary items, laundry and linen, supplies and equipment, utilities, facility and equipment maintenance, and administrative costs. Fixed costs, determined by factors other than facility management, may include equipment rental, insurance, taxes and licenses, interest and finance charges, depreciation, rent, amortization, and other costs. In order to control cost, some states set reimbursement limits only on variable costs since facilities have greater discretion in reducing variables than fixed expenditures.

State Medicaid programs may place ceilings on selected types of costs by "cost center" (a budget category such as dietary costs or nursing wages). States may elect to set a maximum rate for all nursing home reimbursement by individual facility or by class (facilities grouped by characteristics such as size). Spitz (1981b), in his guide for nursing home cost containment, encourages states to set a maximum ceiling for total facility costs, a limit that any nursing home could receive. He considers that this approach gives facilities greater flexibility than does the setting of cost center ceilings. In 1978, 16 states placed a ceiling on total expenditures for facilities; 31 placed limits on some cost centers (AHCA, 1978). In 1983, 14 states reported ceilings on total costs; 24 reported limits on cost centers (AHPC, 1983). These data may suggest that fewer states are using ceilings or may reflect differences in reporting. In any case, states are using both approaches to limit reimbursement to nursing facilities.

Methods of establishing ceilings for cost centers also vary by state. For example, Oklahoma uses 24 cost centers, with a ceiling of the 60th percentile of the cost experience in each peer group of homes (Spitz, 1981b). In establishing ceilings, states frequently use percentage limitations on actual costs or percentage limitations based on the median level of costs. In 1978, 16 states reported cost limitations on a percentage of median actual costs, while 24 used a percentile of actual costs (AHCA, 1978).

Property costs are also a state discretionary option for Medicaid rate setting. Property costs may be a small proportion of a facility's total costs, but policies relative to depreciation, leases, and interest expenses can have important effects on overall state reimbursement rates. In a study of 66 facilities, Birnhaum and others showed that nursing home property and other nonoperating costs typically accounted for 13 percent of the total facility costs, but that there was substantial variation among facilities (Birnbaum, Lee, Bishop, and Jensen, 1981).

States have the option of allowing nursing homes to use either straight-line or accelerated depreciation methods. States using straight-line depreciation for Medicaid reimbursement contend that this policy reduces costs (Spitz, 1981b). However, nursing home providers prefer accelerated methods to allow for faster recovery of investment outlays and for additional interest income (Grimaldi, 1982). Grimaldi's (1982) argument that accelerated depreciation schedules are not significantly higher than straight-line depreciation is based on data from a 1981 Washington state study which showed that accelerated depreciation resulted in a rate of interest only one percentage point higher than rates calculated using straight-line depreciation (McCaffree, 1976). One percentage point could represent a sizable amount of money for states with large Medicaid nursing home expenditures.

Another concern is the time period over which depreciation is calculated. Longer time periods decrease the amount a facility can depreciate each year, while shorter periods increase this amount (Spitz, n.d.). In 1982, 21 states reported reimbursement rate policies imputing a useful lifetime of 40 years to nursing home facilities (IHPP and NGA, 1982). State choice to use 40 or 30 years, for example, affects overall state reimbursement rates.

Assets can be valued on the basis of original or historic costs adjusted for subsequent renovations, replacement costs (cost of rebuilding the facility), market value of the facility (price of the facility on the private market), or an imputed value (state established price independent of cost experience; Spitz, n.d.). For example, Illinois imputes the value based on average cost per bed, adjusted for age and location (Spitz, 1981a). Such policy variations can influence reimbursement rates. The use of historic costs tends to minimize reimbursement, while the use of market value allows for higher asset values and higher reimbursement (Spitz, n.d.; Grimaldi, 1982). New York probably has the most experience with cost-based property reimbursement tied to historic cost and actual debt service (Spitz, 1981a). Spitz (n.d.) recommends to states that the most effective method for controlling the impact of current market value on reimbursement is simply not to recognize it, instead setting the value on a one-time basis, or imputing a cost. In 1978, 45 states used the cost of the present owner as the basis for depreciation. Four states used the original cost of the seller, which is likely to be lower than the present owner cost (AHCA, 1978). By 1983, a telephone survey of state Medicaid agencies found that 24 states used historic costs, 3 used replacement value, 3 used market value, and 9 used other methods (AHPC, 1983).

Interest rate can also be a factor in determining state reimbursement rates. Interest rates vary by the size of the principal borrowed, the interest rate agreed upon, the length of time, the credit-worthiness of the borrower, the loan security, the type of lending institution, whether the facility has loan guarantees, whether there are public bond measures, and by other factors (Spitz, n.d.). Interest-rate allowances may be based upon the rate that borrowers negotiate, or there may be a ceiling at the prevailing interest rate for assets. Some states, such as Massachusetts and Pennsylvania, have imposed limits to discourage excessive borrowing (Grimaldi, 1982). Other states have used the Medicare rate of return (1.5 times the interest rate on short-term certificates in the Hospital Insurance Trust Fund) as the maximum level for reimbursement (Spitz, n.d.).

Leases and rentals constitute another type of cost that states may attempt to control in order to reduce Medicaid costs. In some states, providers have used lease arrangements to circumvent the depreciation and interest-rate allowances. In leaseback arrangements, owners form management corporations and lease the facility from themselves as owners for a fee. This is another way to increase owner profits, since the costs of leases are reimburseable items for Medicaid and Medicare. If rents and leasebacks are financially advantageous, providers have an incentive to develop such systems. Some states have tried to minimize rentals and leases to discourage such leaseback arrangements. Spitz (n.d.) recommends that states not allow reimbursement costs for lease and rental costs. In 1982, 32 states reported that they treat leased and owned facilities in an identical fashion, disallowing costs of leases and rentals (IHPP and NGA, 1982).

Also influencing reimbursement rates are the costs of meeting state and federal licensing and certification requirements (Kurowski and Shaughnessey, 1983). Variations among states in nursing standards and other requirements may have a substantial impact on reimbursement rates. One analysis of nursing homes (Birnbaum et al., 1981) showed both nursing hours per patient day and an index of the provision of rehabilitative services to be highly significant predictors of average operating costs. Birnbaum and others (1981) found that states with stringent life-safety codes and inflexible nurse-staffing requirements also had higher costs. Reimbursement rates are designed to cover cost differentials based on different state requirements for nursing hours per patient day.

State requirements, particularly nursing standards, also affect the level of care provided, with higher professional nursing staff requirements typically required for skilled nursing facilities than for intermediate care facilities. State licensing and certification standards determine the level of care, the type of patients, and the costs. Studies of states suggest that definitions of facility licensing and certification status, and the enforcement of these standards, vary considerably among states (Birnbaum et al., 1981). These variations in standards are expected to result in differential reimbursement rates, with lower ICF reimbursement under Medicaid certification requirements.

State Medicaid programs are required to set reimbursement policies with some relationship to the cost of care, thus requiring periodic adjustments for inflation. Although state reimbursement methodologies have generally been fairly stable over time, most state Medicaid programs adjust their rates for inflation annually, or even semiannually. In 1978, 42 states made annual rate revisions, six made semiannual adjustments, and one made adjustments every third year (ACHA, 1978).

States have several options for making adjustments for inflation, including the consumer price index (CPI), the market basket index (involving only health-related costs), the gross national product (GNP) deflator (a federal inflation index), or the Nursing Home Price Index developed by the U.S. Health Care Financing Administration (HCFA). States have generally been advised to avoid using the CPI because it overestimates some costs (such as housing), underestimates medical care costs, and applies only to metropolitan areas (Spitz, 1981b). Between 1979 and 1981, the CPI was 1-4 percentage points higher than the GNP deflator, and 3.6 percentage points higher than the HCFA index (Spitz and Atkinson, 1982). Spitz and Atkinson (1982) reported that 27 states used the CPI in 1982, 19 used a state composite index (which may include CPI), three used the HCFA nursing home index, and one used the GNP deflator (see also U.S. GAO, 1983). States change their inflation adjustments more frequently than their overall Medicaid reimbursement methods, and such changes significantly affect the rates.

In addition to the factors described above, states have a variety of other policy options in setting rates. Reimbursement rates can be used on size, location, ownership, hospital affiliation, patient characteristics, occupancy rates, and other factors (Bishop, 1980; Schlenker and Shaughnessy, 1981; Birnbaum et al., 1981). Classifying facilities into "class" or peer groups by such characteristics as size is an approach used by some states to assign reimbursement rates. In 1978, 16 states used some type of peer group system to establish reimbursement rates (AHCA, 1978); in 1982, 25 states reported such as approach (IHPP and NGA, 1982). Type of ownership (e.g., for-profit, nonprofit, and public) has been used, as in New York, to allow higher rates to nonprofit facilities than to for-profit facilities. States using this approach may encourage a change in ownership pattern. States that make such distinctions may expect to have higher overall costs than states not making such distinctions (Birnbaum et al., 1981).

State rate setters have also used incentives and disincentives to modify nursing home industry behavior. One of the more popular approaches is to add penalties for low occupancy and/or incentives for high occupancy. The purpose of this approach is to encourage facilities to be more effiicient in their operations under the assumption that caring for larger numbers of patients offers economies of scale. In 1978, 39 states reported a requirement for minimum occupancy levels for all except new facilities (AHCA, 1978). Birnbaum et al. (1981) found that, contrary to expectations, states with occupancy penalties tended to have significantly higher per diem costs—however, this may result from a tendency of states with higher costs to adopt penalty systems. Bishop (1980) argues against occupancy penalties because they may further constrain Medicaid rates and thus impede the access of Medicaid patients to nursing home beds.

Some states have attempted to link reimbursement incentives and disincentives to case mix (term for patient characteristics such as age and disability) and quality of care, as measured by patient outcomes—that is, changes in patient status over given periods of time.[2] Case mix, defined by patient conditions or health problems, is considered to have a major influence on nursing care requirements, staffing requirements, and costs. Heavy patient care requirements are expected to be costly and are thus reimbursed at high rates by some states.[3]

Illinois, West Virginia, and Ohio have implemented Medicaid reimbursement systems for nursing homes that take both quality and case mix into consideration through reimbursement incentives and disincentives (Walsh, 1979; Shaughnessy and Kurowski, 1980; Spitz, 1981a). The Massachusetts reimbursement method makes case mix adjustments for proportion of "heavy care" (those patients with greater nursing care needs than the average patient, as defined by the state), for occupancy rates, and for quality of care as measured by state licensing and certification surveys (Harrington, Pardini, Peguillan-Shea, LaLonde-Berg, and Bogaert, 1983). In 1982, 16 states reported tying reimbursement rates to grades of patient disability (IHPP and NGA, 1982). Several demonstrations have tested different methods of linking reimbursement to quality of care incentives (Kane, Bell, Hosek, Riegler, and Kane, 1983; Meiners, Heineman, and Jones, 1982; Willemain, 1983). Tying reimbursement to individual patient characteristics has been expensive for states to administer because such programs require more frequent assessments of individual patients than other reimbursement systems. Such approaches have been recommended as a method of increasing access for Medicaid patients to nursing home beds because facilities would be more willing to take Medicaid patients with heavy care requirements if the facilities are paid higher rates. This approach, however, has a potential for negative effects by giving facilities incentives to increase patient dependency and level of care requirements in order to maximize reimbursement.

One of the more controversial reimbursement issues concerns profit allowances for proprietary facilities (U.S. HCFA, 1981b). Some states place ceilings on Medicaid reimbursement, without placing limits on profit rates in profit-making facilities. Others allow no profit making for Medicaid—in 1982, 15 states reported no profit allowances in their reimbursement rates (IHPP and HGA, 1982).

Types of Medicaid profit allowances vary considerably. They include return on equity profits, return on assets, owner-operator salaries, and capital gains. Some states use the Medicare guidelines, which provide for a specific amount of return on equity. Contrasting such methods to the regulation of the rate of return on total assets, McCaffree (1976) notes the difficulty of identifying and monitoring return on equity. He also points out the incentives under this arrangement for borrowers to borrow, and for lenders to lend, above market rates.

Many states have limited owner-operator salaries as a means of reducing excessive profit taking. In 1982, 39 states reported some type of cap on administrative salaries (IHPP and HGA, 1982). Other states have attempted to recapture excessive capital gains—in states without recapture provisions, frequent sales and real estate transactions may be used by facility operators to increase reimbursement rates and profits. During 1982, California and Texas used recent reports of high profits for nursing homes (reported at 41% and 34% return, respectively, on net equity) as rationales for not increasing reimbursement rates (Harrington, Pardini, Peguillan-Shea, Wallace, LaLonde-Berg, and Newcomer, 1983; Harrington, Wood, LaLonde-Berg, and Bogaert, 1983). Recently, state Medicaid programs have increased efforts to control profit margins or are refusing to pay for profits entirely (Spitz and Atkinson, 1982).

In summary, public reimbursement policies for nursing homes are complex and include a large number of variables and policy choices. Medicaid reimbursement policies for nursing homes, under broad federal guidelines, provide many discretionary options to the states, with large variations among them. In direct contrast, policies for Medicare are developed for the nation as a whole. Although the implementation of the policies may be applied somewhat differently by fiscal intermediaries throughout the country, state discretion is minimal.

Trends in State Medicaid Reimbursement Methods

Reimbursement methods can be classified in various ways as shown in Table 6.1. One of the most important considerations is whether reimbursement is paid on a retrospective or on a prospective basis.

A retrospective system uses a reimbursement formula based on the expenditures incurred, paying providers for services after they have been provided without limited what will be paid before the costs are incurred. Such a reimbursement system tends to encourage facilities to increase their expenditures in order to increase their revenues from Medicaid or Medicare. The system invites providers to expand staff, raise wages, make capital improvements, and spend on other activities that are fully reimbursed (Grimaldi, 1982). Retrospective systems use cost-based payment methods, which cover general expenditures with few limitations (U.S. DHHS, 1982; Coelen and Sullivan, 1981). Reim-

Type of Reimbursement	Description	Advantages/ Disadvantages
Retrospective method	Reimbursement is paid for services after the service is provided based on the expense incurred	Encourages facilities to increase their expenditures in order to increase their revenues
Prospective method	Reimbursement rates are set in advance before services are rendered based on some formula of past expenditures	Encourages facilities to spend less than the rate set
Facility-specific system	Reimbursement rates are set for each individual facility on either a retrospective or prospective basis	Allows wide differentials in rates based on the historic expenditures of each facility and penalizes efficient facilities
Class-based system (flat rates)	Reimbursement rates are set for groups or types of facilities such as by size or ownership or geographic location	Standardizes rates. Encourages greater similarity in rates. Rewards lower cost facilities

Figure 6.2:   Definitions of Reimbursement Systems

bursement under retrospective systems, however, may be limited by ceilings on cost centers and by constraints on allowable costs.

Under prospective reimbursement methods, payment rates are determined before services are provided and funds expended (Grimaldi, 1982; Dowling, 1974). Such advance determination of rates gives providers an incentive to keep expenditures within the amounts allowed. This may, however, cause providers to reduce services and quality, so that different types of monitoring systems are needed for prospective than for retrospective systems. Some states have developed modified reimbursement systems, sometimes called "combination" systems, that include aspects of both prospective and retrospective reimbursement. Such an approach may include setting a rate in advance but making retrospective adjustments for selected costs. Studies of prospective reimbursement for hospitals have shown states with mandatory programs to be effective in controlling costs (Coelen and Sullivan, 1981; U.S. DHHS, 1982; U.S. GAO, 1980). Prospective nursing home reimbursement systems for Medicaid are likewise intended to control costs.

A second dimension of reimbursement methodology for both retrospective and prospective systems is whether facilities are reimbursed on an individual basis or on a class (or "flat rate") basis. States that use individual-facility rates apply a cost formula to each facility. Flat rates are characteristically determined for peer groups of facilities, or for all facilities in a state, using a method of estimating fixed and variable costs over a designated time period for an expected number of patient days. Flat rates impose limits on the overall expenditures but vary according to the formulas used and the variables taken into account. Such rate systems are instituted by states with the expectation that they will allow for rates to be controlled to a greater extent and with lower administrative costs than under facility-specific systems.

Table 6.1 shows a summary distribution of different types of state Medicaid nursing home reimbursement methodologies from 1978 through 1983. In 1983, 28 states in the U.S. (including the District of Columbia) reported using a prospective facility-specific reimbursement system for skilled nursing facilities; 6 reported a prospective class system; 10 reported a retrospective facility specific system; and 6 reported a combination of systems. During the 1978–1983 period, reimbursement for intermediate care facilities (ICF) was generally the same as for skilled nursing facilities (SNFs). However, 4 states (Iowa, Kentucky, New Hampshire, and Tennessee) had prospective facility-specific reimbursement for intermediate care but retrospective reimbursement for skilled nursing care. In all of these states, the majority of the beds were ICF care, with SNF care representing only a small percentage of the total. The states all have federally approved reimbursement systems that are reasonably cost related.

The pattern of Medicaid reimbursement methods used by states changed somewhat between 1978 and 1983, especially in the last two years of the period, and these changes show a clear shift away from retrospective reimbursement. Table 6.2 shows two state changes in 1979, one state change during 1981, four state changes in 1982, and two changes in 1983 for SNF reimbursement systems. Six of these changes involved the adoption of an alternative system in place of a retrospective system; none involved a shift to a retrospective system. The changing of reimbursement systems by nine states over a five-year period involved large expenditures of funds and may have an important effect on providers of service. Significant changes in Medicaid reim-

TABLE 6.1   SNF and ICF State Medicaid Reimbursement Systems, 1978-1983

| | Number of States with Reimbursement System | | | | | |
Reimbursement System	1978	1979	1980	1981	1982	1983
Skilled nursing						
Retrospective	18	16	16	16	12	10
Prospective						
Facility-specific	25	26	26	25	27	28
Prospective class	4	4	4	5	6	6
Combination	3	4	4	4	5	6
Intermediate care						
Retrospective	14	13	13	13	9	7
Prospective						
Facility-specific	29	29	29	28	30	31
Propsective class	4	4	4	5	6	6
Combination	3	4	4	4	5	6

SOURCE: Adapted from AHPC (1984).
*Missing data for South Carolina were supplemented with data adapted from the American Health Care Association (AHCA), *How Medicaid Pays for Long Term Care.* Washington, DC: AHCA, 1978.

bursement systems are related to increasing state fiscal pressures requiring severe cost constraints in state Medicaid programs.

Trends in State Medicaid Reimbursement Rates

Medicaid rates are the composite (or direct outcome) of state reimbursement policies. Reimbursement rates for nursing home services are generally developed on a cost per diem basis, rather than by cost per length of stay as with some hospital reimbursement methods. State Medicaid rate data are difficult to summarize because states vary considerably in their reporting forms. Some states report weighted average rates for facilities by type, while other states report unweighted averages, or the maximum rates for facilities of various types. Some states have flat rates for facilities of a given type. States also make distinctions based on other factors; for example, one state has a higher rate for government-owned facilities. Other states have higher rates for urban areas.

Table 6.2 shows the national averages of state per diem SNF and ICF reimbursement rates for each year from 1978 to 1983.[4] In 1978,

TABLE 6.2   U.S. Average of State Medicaid, SNF and ICF per Diem Rates
and Changes, 1978-1983 (in dollars)

| | Average State Medicaid per Diem Rates* | | | |
| | SNF | | ICF | |
Rates for Year	Average Rate	Number of States Reporting	Average Rate	Number of States Reporting
1978	$27.33	24	$21.64	27
1979	33.56	46	26.60	46
1980	36.76	47	29.63	47
1981	40.67	50	32.53	50
1982	44.30	47	34.61	45
1983	47.75	38	35.37	38
Average state changes				
Dollar change, 1979-1982	$11.31	44	$ 8.51	42
Percentage change,				
1979-1982	37.8	44	32.7	42

SOURCE: Adapted from AHPC (1984).**
*Averages calculated across states based on state weighted average rates.
**Missing data on rates supplemented with data adapted from La Jolla Management
Corporation (1982).

the national average of state Medicaid SNF reimbursement rates was
$27.33 and $21.64 for ICF services. In 1983, the national average
of state rates for SNF services was $47.75 and for ICF facilities was
$35.37. Nursing home rates show considerable variation across states
with Indiana reporting $28.72 for ICF rates for 1983 compared with
$119.31 in Alaska (not shown in the table) (AHPC, 1984). The inter-
state variation might be explained by reimbursement systems as well
as by other factors.

Changes in reimbursement rates can be examined both by comparing
percentage increases between years, and by considering absolute changes
over time. Table 6.2 shows average state changes in rates for 1978
through 1983, but since the sample size is small for 1978 and for
1983, the change rates for the period of 1979–1982 are compared.
During the three-year period, SNF rates showed an average increase
of $11.31 (38%); ICF rates, an average increase of $8.51 (33%). Inter-
state variation on these change measures might be explained by the
reimbursement systems, as well as other factors.

Relationship Between Reimbursement Methods and Rates

Although average nursing home rates are influenced by state policy, rates cannot be seen as completely manipulable factors. Nursing home rates must be set taking into consideration nursing home costs, customary levels of reimbursement, and some level of cooperation by nursing home operators. Moreover, state rate setting generally takes place in an environment of strong industry influence, including lobbying by one or more nursing home associations. Thus, it is reasonable to expect that the form of reimbursement system used would influence rate setting, especially the state's ability to contain increases in rates. Likewise, states experiencing rapid increases in rates might be expected to adopt reimbursement systems that would aid in containing rate increases.

Reimbursement rates and changes in rates can be considered by reimbursement system. Table 6.3 presents the U.S. average of state Medicaid SNF and ICF reimbursement rates by reimbursement system for 1978 to 1983. The average rates are somewhat higher for states with retrospective reimbursement systems—SNF rates for each year 1979–82, varying between $8 and $13 higher and ICF rates between $9 and $19 higher.

There is evidence that rate increases are larger for state with retrospective systems than for those with prospective facility-specific systems, although the differences are not as great as might have been expected.[5] States with combination systems appear to experience rate increases as great as or greater than those for retrospective systems.

A recent study by Harrington and Swan (1984) shows that prospective facility-specific, prospective class, and combination systems had significantly lower rates than did retrospective systems. States that changed from retrospective to prospective systems in the period 1978–82 had significantly lower rates than did those maintaining retrospective systems. States with prospective reimbursement systems, particularly facility-specific reimbursement, had significantly lower increases in SNF rates over the 1979–81 period. These findings indicate that (1) prospective reimbursement systems allow states to constrain nursing home rates, and (2) retrospective reimbursement states that adopt alternate systems tend to be among those with lower initial rates (Harrington and Swan, 1984).

TABLE 6.3 U.S. Average of State Medicaid SNF and ICF Reimbursement Rates by Reimbursement System, 1978-1983

Reimbursement System for: *Skilled Nursing*	*SNF Reimbursement Rates (in dollars)*						*1979-1982 Changes**	
	1978	*1979*	*1980*	*1981*	*1982*	*1983*	*Dollar*	*Percentage*
Retrospective	25.55	38.97	41.54	46.25	55.77	66.65	13.07	43.7
Throughout 1978-1982	27.82	40.77	43.40	48.52	55.77	66.65	13.62	43.3
Changed by 1982	18.74	31.78	34.73	39.43			11.06	45.3
Prospective								
Facility-specific	28.39	31.78	35.37	38.57	42.28	44.90	10.29	33.5
Prospective class	24.16	25.86	28.81	34.04	34.06	37.62	7.80	31.6
Combination	34.19	31.06	37.14	39.77	41.14	42.53	15.57	51.9

Intermediate Care	*ICF Reimbursement Rates (in dollars)*						*1979-1982 Changes**	
	1978	*1979*	*1980*	*1981*	*1982*	*1983*	*Dollar*	*Percentage*
Retrospective	21.45	31.52	35.99	38.42	50.90	55.66	11.45	35.8
Throughout 1978-1982	24.19	34.15	40.15	43.46			13.18	36.8
Changed by 1982	15.98	23.63	24.90	27.08			7.41	33.3
Prospective								
Facility-specific	21.93	25.24	28.02	30.64	31.96	33.28	7.74	32.1
Prospective class	19.16	21.82	23.80	28.51	28.32	30.22	5.53	25.7
Combination	25.43	25.59	29.68	31.70	33.59	34.03	9.11	37.1

SOURCE: Adapted from AHPC (1984).
*The change rates were calculated for 44 states for the period of 1979-1982, because the number of states with available data was too small for 1978 and for 1983.
**Missing data were supplemented with data adapted from La Jolla Management (1982) and by AHCA (1978).

143

The historical data regarding reimbursement rates and systems are important, but cannot tell the whole story or predict what will happen in the future as states introduce new systems. Since retrospective reimbursement systems do not allow for cost constraints as well as do existing prospective reimbursement systems and have been largely abandoned by state Medicaid programs, the question for the future may be the relative merits of class and facility-specific prospective systems.

Nursing Home Expenditures

The test of cost constraint is not so much in the restraint of rate increases as in the control of expenditure increases. The bottom line for state policymakers is controlling overall costs, which involves restraining the number of units of service delivered as well as reimbursement rates. A meaningful measure of state Medicaid expenditures for nursing homes would be SNF and ICF services per patient day. Unfortunately, there are inadequate data on numbers of days covered by Medicaid reimbursement. For this reason, total expenditures per recipient per year are examined.

Table 6.4 gives expenditures per recipient and changes between 1978 and 1982 by reimbursement system. Reflecting a policy shift in utilization of services from SNF and ICF care, overall ICF expenditures increased at a much more rapid rate (103%) than did such expenditures per recipient (59%), while total SNF expenditures increased at a lower rate (29%) than did such expenditures per recipient (51%). There is substantial variation among the states on these measures, however, and in some states the increase in total expenditures was greater for SNF than for ICF care. Although SNF rates are generally higher than ICF rates, ICF expenditures per recipient average higher than SNF expenditures per recipient, because ICF services are often of longer duration than are SNF services.

Since there is considerable inter-state variation on changes in SNF and ICF expenditures per recipient, the question is whether these can be accounted for in part by the types of reimbursement systems employed by states. Given the findings that alternate reimbursement systems allowed for constraints on rate increases, it might be expected that these same alternative reimbursement methodologies would also allow for restraints on increases in costs per recipient. It should be

TABLE 6.4   U.S. Medicaid SNF and ICF Expenditures per Recipient and
Changes Over Time by Reimbursement System, 1978-1982

Reimbursement for: Skilled Nursing, 1978	Total % Change 1978-1982	Medicaid SNF Expenditures		% Change 1978-1982	Sample Size
		Dollars Per Recipient			
		1978	1982		
State average for U.S.*	29.4	3797**	5331	51.2**	50
Retrospective, 1982	68.1	3793***	6057	91.5	12
Prospective					
Family specific	17.8	3853**	5341	41.6**	25
Prospective class	−13.2	3446	3695	25.6	4
Combination	38.0	3848	5848	53.9	3
Changed from m retrospective, 1978-1982	24.6		4670	25.1	6
Intermediate Care, 1978		Medicaid ICF Expenditures			
State average for U.S.*	102.8	4584**	7089	58.7**	50
Retrospective, 1982	88.6	4970***	9042	79.5	9
Prospective					
Facility specific	102.8	4604**	6823	52.9**	29
Prospective class	46.0	3627	5119	38.2	4
Conbination	159.3	3882	6908	76.5	3
Changed from retrospective, 1978-1982	139.9		6798	59.7	5
Intermediate Care, 1978		Medicaid SNF Plus ICF Expenditures			
State average for U.S.*	74.0	4535**	7149	62.1**	50
Retrospective, 1982	83.2	4824***	8893	86.5	9
Prospective					
Facility specific	70.9	4559**	6931	55.8**	29
Prospective class	52.5	3844	5732	49.8	4
Combination	98.2	3889	7021	80.7	3
Changed from retrospective, 1978-1982	78.2		6488	52.1	5

SOURCES: Adapted for U.S. HCFA (1984) and AHPC (1984).
*States are weighted equally.
**One case is missing for 1978 expenditures per recipient, so also for 1978-1982
change in expenditures per recipient. The N is one less than that stated.
***For change measures and for 1982 expenditures per recipient, states with retro-
spective reimbursement in 1978 are separated into those with such reimbursement in
1982 and those that changed to another system between 1978 and 1982. However,
for 1978 expenditures per recipient, these states are combined into those with
retrospective reimbursement in 1978. The N is 18 for SNF and 14 for ICF reimbursement systems.

noted, however, that constraints on increases in expenditures per diem would not necessarily be translated into increases in expenditures per recipient unless the average days of care per recipient remained constant. An increase in average days of care (length of stay) is especially likely after a shift in utilization away from SNF to ICF care for Medicaid patients, because those remaining in SNF facilities are likely to be patients with heavy nursing needs.

In Table 6.4 it can be seen that the rate of increasing costs in SNF expenditures for the 1978 to 1982 period was much higher in retrospective states (68%) than in prospective-reimbursing states. The picture is somewhat different for ICF expenditures, where increases in retrospective expenditures are slightly lower than those in prospective facility-specific states, although changes appear to be lower for prospective class states. Table 6.4 also gives the breakdowns by ICF reimbursement system for total (SNF and ICF) expenditures. The 1982 expenditures per recipient are $1900 lower for states with prospective facility-specific systems, and $3100 lower for those with prospective class systems, than for states with retrospective systems.

These results suggest that alternative reimbursement systems may allow for restraints on increases in expenditures per recipient. The picture is clouded by the question of changes in average days of care per recipient, and by the shift in many states from SNF toward ICF care for Medicaid patients, but expenditure per recipient differences nevertheless appear by reimbursement system even in the face of these other changes. Overall, then, it would appear that prospective reimbursement states experience much slower increases in nursing home reimbursement per recipient than do retrospective states.

Conclusion

States are given considerable discretion in establishing Medicaid reimbursement policies for nursing home care. State policymakers are utilizing reimbursement policies to control overall Medicaid nursing home expenditures and to achieve public policy objectives to improve access and quality. While public nursing home reimbursement policies for Medicaid are extremely complex, policymakers are using multiple means to reduce costs.

A strong trend toward adoption of prospective reimbursement methods is one major effort by states to control costs. While trends in state reimbursement rates have been toward steady increases, there is evidence that cost containment efforts are showing some results, even though the variability in policies and rates across states are great. While adoption of cost containment policies appear to be slowing the growth of overall nursing home expenditures, states must balance their need for controlling costs against the effects of such controls on reducing quality and access to care.

All of the existing state reimbursement systems are based on fee-for-service payments on a per diem basis. For-fee-service per diem payment gives providers incentives to increase the number of services offered and the number of days of care provided. For the most part, state Medicaid programs have not examined the feasibility of paying for care on a prepaid capitated basis.

At this time, new demonstration projects for long term care services on a prepaid capitated basis, entitled Social Health Maintenance Organizations (S/HMOs), show great promise. These demonstrations, established by HCFA and Brandeis University, are being closely evaluated during the next three years to determine the effects of this type of reimbursement on utilization, quality, access, and costs of the program. Such demonstrations may prove not only to control costs and nursing home utilization but also to ensure access and quality. Approaches that address changes in both the delivery and financing of nursing home services to correct the current problems in the delivery of nursing home care are more attractive than current efforts by policymakers to fine-tune the fee-for-service reimbursement system (see Chapter 12 for discussion).

At the same time, states are establishing new community-based waiver programs to establish alternatives to nursing home care (see Chapter 9). Such programs propose to offer alternatives to nursing homes, but have not developed reimbursement alternatives to the standard fee-for-service arrangements. Until new approaches that go beyond the fee-for-service arrangement, state reimbursement policies will probably only have limited impacts on controlling the overall growth of nursing home expenditures.

Unfortunately, most efforts to control costs are not combined with quality assurance and access policies. As a result, the trend for nursing homes to continue high profits and further take-over by large proprietary chains continues. Quality of care problems are still considered by many in the field to be serious. Increasing reimbursement rates would not necessarily have any impact on improving either quality or access for those on Medicaid.

The efforts to tie reimbursement to quality of care and patient mix are of interest. These efforts unfortunately are limited to fee-for-service reimbursement and have yet to show that they can control utilization or quality. Other efforts to contract for Medicaid beds would address the access problems. Quality may be improved by stricter regulation with ties to reimbursement.

Notes

1. ICF-MR services are used predominantly by the retarded, with only 3 percent of the total 1982 Medicaid ICF-MR expenditures going for services to the aged (U.S. HCFA, 1984).

2. For discussions of the concept of quality care, see Chekryn and Roos (1979) and Brook and Avery (1977).

3. For discussions of the concept of case mix, see Brook and Avery, 1977; McAuliffe, 1979; Brook, 1979; Donabedian, 1980; Shaughessy and Kurowski, 1980; Willemain, 1980.

4. The AHPC telephone survey data (1984) were collected in part because of a concern with the accuracy of the existing data on reimbursement rates and methods, and in an effort to build as complete a data set as possible for the period 1978 through 1983. As expected, the AHPC telephone survey data do differ from the earlier data collected on reimbursement systems and rates reported by La Jolla Management Corporation (1982) and with that on reimbursement methods reported by the National Governors' Association (1982) and the American Health Care Association (1978). For reimbursement systems, the telephone survey data differ in seven states from that previously available; and for reimbursement rates, the 1979–81 SNF data differ from the previously available figures for 27 states, and the ICF data for 24 states. Where data were unavailable from the AHPC telephone survey, the "best available data" were taken from the La Jolla data and included in the figures reported in Table 6.2.

5. States with higher base rates would be expected to have greater dollar increases in rates and smaller percentage increases in rates, all else being equal. Thus, in order to test for differences between systems, the change measures should be adjusted for the base rates.

References

Aging Health Policy Center (AHPC). Unpublished telephone survey of state Medicaid agencies. San Francisco, CA: AHPC, University of California, 1983.

Aging Health Policy Center (AHPC). Unpublished telephone survey of states, Medicaid reimbursement policy. San Francisco, CA: AHPC, University of California, 1984.

American Health Care Association (AHCA). *How Medicaid Pays for Long Term Care*. Washington, DC: American Health Care Association, 1978.

Birnbaum, H., A. J. Lee, C. Bishop, and G. Jensen. *Public Pricing of Nursing Home Care*. Cambridge, MA: Abt Books, 1981.

Bishop, C. E. "Nursing Home Cost Studies and Reimbursement Issues." *Health Care Financing Review*, 1, No. 3, (Winter 1980), 47–64.

Brook, R. H. "Studies of Process-Outcome Correlations in Medical Care Evaluations." *Medical Care*, 17, No. 8 (August 1979), 868–873.

Brook, R. H. and A. D. Avery. *Quality of Medical Care Using Outcome Measures*. DHEW Pub. No. HRA-77-3175. Rockville, MD: U.S. Department of Health, Education, and Welfare, 1977.

Chekryn, J., and L. L. Roos. "Auditing the Process of Care in a New Geriatric Unit." *Journal of the American Geriatrics Society*, 27, No. 3 (March 1979), 107–111.

Coelen, C., and D. Sullivan. "An Analysis of the Effects of Prospective Reimbursement Programs on Hospital Expenditures." *Health Care Financing Review*, 2, No. 3 (Winter 1981), 1–53.

Commerce Clearing House (CCH). Medicare-Medicaid Administrative and Reimbursement Reform Act of 1979 (H. R. 934, December 12, 1979). In *Medicare and Medicaid Guide*. Chicago, IL: CCH, 1981–1984.

Donabedian, A. *The Definition of Quality and Approaches to Its Assessment*. Ann Arbor, MI: Health Administration Press, 1980.

Dowling, W. L. "Prospective Reimbursement of Hospitals." *Inquiry*, 11, No. 3 (September 1974), 163.

Feder, J., and W. Scanlon. "Regulating the Bed Supply in Nursing Homes." *Milbank Memorial Fund Quarterly/Health and Society*, 58, No. 1 (Winter 1980), 54–88.

Gibson, R. M., D. R. Waldo, and K. R. Levit. "National Health Expenditures, 1982." *Health Care Financing Review*, 5, No. 1 (Fall 1983), 1–31.

Grimaldi, P. L. *Medicaid Reimbursement of Nursing-Home Care*. Washington, DC: American Enterprise Institute for Public Policy Research, 1982.

Harrington, C., A. Pardini, V. Peguillan-Shea, G. R. LaLonde-Berg, and M. P. Bogaert. *Massachusetts: State Discretionary Policies and Services in the Medicaid, Social Services, and Supplemental Security Income Programs*. San Francisco, CA: Aging Health Policy Center, University of California, 1983.

Harrington, C., A. Pardini, V. Peguillan-Shea, S. P. Wallace, G. R. LaLonde-Berg, and R. J. Newcomer. *California: State Discretionary Policies and Services and Services in the Medicaid, Social Services, and Supplemental Security Income Programs*. San Francisco, CA: Aging Health Policy Center, University of California, 1983.

Harrington, C., and J. Swan. "Medicaid Reimbursement Policies, Rates, and Changes in Rates." *Health Care Financing Review*, in press (1984).

Harrington, C., J. B. Wood, G. R. La-Londe-Berg, and M. P. Bogaert. *Texas: State Discretionary Policies and Services in the Medicaid, Social Services, and Supplemental Security Income Programs*. San Francisco, CA: Aging Health Policy Center, University of California, 1983.

Intergovernmental Health Policy Project (IHPP), and National Governors' Association (NGA) State Medicaid Information Center. *Recent and Proposed Changes in State Medicaid Programs: A Fifty State Survey*. Washington, DC: IHPP, 1982.

Kane, R. L., R. M. Bell, S. D. Hosek, S. Z. Riegler, and R. A. Kane. *Outcome-Based Reimbursement for Nursing Home Care.* Santa Monica, CA: Rand, 1983.

Kurowski, B. D., and P. W. Shaughnessey. "The Measurement and Assurance of Quality." In *Long-Term Care: Perspectives From Research and Demonstration.* Ed. R. J. Vogel and H. C. Palmer. Washington, DC: U.S. Health Care Financing Administration, 1983.

La Jolla Management Corporation. *Medicaid Program Characteristics: Summary Tables.* Volume 1. Washington, DC: U.S. Health Care Financing Administration, Office of Research and Demonstrations, 1982.

McAuliffe, W. E. "Response to Dr. Brook." *Medical Care,* 17, No. 8 (August 1979), 847–877.

McCaffree, K. M. *A Study of Alternative Depreciation Methods and Their Impact on the Rates of Return of Equity Capital and Reimbursement Levels for Nursing Home Care.* Seattle, WA: Battelle Human Affairs Research Center, 1976.

Meiners, M. R., G. D. Heinemann, and B. J. Jones. "An Evaluation of Nursing-Home Payments Designed to Encourage Appropriate Care for the Chronically Ill: Some Preliminary Findings." Paper Presented to the American Economic Association, New York, December 1982.

National Governors' Association (NGA). The State Medicaid Program Information Center. *A Catalogue of State Medicaid Program Changes.* Washington, DC: NGA, 1982.

Scanlon, W. J. "Nursing Home Utilization Patterns: Implications for Policy." *Journal of Health Politics, Policy and Law,* 4, No. 4 (Winter 1980a), 619–641.

———. "A Theory of the Nursing Home Market." *Inquiry,* 17, No. 2 (Spring 1980b), 25–41.

Schlenker, R., and P. Shaughnessy. *A Framework for Analyzing Nursing Home Cost, Case Mix and Quality Interrelationships.* Working Paper No. 7. Denver, CO: Center for Health Services Research, University of Colorado Health Sciences Center, 1981.

Shaughnessy, P., and B. Kurowski. *Quality Assurance Through Reimbursement.* Working Paper No. 8. Denver, CO: Center for Health Services Research, University of Colorado Health Sciences Center, 1980.

Spitz, B. *Medicaid Nursing Home Reimbursement: New York, Illinois, California Case Studies.* Baltimore, MD: U.S. Health Care Financing Administration, 1981a.

———. *State Guide to Medicaid Cost Containment.* Washington, DC: Intergovernmental Health Policy Project, Center for Pólicy Research, National Governors' Association, 1981b.

———. *State Options for Reimbursing Nursing Home Capital.* Washington, DC: Urban Institute, n.d.

Spitz, B., and G. Atkinson. *Nursing Homes, Hospitals and Medicaid: Reimbursement Policy Adjustments 1981–82.* Washington, DC: National Governors' Association, 1982.

Spitz, B., G. Engquist-Seidenberg, F. Teitelbaum, and R. Curtis. *State Guide to Medicaid Cost Containment.* Washington, DC: Center for Policy Research, Office of Research Studies, National Governors' Association, 1980.

U.S. Department of Health and Human Services (DHHS), Office of the Secretary. "Hospital Prospective Payment for Medicare." A Report to Congress Required by the Tax Equity and Fiscal Responsibility Act of 1982. Washington, DC: U.S. Government Printing Office, 1982.

U.S. General Accounting Office (GAO). *Medicaid and Nursing Home Care: Cost Increases and the Need for Services Are Creating Problems for the States and the Elderly.* Report to the Chairman of the Subcommittee on Health and the Environment, Committee on Energy and Commerce, House of Representatives. Washington, DC: U.S. GAO, 1983.

———. *Rising Hospital Costs Can Be Restrained by Regulating Payments and Improving Management.* Report to the Congress by the Comptroller General of the United States. Washington, DC: U.S. GAO, 1980.

U.S. Health Care Financing Administration (HCFA). *An Overview of Medicaid Nursing Home Reimbursement in Seven States.* Health Care Financing Grants and Contracts Report. Office of Research, Demonstrations, and Statistics, Washington, DC: U.S. Department of Health and Human Services, 1981a.

———. *Profits, Growth and Reimbursement Systems in the Nursing Home Industry.* Washington, DC: U.S. Department of Health and Human Services, 1981b.

———. Medicaid Program Data Branch. *National Medicaid Statistics: Fiscal Years 1975 to 1982.* State 2082 Tables data tape. Baltimore, MD: U.S. Department of Health and Human Services, 1984.

U.S. National Center for Health Statistics (NCHS), and A. Sirrocco. "Nursing and Related Care Homes as Reported From the 1980 NMFI Survey." *Vital Statistics, Series 14,* No. 29. DHHS Pub. No. (PHS)84-1824. Hyattsville, MD: U.S. Department of Health and Human Services, December, 1983.

U.S. Public Law 92-603. *Social Security Amendments of 1972.* Washington, DC: U.S. Government Printing Office, 1972.

U.S. Public Law 96-499. *Omnibus Reconciliation Act of 1980.* Washington, DC: U.S. Government Printing Office, 1980.

Walsh, T. J. "Patient-Related Reimbursement for Long-Term Care." In *Reform and Regulation in Long-Term Care.* Ed. V. LaPorte and J. Rubin. New York: Praeger, 1979.

Willemain, T. R. "Nursing Home Levels of Care: Reimbursement of Resident Specific Costs." *Health Care Financing Review,* 2, No. 2 (Fall 1980), 47–52.

———. "Survey-based Indices for Nursing Home Quality Incentive Reimbursement." *Health Care Financing Review,* 4, No. 3 (March 1983), 83–90.

CHAPTER 7

INSTITUTIONAL LONG TERM CARE SERVICES

Charlene Harrington
James H. Swan

In the United States, the term "long term care services" has often been synonymous with the concept of institutional services (i.e., nursing home services) as observed in Chapter 1. This misnomer occurs in part because nursing home services represent a major proportion of the total public expenditures for long term care services. Institutional long term care services are provided primarily by nursing homes, although some general hospitals and chronic disease hospitals also provide long term care services.

Institutional care is the subject of intense public debate for many reasons, including the rapid growth in overall expenditures, complaints about poor quality of care, and an expanding demand for services beyond the supply of beds. The industry has grown to the point that in 1982 the nation spent 27 billion dollars on nursing home services representing 9.5 percent of total personal health care dollars spent in the U.S. that year. A fiscal crisis in the Medicaid program at both federal and state levels has focused intense attention on nursing home expenditures (U.S. CBO, 1977; U.S. HCFA, 1981). Problems in regulating quality of institutional care are also of concern to state and federal officials as well as to the public. As public financing has become available, concern for improving the quality of institutional care has grown. Others were interested in limiting state funds, public policymakers were brought into conflict with providers and consumers.

Authors' Note: The research on which this chapter is based was funded by the National Center for Health Services (Research Grant No. HS04042) and the Health Care Financing Administration (Grant No. 18-P9762019).

A broad overview is needed to understand the nature of the institutional long term care problem and state approaches to it. This chapter discusses the growth of institutional long term care services in the U.S., and considers state variations and changes in supply over time. Factors that influence the supply and demand of nursing home beds are identified. Of particular importance are those policies that states employ in an attempt to control the growth of institutional long term care beds.

Historical Background

The nursing home industry is a multibillion dollar business in the United States, with one of the highest growth rates in expenditures among all health services. In 1980, there were about 23,000 nursing homes in the country serving 1.54 million residents (U.S. NCHS, 1983). Most of these residents are old and disabled. Although only about 5 percent of the total aged population is institutionalized at any point in time, one in five individuals living past the age of 65 will spend some time in a nursing home (Vladeck, 1980).

Nursing homes were a small cottage industry that began to receive a stable source of income after 1935 when the Old Age and Survivors Insurance and the Old Age Assistance programs were enacted, providing cash assistance to older people (Waldman, 1983; Birnbaum, Lee, Bishop, and Jensen, 1981; Vladeck, 1980). Medicaid and Medicare programs established in 1965 provided a steady source of income for nursing homes and thus encouraged the subsequent rapid growth in supply of beds. The growth rate in U.S. nursing home beds was 197 percent for the 1963–1980 period (U.S. NCHS, 1965; 1983). The primary source of financing shifted from 80 percent private funding in 1960 to 56 percent public funding in 1982 (Birnbaum et al., 1981; Gibson, Waldo, and Levit, 1983).

Levels of Nursing Home Care

Four types of nursing home care can be distinguished: skilled nursing, intermediate care, intermediate care for the mentally retarded, and personal care. The National Center for Health Statistics (NCHS) defines a skilled nursing facility (SNF) as an institution in which 50 percent or more of the residents receive nursing care during the week and where at least one full-time registered nurse (RN) or licensed practical nurse (LPN) is employed (U.S. NCHS, 1979). An intermediate care facility (ICF) can be defined as one in which some residents, but fewer than 50 percent, receive some nursing care during the week and where at least one full-time RN or LPN is employed (U.S. NCHS, 1979). A personal care home (sometimes called boarding, domiciliary care, or residentual care home) is one in which some residents receive nursing care during the week; no full-time RN or LPN is employed; and administration of medicines or supervision of self-administered medicines or assistance with activities of daily living is provided (U.S. NCHS, 1979). Intermediate care facilities for the mentally retarded (ICF-MRs) are designed to provide care and training in activities of daily living and social skills to the mentally retarded and those persons with related conditions. No specific nursing staff ratios are required.

The current classification system for residents and services fills three purposes: identifying level of care needs for residents; identifying the level of care that providers are authorized to provide; and allowing for public payments to vary according to the type of service offered and the residents served (Bishop, Plough, and Willemain, 1980).

Facilities are licensed by states, and they must receive certification in order to receive Medicare and Medicaid patients and payments. Licensure is the process by which states grant organizations or individuals permission to operate, after meeting predetermined state qualifications (Kurowski and Shaughnessy, 1983). Certification allows facilities to be reimbursed by Medicare and Medicaid, after they have been surveyed and found to meet specific federal criteria called "conditions of participation." The conditions are generally based on structural requirements intended to ensure the capacity to provide adequate care—such as availability of certain services, educational requirements of the staff, minimal staffing patterns, and fire and safety codes (Kurowski and Shaughnessy, 1983).

Medicaid and Medicare standards for certification require that SNFs offer continuous skilled nursing services, but no acute care that requires hospitalization. ICF care is not paid for or certified by Medicare, but is an optional service in the Medicaid program. The ICF program was first established in 1967 for payments under the cash assistance titles of the Social Security Act. In 1971 ICFs were authorized for Medicaid coverage for the aged, blind, and disabled and the mentally retarded (Dunlop, 1979). Medicaid established for ICFs similar but lower standards than for SNFs, and set ICF reimbursement not to exceed 90 percent of SNF reimbursement (Dunlop, 1979; Waldman, 1983). Both Medicare and Medicaid prohibit certification of and reimbursement to personal care homes, because they do not offer professional nursing services.

The Medicare program was designed to provide skilled nursing for a limited period of time to persons recently discharged from a hospital. The original term for this category of care was "extended care," limited to individuals who spent three or more days in a hospital, who transferred to a nursing home within 14 days of discharge from the hospital, and who received a maximum of 100 days of care. After the program was established, the utilization of extended care expanded rapidly. In response, the Medicare program enacted new restrictive regulations in 1969 that narrowed the definition of skilled nursing (Vladeck, 1980; Waldman, 1983). In 1972, Medicare extended care facilities were reclassified as skilled nursing facilities, and a single set of standards was developed for SNFs by Medicare and Medicaid (Vladeck, 1980; Waldman, 1983). Recent changes in Medicare legislation removed the three-day hospitalization requirement, among other requirements. Even so, less than 2 percent of all Medicare expenditures are for skilled nursing services (Gibson et al., 1983).

The ICF program for the Mentally Retarded (ICF-MR) has been rapidly expanded within the last five years by many state Medicaid programs. Some states have their own licensing requirements for ICF-MRs while others simply use the federal certification requirements for ICF-MRs, in conjunction with ICF licensing.

The states have considerable discretion in designating which facilities will be licensed and certified as skilled or as intermediate care. After the ICF program was established, in fact, many states reclassified patients and facilities from SNF to ICF in a somewhat arbitrary fashion, principally to reduce costs to the Medicaid program (Vladeck, 1980). Intermediate care facilities now represent roughly half of the nation's nursing homes.

Patient misclassification and inappropriate placement are widespread problems. The General Accounting Office reported that 40 percent of SNF patients did not need skilled nursing care (U.S. GAO, 1972). In 1977, the Congressional Budget Office (U.S. CBO, 1977) reported that 10-20 percent of SNF patients and 20-40 percent of ICF patients were not placed at the appropriate level (See also U.S. Senate, 1977-78; Liu and Mossey, 1980; U.S. NCHS, 1979; U.S. HCFA, 1980).

Other studies show inconsistencies in patient classification among and within states (CRA, 1976). Certain ICFs in some states are considered to be more like SNFs in other states in terms of the level of care needs of residents. The percentage of patients in SNFs compared to ICFs varies considerably among states, in part because the definitions and standards are not uniform. State discretionary policies clearly play an important role in the type of patients and facilities classified as ICF and SNF. Various studies have confirmed that SNFs have higher expenditures than do ICFs, but that this differential varies considerably among states (Birnbaum et al., 1981; Mennemeyer, 1979; Bishop, 1979; Bishop, 1980; Reis and Christianson, 1977; Jensen and Birnbaum, 1979; Deane and Skinner, 1978). These differences are expected, since federal requirements for nursing care are less intense for ICF than for SNF services and patients.

Nursing Home Bed Supply

NUMBER OF LICENSED BEDS

National statistics on nursing home beds have not been reported or collected on a regular basis since 1976. The Aging Health Policy Center collected data directly from states to examine trends in bed supply over time.[1] Table 7.1 shows the number of beds by state for the time period of 1978 through 1983. During this period there was an expansion of nursing home beds, and almost all states reporting showed increases. The growth rate, however, slowed substantially in the 1981-83 period in comparison to the 1978-81 period.

BEDS PER POPULATION

Table 7.2 shows that for the period 1978-1981 states range from 20 to 96 beds per 1,000 residents aged 65 and older. States at the low end tend to be those with large younger retirement populations such as Arizona and Florida. Southern states also tended to have lower beds per population. States at the high end of the range tend

TABLE 7.1 Total Nursing Home Beds and Percentage Change by State, 1978-1983*

| | Number of Nursing Home Beds | | | | | | % Change | |
| | Number of Beds in Year | | | | | | | |
State	1978	1979	1980	1981	1982	1983	1978-1981	1981-1983
AL	19,954	20,200	20,522	21,135	21,306	21,476	5.9	1.6
AK	823	823	823	718	821	814	-12.8	13.4
AZ	5,354	5,534	6,197	6,904	7,148	7,834	29.0	13.5
AR	18,548	18,778	19,111	19,838	19,981	20,405	7.0	2.9
CA	110,826	109,329	111,556	111,305	112,922	113,612	0.4	2.1
CO	20,066	18,131	18,305	18,347	18,203	18,030	-8.6	-1.7
CT	24,169	25,713	26,127	26,248	26,221	26,395	8.6	0.6
DE	2,997**	3,305****	3,646	3,787	4,034	4,269	26.4	12.7
DC	1,881**	2,057	1,748	1,793	1,973	2,573	11.2	43.5
FL	34,003	35,479	37,420	37,803	41,578	44,745	11.2	18.4
GA	31,496	32,881	32,881	33,753	36,427	36,689	7.2	8.7
HI	2,171	2,505	2,620	2,623	2,624	2,605	20.8	-0.7
ID	4,454	4,471	4,637	4,805	4,690	4,645	7.9	-3.3
IL	85,888	87,674	87,284	88,095	87,193	87,918	2.6	-0.2
IN	41,010***	42,817	42,445	44,853	50,414	50,078	9.4	11.6
IA	32,125	32,389	32,277	32,964	33,961	34,021	2.6	3.2
KS	26,227	26,020	25,793	26,233	26,322	26,536	0.0	0.5
KY	16,167	17,053	18,154	18,850	18,487	18,884	16.6	0.2
LA	22,541	24,496	25,600	25,293	26,100	26,980	12.2	6.7
ME	8,693	8,812	8,872	8,898	8,919	9,191	2.4	3.3
MD	19,322***	19,529	20,582	21,603	22,259	23,056	11.8	6.7
MA	45,300	47,331	46,830	46,248	46,562	46,050	2.1	-0.4
MI	46,026	46,517	46,477	46,348	46,128	48,275	0.7	4.2
MN	44,492	44,846	45,681	45,658	45,760	44,940	2.6	-1.6
MS	12,399	13,417	12,245	13,455	13,793	14,201	8.5	5.5
MO	34,706	38,051	38,142	40,282	43,173	45,134	16.1	12.0
MT	6,270	6,173	6,267	6,104	6,124	6,317	-2.6	3.5
ND	5,956	6,026	6,277	6,482	6,599	6,757	8.8	4.2

NE	18,284	18,194	18,108	18,674	18,325	18,536	2.1	-0.7
NV	2,009	2,130	2,170	2,243	2,256	2,470	11.6	10.1
NH	6,253	6,486	6,696	6,983	6,928	6,981	11.7	-0.0
NJ	26,790	28,522	29,659	30,828	31,233	31,229	15.1	1.3
NM	2,910	3,301	3,276	3,984	4,075	4,531	36.9	13.7
NY	90,178	91,513	92,162	93,504	94,210	95,727	3.7	2.4
NC	17,424	19,259	19,652	21,166	21,869	21,880	21.5	3.4
OH	65,126	67,664	70,714	72,650	74,164	74,334	11.6	2.3
OK	28,122	27,811	28,944	29,472	29,807	29,797	4.8	1.1
OR	14,653	14,610	14,922	15,142	15,221	15,254	3.3	0.7
PA	66,673	68,940	72,205	73,776	75,183	78,632	10.7	6.6
RI	8,228	8,821	8,685	8,724	8,851	9,252	6.0	6.1
SC	9,875	10,200	11,362	11,795	12,462	12,899	19.4	9.4
SD	7,386	7,507	7,589	7,745	7,701	7,731	4.9	-0.2
TN	18,505	20,510	23,003	25,218	26,206	26,596	36.3	5.5
TX	99,000	100,687	101,101	102,788	102,724	100,986	3.8	-1.8
UT	5,758	5,797	5,548	5,423	5,406	5,600	-5.8	3.3
VT	2,852	2,811	2,826	3,069	2,970	3,111	7.6	1.4
VA	16,283	17,698	19,177	20,313	21,477	22,625	24.7	11.4
WA	28,225	26,811	26,876	27,307	27,378	27,379	-3.3	0.3
WI	50,542	50,737	51,689	52,700	52,378	53,627	4.3	1.8
WV	4,789	4,774	5,086	5,668	6,316	7,038	18.4	24.2
WY	1,962	1,988	2,050	2,060	2,098	2,098	5.0	1.8
U.S. Total	1,315,691	1,347,128	1,372,019	1,401,657	1,428,960	1,450,413	6.5	3.5

SOURCE: Adapted from AHPC, 1984.
*These statistics include all skilled nursing and intermediate care beds but exclude all intermediate care beds for the mentally retarded. The statistics also include all SNF and ICF beds whether in free-standing or hospital-based facilities.
**Data adapted from U.S. GAO, 1983.
***Data adapted from U.S. NCHS, 1980.
****Data Imputed.

to be in the Midwest, and some of them have fairly high proportions of aged residents. The ratio of beds per population thus shows regional patterns and significant differences among states (U.S. GAO, 1983).

Changes in number of beds should be examined relative to changes in populations served—i.e., the aged (U.S. GAO, 1983; Lane, 1984). Table 7.2 shows that expansion in number of beds has not kept up with the increases in the aged population. While most states had increases in total number of beds, they actually showed declines in their beds per 1,000 aged residents.

TYPE OF CARE

The type of care for which beds are available varies by state. The percentages of nursing home beds licensed for skilled nursing care are shown in Table 7.3.[2] In some states (such as Alaska, Arizona, California, Florida, Idaho, Mississippi, and Wisconsin) SNF beds clearly predominate, while in other states (such as Iowa, Kansas, Louisiana, Maine, Nebraska, New Mexico, and Oklahoma) ICF beds greatly outnumber SNF beds. The states with available data are about evenly split between emphasis on SNF versus on ICF beds. There was no pronounced overall pattern of change in state percentages of SNF and ICF beds over time. Those few states that shifted from SNF to ICF care tended to do so earlier in the 1978–83 period, while the shifting from ICF to SNF tended to have continued throughout the period.

MEDICAID CERTIFICATION OF BEDS

More beds are generally licensed in states than are certified for Medicaid or for Medicare reimbursement. Table 7.3 shows the number of certified beds by state. Most states (36) had at least 90 percent of their beds Medicaid certified in each year for which data are reported. States differ on changes in percentage certified, with 7 states decreasing and 11 increasing by one percent. There was a tendency for more decreases in percentage certified in the 1981-83 period than in the 1978-81 period (not shown in the table).

TABLE 7.2   Nursing Home Beds and Percentage Change per 1000 Aged: 1978-1981*

| | Beds per 1000 Aged 65+ | | |
State	1978	1981	% Change 1978-1981
AL	48.8	46.8	−4.2
AK	82.3	59.8	−27.3
AZ	19.8	21.2	7.2
AR	63.5	62.0	−2.4
CA	49.3	44.6	−9.4
CO	86.5	71.9	−16.8
CT	69.5	69.8	0.5
DE	54.5	62.1	13.9
DC	26.1	24.2	−7.3
FL	22.3	21.5	−3.7
GA	66.6	69.2	3.9
HI	32.4	32.4	−0.0
ID	51.2	49.0	−4.2
IL	71.3	68.3	−4.3
IN	73.1	74.6	2.1
IA	85.2	83.5	−2.1
KS	88.3	84.4	−4.5
KY	41.8	45.1	7.9
LA	60.9	61.1	0.3
ME	65.4	61.8	−5.5
MD	52.2	52.8	1.1
MA	64.7	62.6	−3.3
MI	53.0	49.3	−7.0
MN	96.3	93.2	−3.2
MS	45.9	45.6	−0.7
MO	55.4	61.2	10.6
MT	77.4	70.2	−9.4
NE	90.5	89.8	−0.8
NV	35.6	31.2	−13.2
NH	65.1	65.9	1.1
NJ	32.5	34.9	7.4
NM	28.0	32.9	17.7
NY	43.0	42.8	−0.7
NC	31.6	33.7	6.6
ND	76.4	79.1	3.5
OH	57.9	60.5	4.5
OK	79.0	76.8	−2.8
OR	51.4	48.1	−6.5
PA	45.6	47.0	2.9
RI	68.0	67.1	−1.3
SC	38.3	39.3	2.7
SD	83.0	84.2	1.4
TN	38.7	47.3	22.2
TX	78.3	72.8	−7.0
UT	56.5	47.6	−15.7
VT	51.9	52.0	0.3

(continued)

TABLE 7.2 Continued

| | Beds per 1000 Aged 65+ | | |
State	1978	1981	% Change 1978-1981
VA	34.8	38.8	11.6
WV	21.6	23.3	8.1
WA	70.4	61.0	−13.4
WI	92.7	91.2	−1.7
WY	54.5	54.2	−0.5
U.S. Total	57.4	56.0	−2.5

SOURCE: Adapted from AHPC (1984).
*Statistics computed using data from Table 7.1 and figures from the Bureau of the Census.

HOSPITAL-BASED AND NONHOSPITAL-BASED BEDS

Nursing home beds can be classified by type of facility: free-standing facilities, or hospital-based (either chronic disease hospitals, or general hospitals).[3] Table 7.3 reports the percentages of total beds that were hospital-based in 1983. Of the states reporting, 7 had 10 percent or more of their nursing home beds located in hospitals and 7 more had between 5 and 10 percent hospital-based beds. Eleven states had no hospital-based beds. There were few pronounced changes in the percentages of hospital-based beds among the states.

Factors Affecting Nursing Home Bed Supply

A number of factors are considered to affect nursing home bed supply, either positively by stimulating supply or negatively by constraining it. Recent factors that stimulate supply are described by Lane as those that encourage investments, including: private bond market financing, growth of chain structure for investor-owned and tax-exempt providers, leasing and mergers by investor-owned chains, market speculation, creative financing for new services, greater acceptance of a business approach, improved debt and liquidity of existing facilities, rapid growth of public companies, strong demand for long term care services, and diversification (Lane, 1981; 1984).

Lane (1984) reports that as growth rates have slowed, the financial viability of the industry has improved considerably in recent years. In part, this is because assets are more liquid than before. The ratio

TABLE 7.3   Percentage of Nursing Home Beds SNF-Licensed; Medicaid-Certified; Hospital-Based, 1983

State	SNF-Licensed Beds*	Medicaid-Certified Beds**	Hospital-Based Beds
AL	71.0	97.8	7.0
AK	96.7	65.4	13.4
AZ	86.0	–	2.8
AR	54.7	98.3	0.0
CA	–	(93.0)	–
CO	65.4	78.6	5.8
CT	81.9	96.3	0.0
DE	57.1	82.1	0.0
DC	15.0	79.6	0.0
FL	–	85.4	0.0
GA	76.0	100.0	0.4
HI	65.9	95.4	26.7
ID	95.3	97.6	13.4
IL	–	–	–
IN	20.1	74.6	1.1
IA	–	–	–
KS	10.2	100.0	4.5
KY	23.5	97.9	1.9
LA	6.6	96.8	0.0
ME	4.4	100.0	2.7
MD	–	97.1	2.8
MA	41.4	94.8	0.0
MI	–	94.2	4.2
MN	60.7	99.9	0.0
MS	87.7	94.8	1.1
MO	51.1	64.3	0.0
MT	54.3	99.5	25.6
NE	19.6	97.3	10.5
NV	71.5	100.0	3.8
NH	–	96.8	–
NJ	–	100.0	0.0
NM	7.5	95.4	9.0
NY	74.2	98.9	–
NC	46.5	97.5	6.1
ND	–	–	–
OH	–	85.3	1.2
OK	3.0	95.7	0.5
OR	–	84.6	2.2
PA	70.2	–	–
RI	24.9	98.9	0.0
SC	66.2	97.4	5.5
SD	49.7	99.1	13.8
TN	–	92.6	9.9
TX	–	–	–
UT	–	97.9	7.3
VT	22.7	93.1	13.1

(continued)

TABLE 7.3   Continued

State	SNF-Licensed Beds*	Medicaid-Certified Beds**	Hospital-Based Beds
VA	–	92.4	1.7
WA	–	92.7	1.4
WV	–	–	–
WI	–	–	–
WY	78.7	100.0	16.2

SOURCE: Adapted from AHPC (1984).
*The number of "nursing home beds" upon which the percentages are based is the sum of the SNF plus the ICF beds—this sum will differ from the total nursing home beds reported in Table 7.1 wherever there are beds licensed as "nursing home" or as "SNF/ICF" that could not be identified as either SNF or ICF.
**Percentage for California in 1982. Fewer beds are listed as licensed than are listed as certified in 1983 for states with 100% rates. More SNF or ICF beds are certified than licensed for some states because the same beds are certified differently than they are licensed.

of debt to net worth fell to a nine-year low during 1981, and profit margins for the year ending 1982 were the third highest in fifteen years (Lane, 1984).

Tax-exempt financing has become a major source of capital for the nursing home industry. Section 232 of the Federal Home Administration Mortgage Insurance Program for nursing homes has recently shown new financial support for construction and this combined with tax-exempt bonds has stimulated growth (Lane, 1984). Nursing homes have moved rapidly toward larger growth and proprietary ownership. Proprietary owners operated 81 percent of the nursing homes in the U.S. (U.S. NCHS, 1983). While most nursing homes are small in size, the majority (61 percent) of beds are located in facilities with 100 beds or more (U.S. NCHS, 1983).

Many nursing homes are now owned by chains, and a growing number of these chains are publicly held corporations, bringing new capital to expand growth. The nursing home industry is consolidating into larger corporations with mergers and acquisitions by larger multi-facility groups. Blyskal (1981) reported that the ten largest nursing home chains accounted for 10 percent of the total beds in the United States, and 32 corporations controlled 17 percent of the beds in 1983 (LaViolette, 1983). These largest chains included Beverly Enterprises, ARA Services, National Medical Enterprises (which bought National

Health Enterprises), and Cenco Inc. The top corporations are listed on the New York Stock Exchange and the American Stock Exchange. In 1983, chain ownership increased by 30.4 percent over the previous year, primarily through acquisition of existing homes, and not through new construction (LaViolette, 1983). This trend, called horizontal growth, is expected to continue to the point that 5–10 nursing home corporations will own 50 percent of all the beds in the United States by 1990.

Nursing homes are moving quickly to diversify investments. Most nursing home chains control other types of businesses, such as pharmaceutical suppliers and respiratory therapy companies. This trend is called vertical integration. The latest activity of nursing homes has been to develop other long term care businesses, including home-health care corporations and residential care facilities (Lane, 1984; Vladeck, 1980). Banks are the real owners of nursing homes since most owners have large mortgages and little equity in their facilities. Banks and investment corporations are promoting the move toward consolidation of the nursing home industry (Lane, 1984).

High profit rates have stimulated growth and investment in nurisng homes. The ratio between price and earnings in the industry is commonly between 14 and 18 percent. Beverly Enterprises, with 450 million dollars in business in 1982, reported a growth rate in earnings of 700 percent from 1978 to 1982. In 1982, the corporation increased by 10,000 beds, thus growing by 25 percent (Blyskal, 1981; Keppel, 1982). Moskowitz (1983) reported that 10,000 dollars invested at the start of 1982 in any of the four top health care corporations (including hospitals and nursing homes) was worth 18,000 dollars at the end of the year. An investment of 10,000 dollars five years ago would have been worth over 100,000 dollars in 1983 (Moskowitz, 1983). State studies such as one in California showed a 41 percent profit on net equity on average for all nursing homes in the stae in 1978–79 (CHFC, 1981); Texas showed 34 percent on net equity for 1978 (Harrington, Wood, LaLonde-Berg, and Bogaert, 1983). Lane (1984) reports pretax profit margins of 6–7 percent while other reports are lower at 3.3–5.5 percent.

Nursing home bed supply increased at a rate of about 8 percent per year between 1963 and 1973, but began to slow between 1976 and 1980 to an annual rate of about 2.9 percent (U.S. GAO, 1983; see also Table 7.1). The reduction in the rate of growth has been widely attributed to state policies that constrain bed growth. Conditions such as high interest rates and high costs of construction may have been equally important in reducing the rate of growth (Lane, 1984). Other relevant factors indentified by Lane (1984) are: continued media attention to investigations, 1977 legislation controlling fraud and abuse, major increases in federal minimum wage laws, the promotion of alternative care models including home care, and attention to antitrust laws. All these factors may have had a dampening effect on nursing home growth in the last ten years.

State Policies to Control Nursing Home Bed Supply

State policies have had mixed effects in reducing the supply of nursing home beds. One of these policies is state Certificate of Need (CON) laws requiring state approval of new construction or bed expansion. In a qualitative study of the effects of nursing home certificate-of-need requirements on bed supply, Feder and Scanlon (1980) suggest that CON has been successful in limiting the supply of nursing home beds and that states use CON primarily as a tool to limit their total expenditures on nursing home care. On the other hand, Cohodes, Pardini, and Cohen (1980) found little evidence that denials of CON applications have directly reduced the growth rate of new nursing homes, because states have approved the vast majority of CON requests. Other studies of the effect of CON on hospital bed supply have not shown CON to be effective in constraining growth in hospital assets or overall hospital costs, although the supply of beds grow at a slower rate than would have been expected (Salkever and Bice, 1979; Sloan and Steinwald, 1980). Thus, it is not likely that CON has a great effect on controlling nursing home growth.

Birnbaum (1981) found that states with strict life safety codes had higher costs and that states with inflexible nursing staff requirements had higher costs. Similarly, occupancy penalties imposed by state rate-setting agencies were significantly associated with higher costs. It might be inferred that states with strong regulations may impede growth in bed supply, but this has not be shown empirically.

Reimbursement rates are probably one of the most important of all state policy variables in influencing supply (Salkever, 1972; Pauly and Drake, 1971; Dowling, 1974; Berry, 1976; Geomet, 1976; Gaus and Hellinger, 1976). Increases in reimbursement rates can encourage entry into the industry, and/or the expansion of existing services. Increases in Medicaid reimbursement rates are incentives for providers to treat Medicaid patients (Paringer, 1980; Hadley and Lee, 1978; Rice, 1978). In his study of state nursing home utilization, Scanlon (1980a and 1980b) found that the nursing home market first accepts patients with sufficient private funds to pay for care and then fills the remaining beds with publicly paid residents once the private demand has been satisfied. This occurs because Medicaid reimbursement rates, established by state governments, are usually lower than private rates.

Demand for Nursing Home Services

Demand for nursing home services is closely associated with both state characteristics and patient characteristics. Demand is an economist's term for the number of persons who wish to use a service at a specified time and price. Demand is dependent upon consumer preference and ability to purchase services (Scanlon, Difederico, and Stassen, 1979) and other factors. Need for nursing home service is an imprecise term used to refer to the number of beds for persons that experts believe require institutional care. Objective need determinations may be quite different from the demand for services (Feder and Scanlon, 1980).

Planners typically use one of two methods of determining state need for beds. One method projects the number of beds needed in the future from the number in current use, adjusted for expected changes in the size of the elderly population and for current occupancy rates. The other method establishes a norm or target ratio of beds to population that is independent of the current use of beds (Feder and Scanlon, 1980). All methods of determining need are subject to criticism, and to manipulation by planners and policymakers. Factors that are empirically important can be determined by examining relationships among the number of beds available, utilization of nursing home services, and expenditures, as well as relationships of these factors to state and to patient characteristics.

The age of a state's population is highly associated with demand for and utilization of services. Scanlon (1980a and 1980b) showed in an analysis of national data on states for 1969–1973 that age is the most important factor affecting nursing home utilization. In particular, the percentage of the elderly population in a state above 85 years of age is highly significant in estimating utilization. The percentage of those aged 85 and over using nursing homes is four times greater than that for all elderly. Similar findings resulted from analyses conducted by Dunlop (1976) and Chiswick (1976).

Climate was found to be a significant factor in Scanlon's (1980a and 1980b) analysis, with warmer states showing lower nursing home utilization. States with high proportions of blacks in the population had lower utilization rates, but the differences were not significant, and any such differences can be attributed to the fact that blacks are concentrated in low-income states in the Southeast, which have more restrictive eligibility policies and restrictive policies on nursing home supply (Scanlon, 1980a and 1980b; Dunlop, 1976).

The percentage of state population that is married is negatively related to nursing home utilization (Dunlop, 1976; Scanlon, 1980a and 1980b). A positive relationship was found between female labor force participation and nursing home utilization (Chiswick, 1976). These findings are attributed to the higher likelihood that married rather than single children, and that women rather than men, will be able to provide care for their parents as an alternative to nursing home institutionalization.

The percentage of state population living in urban areas is also positively related to utilization (Dunlop, 1976; Chiswick, 1976; and Scanlon, 1980a and 1980b). This indicates that individuals living in rural environments may have fewer alternatives to nursing home care, particularly if they are geographically isolated from children, family, or friends.

The percentage of state elderly population with low incomes was found to be positively related to nursing home utilization (Dunlop, 1976; Chiswick, 1976). Scanlon (1980a and 1980b) found a negative association of the higher number of low-income aged with nursing home utilization, and considered this to reflect the fact that wealthier states support larger nursing home populations.

Disability levels have been found to be associated with costs of care in nursing homes. The higher the disability levels, as measured by activities of daily living, the higher the average operating and total costs in nursing homes (Bishop, 1980; Bishop, 1979; Walsh,

1979; Jensen and Birnbaum, 1979; Birnbaum et al., 1981; Deane and Skinner, 1978). Thus, disability levels may also be related to nursing home bed supply differences among states.

Policies Affecting Demand for Nursing Home Services

Within the literature and policy arena, there is a continuing controversy over whether or not the demand for nursing home services exceeds the nursing home bed supply. Scanlon (1980a and 1980b) for example, argues that there is a demand for beds that exceeds the supply. Accurate occupancy rates (percent of beds occupied by patients during a one-year period) are extremely difficult to obtain since precise counts of beds and patient days are not available. In one estimate, the Master Facility Inventory (U.S. NCHS, 1980) reported an average occupancy of 89 percent in 1978 for those nursing homes reporting nationally. Some reports indicate that occupancy rates are increasing, but national data to support these contentions are not available.

State Medicaid programs have become increasingly concerned about the increase in demand for nursing home services. States have adopted certain policies designed to reduce utilization and expenditures for nursing home services by controlling demand for services. For example, the adoption of a medically needy program results in the granting of Medicaid eligibility to some who previously faced the private price for such services. Reductions in Medicaid eligibility and the imposition of copayments exert negative impacts on demand for services (Helms, Newhouse, and Phelps, 1978). Changes in state policies with respect to non-nursing home service coverage, and limits on such coverage, can also affect demand for care. Policies that reduce demand for one type of service may increase demand for substitute services (e.g., limits on the number of hospital days may increase demand for nursing home beds; Averill and McMahon, 1977).

The effectiveness of these strategies has yet to be empirically verified. For example, in a study using 1969 and 1973 national nursing home state data from the Master Facility Inventory and from the National Nursing Home Surveys of 1969 and 1973, Scanlon (1980a and 1980b) analyzed the effects of state policies (including the presence or absence of a medically needy program, the income standard level of Medicaid coverage in a nursing home, state ICF coverage, presence of a Medicaid program, and presence of state preadmission screening for nursing home care) on nursing home utilization. He found that only the presence of state preadmission screening criteria was significantly related to increased use of nursing homes. Since preadmission screening is designed by states as a barrier to care, the positive coefficient was only interpretable as reflecting state use of such screening as a response to previously high utilization patterns.

Another area considered important is that of the availability of services that provide alternatives to nursing home care (Palmer, 1983). Because it is difficult to measure the availability of alternative services, relationships between alternatives and nursing home utilization have not been extensively studied. Moreover, the use of such alternatives has been somewhat restricted. This is partially due to the fact that nursing home care is reimbursed by Medicaid, whereas most alternatives are not as likely to be covered by public payers. The limited availability of alternatives in many communities is another factor that restricts their use (Scanlon, 1980a).

Dunlop (1976) found that the percentage of state elderly population in mental hospitals is negatively related to nursing home utilization. Home health services are also used as substitutes for nursing home placement. As more home-health services are used by Medicare beneficiaries, there is a decrease in nursing home services used (Dunlop, 1976). States that offer ICF services were also found to provide fewer SNF services (Dunlop, 1976), indicating some substitution between the two types of services. The more personal care beds available for the elderly, the less likely that nursing homes will be used (Scanlon, 1980a and 1980b).

Scanlon (1980a and 1980b) argues that state eligibility and reimbursement rate policies do not affect nursing home utilization because the nursing home market is not in equilibrium. His argument that demand greatly exceeds supply is demonstrated by his analysis of the private nursing home utilization market. When markets are in equilibrium, increases in either demand or supply should result in increased utilization of services, and reductions in demand or supply should similarly lead to reductions in observed utilization (Fair and Jaffe, 1972; Paringer, 1983; Nadiri and Rosen, 1973). However, when excess demand is present, and when providers are financially motivated to prefer private patients to public beneficiaries, state policies are not likely to alter service utilization (see Chapter 11).

Conclusion

The structure of institutional services is a product of federal certification, reimbursement, and level-of-care policies. But states are also given a great deal of discretion in managing their Medicaid programs, and their policies have varied effects on supply and demand for nursing home services. Further, there is considerable variation among states in the number of and types of beds available. A great many variables are needed to explain these variations among states, as well as the variation in utilization and expenditure patterns among facilities. Certainly, state demographic variables, particularly population age structure and patient characteristics, are important factors in the supply and utilization of services.

States will clearly continue to use state policies in attempts to influence supply and demand for nursing home services. The effectiveness of these policies will be tested where demand for services outweighs supply. Policymakers will have to determine what goals they wish to pursue in expanding the number of nursing home beds, the number of alternatives to institutional services, or both to meet growing demand. The issues are becoming clear only now, with an understanding of the complexity of the nursing home market.

The solutions are not as clear as are the problems. The demand for long term care services appears to be growing and to exceed the services available. Expansion of the supply of nursing home beds to meet the demand for care would be costly to government. The more nursing home beds built in states, the more individuals will likely use the beds, and the greater the cost to government. If Medicaid rates for nursing home services were reduced relative to rates for alternatives, this might reduce demand for institutional services, but this could have negative consequences for public patients who might then be denied access to nursing home services in favor of private patients. Expansion of the nursing home bed supply may not be appropriate in terms of the type of long term care services needed by frail elderly.

The development of alternatives to nursing home care are essential to plans for reducing demand for institutional care and providing more appropriate care. Chapter 9 discusses alternatives to institutional care. On the other hand, expansion of alternatives to institutional care may also not be able to meet the growing demand, and would add to the costs of government in addition to the costs for institutional services. Unless the delivery and financing of long term care services are changed, the current problems will no doubt exacerbate. Policy options that would provide greater incentives for cost containment, ensuring access and quality, and encouraging appropriate utilization of services are needed. These options will be discussed in Chapter 12.

Notes

1. The National Center for Health Statistics collected Master Facility Inventory (MFI) data in 1976, 1978, and 1980 by telephone surveys of states. The surveys tend to overstate the number of beds because they include some personal care beds along with the skilled and intermediate care beds. Problems of inconsistent reporting by states also made the data somewhat unreliable. Another source of data is the Medicare-Medicaid Automated Certification System (MMACS), which provides certification statistics on the number of beds. However, the MMACS data double counted the Medicare and Medicaid certified beds (U.S. NCHS, 1982; U.S. GAO, 1983). The U.S. GAO (1983) completed a telephone survey of the states regarding nursing home beds for the period 1976 to 1980, but these data were so incomplete that their utility is questionable. As a result of these problems, the Aging Health Policy Center (AHPC) collected its own data on nursing home beds for the period 1978 to 1983, and these data are presented in this chapter. There are some states with missing data, but data are completely lacking in no state. Nevertheless, these data represent the most complete data set available for recent years, and are believed to be more accurate than other data sets.

2. AHPC data collection and tabulation are concerned with the determination of how many beds were actually licensed as SNF beds in institutions that also had other types of beds—in the MFI, all beds in such institutions tended to be counted as SNF beds. Complicating this was the practice of some states of licensing some beds as SNF/ICF in addition to licensing others as simply SNF or ICF. In most such cases, the dual-licensed beds have been counted as SNF beds, though further division into SNF and ICF beds was sometimes possible. In some cases, not all beds could be assigned to either SNF or ICF categories, and it is for this reason that the total figures sometimes differ from the sums of the SNF and ICF figures. This is the case with noncertified comprehensive (private-pay only) beds in Indiana, with hospital-based long term care beds in Kansas and Nebraska, and with nursing home-based long term care beds in New Mexico. In some states, only the total figure was available; and in a few cases only SNF or ICF, but not both, and no total figures are available.

3. In the past, such accounting has been difficult because data from sources such as the Master Facility Inventory (MFI) do not distinguish between free-standing or hospital-based facilities. In a 1983 study, the GAO attempted to make this distinction, obtaining

data on hospital-based facilities in 31 states (U.S. GAO, 1983, p. 31). The American Hospital Association provides their own data on hospital-based long term care beds. These beds (classified as skilled nursing or intermediate care) are based in either general hospitals or chronic hospitals. In its Telephone Survey, the AHPC attempted to distinguish hospital-based from nonhospital-based SNF and ICF beds.

References

Aging Health Policy Center (AHPC). Unpublished telephone survey of states, Nursing Home Supply Data. San Francisco, CA: AHPC, University of California, 1984.

Averill, R., and L. McMahon. "A Cost Benefit Analysis of State Certification." *Medical Care,* 15, No. 2 (February 1977), 158-173.

Berry, R. "Prospective Reimbursement and Cost Containment: Formula Reimbursement in New York." *Inquiry,* 13, No. 3 (September 1976), 288-301.

Birnbaum, H., A. J. Lee, C. Bishop, and G. Jensen. *Public Pricing of Nursing Home Care.* Cambridge, MA: Abt, 1981.

Bishop, C. "Nursing Home Costs in Massachusetts." In *Reimbursement Strategies for Nursing Home Care: Developmental Cost Studies, Final Report.* Ed. H. C. Birnbaum, C. Bishop, G. Jensen, A. J. Lee, and D. Wilson. Cambridge, MA: Abt, 1979.

Bishop, C. E. "Nursing Home Cost Studies and Reimbursement Issues." *Health Care Financing Review,* 1, No. 4 (Spring 1980), 47-64.

Bishop, C. E., A. L. Plough, and T. R. Willemain. "Nursing Home Levels of Care: Problems and Alternatives." *Health Care Financing Review,* 2, No. 2 (Fall 1980), 33-45.

Blyskal, J. "Gray Gold." *Forbes* (November 23, 1981), 80-81.

California Health Facilities Commission (CHFC). *Economic Criteria for Health Planning Report, FY 1981-82/FY 1982-83.* Vol. 2. Draft report. Sacramento, CA: CHFC, 1981.

Chiswick, B. "The Demand for Nursing Home Care: An Analysis of the Substitution Between Institutional and Non-Institutional Care." *Journal of Human Resources,* 11, No. 3 (Summer 1976), 295-316.

Cohodes, D. R., A. Pardini, and A. B. Cohen. *Analysis of Interstate Certificate of Need Program Variation.* Cambridge, MA: Urban Systems Research and Engineering, 1980.

Community Research Applications (CRA). *A National Study of Levels of Care of Intermediate Care Facilities.* Report to the Health Services Administration, New York, NY: CRA, 1976.

Deane, R., and D. Skinner. "Development of a Formula Incentive Reimbursement System for Long-Term Care." Washington, DC: Applied Management Sciences, 1978.

Dowling, R. "Prospective Reimbursement of Hospitals." *Inquiry,* 11, No. 3 (September 1974), 163-180.

Dunlop, B. D. "Determinants of Long Term Care Facility Utilization by the Elderly: An Empirical Analysis." Working Paper. Washington, DC: Urban Institute, 1976.

Dunlop, B. D. *The Growth of Nursing Home Care.* Lexington, MA: D. C. Heath, 1979.

Fair, R., and D. M. Jaffe. "Methods of Estimation for Markets in Disequilibrium." *Econometrica,* 40, No. 3 (May 1972), 497-514.

Feder, J., and W. Scanlon. "Regulating the Bed Supply in Nursing Homes." *Milbank Memorial Fund Quarterly/Health and Society,* 58, No. 1 (Winter 1980), 54-88.

Gaus, C., and F. Hellinger. "Results of Prospective Reimbursement." *Topics in Health Care Financing,* 3, No. 2 (Winter 1976), 83-96.

Geomet, Inc. "Analysis of the New Jersey Hospital Prospective Reimbursement System: 1968-1973." Final Report under contract No. HEW 05-74-268. Washington, DC: U.S. Social Security Administration, 1976.

Gibson, R. M., D. R. Waldo, and K. R. Levit. "National Health Expenditures, 1982." *Health Care Financing Review,* 5, No. 1 (Fall 1983), 1-43.

Hadley, J., and R. Lee. "Physicians' Price and Output Decisions: Theory and Evidence." Working Paper. Washington, DC: Urban Institute, 1978.

Harrington, C., J. B. Wood, G. R. LaLonde-Berg, and M. P. Bogaert. *Texas State Discretionary Policies and Services in the Medicaid, Social Services, and Supplemental Security Income Programs.* San Francisco, CA: Aging Health Policy Center, University of California, 1983.

Helms, J., J. Newhouse, and C. Phelps. "Copayments and Demand for Medical Care: The California Medicaid Experience." *Bell Journal of Economics,* 9, No. 1 (Spring 1978), 192-208.

Jensen, G., and H. Birnbaum. "An Analysis of Nursing Home Costs Based on a National Sample." In *Reimbursement Strategies for Nursing Home Care: Developmental Cost Studies, Final Report.* By H. Birnbaum et al. Cambridge, MA: Abt, 1979.

Keppel, B. "Multihospital Affiliation in Hand, Beverly Aims to Double Its Size. *Modern Healthcare,* 12, No. 6 (June 1982), 70-72.

Kurowski, B. D., and P. W. Shaughnessy. "The Measurement and Assurance of Quality." In *Long-Term Care: Perspectives from Research and Demonstrations.* Ed. R. J. Vogel and H. C. Palmer. Washington, DC: U.S. Department of Health and Human Services, Health Care Financing Administration, 1983.

Lane, L. F. "Developments in Facility-Based Services." Paper prepared for the National Institute of Medicine, Nursing Home Study Committee, January 1984.

Lane, L. F. "The Nursing Home, Weighing Investment Decisions." *Hospital Financial Management,* 35, No. 5 (May 1981), 30-45.

LaViolette, S. "Nursing Home Chains Scramble for More Private-Paying Patients." *Modern Healthcare,* 13, No. 5 (May 1983), 130-138.

Liu, K., and J. Mossey. "The Role of Payment Source in Differentiating Nursing Home Residents, Services, and Payments." *Health Care Financing Review,* 2, No. 1 (Summer 1980), 51-61.

Mennemeyer, S. "Long-Term Care Costs in New York State." Buffalo: State University of New York, Department of Economics, 1979.

Moskowitz, M. "The Health Care Business is Healthy." *San Francisco Chronicle* (March 28, 1983), 50.

Nadiri, M., and S. Rosen. *A Disequilibrium Model of Demand for Factors of Production.* New York: NY: Columbia University Press, 1973.

Palmer, H. C. "The Alternatives Question." In *Long-Term Care: Perspectives from Research and Demonstrations.* Ed. R. J. Vogel and H. C. Palmer. Washington, DC: U.S. Department of Health and Human Services, Health Care Financing Administration, 1983.

Paringer, L. "Economic Incentives in the Provision of Long-Term Care." In *Market Reforms in Health Care: Current Issues, New Directions, Strategic Decisions.* Ed. J. A. Meyer. Washington, DC: American Enterprise Institute, 1983, pp. 119-143.

Paringer, L. "Medicare Assignment Rates of Physicians: Their Response to Changes in Reimbursement Policy." *Health Care Financing Review,* 1, No. 3 (Winter 1980), 75-90.

Pauly, M., and D. Drake. "Effect of Third-Party Methods of Reimbursement on Hospital Performance." In *Empirical Studies in Health Economics.* Ed. H. E. Klarman. Baltimore, MD: Johns Hopkins Press, 1971.

Reis, B., and J. B. Christianson. "Nursing Home Costs in Montana: Analysis and Policy Applications." Bozeman, MT: Montana Agricultural Experiment Station, Research Report 117, 1977.

Rice, T. "Economic Incentives and Physician Practice: An Examination of Medicare Participation Decisions and Physician Induced Demand." Unpublished Ph.D. dissertation, University of California, Berkeley, September 1978.

Salkever, D. "A Microeconomic Study of Hospital Cost Inflation." *Journal of Political Economy,* 80, No. 6 (November–December 1972), 1144-1166.

Salkever, D., and T. Bice. *Hospital Certificate-of-Need Controls: Impact on Investment, Costs and Use.* Washington, DC: American Enterprise Institute for Public Policy Research, 1979.

Scanlon, W. J. "Nursing Home Utilization Patterns: Implications for Policy." *Journal of Health Politics, Policy and Law.* 4, No. 4 (Winter 1980a), 619-641.

Scanlon, W. J. "A Theory of the Nursing Home Market." *Inquiry,* 17, No. 1 (Spring 1980b), 25-41.

Scanlon, W. J., E. Difederico, and M. Stassen. *A Framework for Analysis of the Long Term Care System.* Washington, DC: Urban Institute, 1979.

Sloan, F., and B. Steinwald. *Insurance Regulation and Hospital Costs.* Lexington, MA: D.C. Heath, 1980.

U.S. Congressional Budget Office (CBO). *Long Term Care: Actuarial Cost Estimates.* Technical Analysis Paper. Washington, DC: U.S. Government Printing Office, 1977.

U.S. General Accounting Office (GAO). *Medicaid and Nursing Home Care: Cost Increases and the Need for Services are Creating Problems for the States and the Elderly.* Washington, DC: U.S. GAO, 1983.

U.S. General Accounting Office (GAO). *Problems in Providing Guidance to States In Establishing Rates of Payment for Nursing Home Care Under Medicaid Programs.* Washington, DC: U.S. GAO, 1972.

U.S. Health Care Financing Administration (HCFA). *Long Term Care: Background and Future Directions.* Washington, DC: U.S. Government Printing Office, 1981.

U.S. Health Care Financing Administration (HCFA). "Nursing Home Utilization in California, Illinois, Massachusetts, New York and Texas: 1977 National Nursing Home Survey. *Vital and Health Statistics,* Series 13, No. 48. DHHS Pub. No. (PHS) 81-1799. Washington, DC: U.S. Department of Health and Human Services,

U.S. National Center for Health Statistics (NCHS). "Characteristics of Residents in Institutions for the Aged and Chronically Ill, United States, April –June 1963." *Vital and Health Statistics: Data from the National Health Survey,* Series 12, No. 2. Washington, DC: U.S. Department of Health, Education and Welfare, 1965.

U.S. National Center for Health Statistics (NCHS). *Master Facility Inventory, 1978.* Unpublished tables. Washington, DC: U.S. Department of Health and Human Services, 1980.

U.S. National Center for Health Statistics (NCHS). *Master Facility Inventory, 1980.* Unpublished tables. Washington, DC: U.S. DHHS, PHS, 1982.

U.S. National Center for Health Statistics (NCHS). *The National Nursing Home Survey 1977 Summary for the United States.* Vital & Health Statistics, Series 13, No. 43. Washington, DC: U.S. Government Printing Office, 1979.

U.S. National Center for Health Statistics (NCHS), and A. Sirrocco. "Nursing and Related Care Homes as Reported from the 1980 NMFI Survey." *Vital and Health Statistics,* Series 14, No. 29. DHHS Pub. No. (PHS) 84-1824. Washington, DC: U.S. Government Printing Office, 1983.

U.S. Senate Special Committee on Aging. *Health Care for Older Americans: The "Alternatives" Issue.* Parts 1-7. Washington, DC: U.S. Government Printing Office, 1977-78.

Vladeck, B. C. *Unloving Care: The Nursing Home Tragedy.* New York: Basic Books, 1980.

Waldman, S. "A Legislative History of Nursing Home Care." In *Long-term Care: Perspectives from Research and Demonstrations.* Ed. R. J. Vogel and H. C. Palmer. Washington, DC: U.S. Department of Health and Human Services, Health Care Financing Administration, 1983.

Walsh, T. J. "Patient-Related Reimbursement for Long-Term Care." In *Reform and Regulation in Long-Term Care.* Ed. V. LaPorte and J. Rubin. New York: Praeger, 1979.

CHAPTER 8

THE STATE ROLE IN BOARD AND CARE HOUSING

Robyn Stone
Robert J. Newcomer

Board and care facilities have existed for many years to provide food, shelter, and some degree of protection for chronically impaired, dependent elderly and disabled individuals. During the past decade a combination of factors, including increasing fiscal constraints on state and local governments, deinstitutionalization of mental hospital patients, and the serious consideration of community-based alternatives to nursing homes has stimulated interest in board and care housing. Maintenance of the chronically impaired elderly and disabled in such housing is seen as a means to reduce the costs of institutionalization, promote independence, and enhance quality of life (Harmon, 1982).

While board and care housing represents a potentially large resource in the long term care service continuum, the diverse and frequently elusive nature of the board and care "industry" also poses a dilemma for state and local governments. This dilemma can be attributed, in large part, to the fact that the typical home, inconspicuously located among private dwellings, tends to be a "mon and pop" operation with provider(s) often lacking the requisite administrative skills and substantive knowledge to address the special needs of residents (Harmon, 1982). In addition, the housing stock frequently fails to meet all appropriate safety standards.

These problems began to receive national attention in the early 1970s, after a rash of boarding home fires and exposure of substandard

Authors' Note: The contents of this chapter are drawn from research supported by the U.S. Department of Health and Human Services, Administration on Aging, under cooperative agreement no. 90AP0003.

conditions and resident abuse and exploitation (U.S. GAO, 1979; U.S. House, 1981a; 1981b). A series of federal initiatives was designed to help ameliorate these problems. The first of these was the Keys Amendment to the Social Security Act in 1976 (Section 161(e) of the Act). The Keys Amendment, though not providing for direct federal regulation of quality of care or life safety standards, attempted to stimulate state efforts to regulate and monitor board and care by requiring states to set and enforce standards concerning admission policies, life safety, sanitation, and civil rights protection for board and care facilities where three or more SSI recipients reside (U.S. House, 1981b).

While this legislation encouraged many states to clarify the language in their standards and regulations (Stone, Newcomer, and Saunders, 1982; Reichstein and Bergofsky, 1983), there appears to be little demonstrable improvement in life safety or quality of care. For example, in 1979 a U.S. General Accounting Office (U.S. GAO, 1979) investigation of boarding homes cited unsafe and unsanitary living conditions in facilities housing SSI recipients. Several studies found that existing regulations largely exclude personal care and social needs, areas which are often more subject to abuse or quality variability than physical features of the housing (Mellody and White 1979; Dittmar and Smith, 1983). The U.S. Select Committee on Aging, through its hearings, has also reported "widespread instances of poor living conditions and negligent care for a population which is, for the most part, indigent or elderly, and many of whom are former patients in mental institutions" (U.S. House, 1981b, p. 5).

Another federal measure designed to strengthen state capability in enforcement and monitoring of board and care housing was a 1978 amendment to the Old Americans Act (OAA) that encouraged nursing home ombudsman programs to include advocacy for board and care residents. Only a few states, such as Florida and New Jersey, officially expanded the responsibilities of their ombudsman programs to include board and care under this voluntary program (U.S. AoA, 1981). Congress has since added a provision in the 1981 OAA amendments requiring state nursing home ombudsmen to investigate complaints about board and care homes.

More recent federal efforts have been initiated in response to findings by the Office of the Inspector General of the U.S. Department of Health and Human Services (U.S. DHHS, 1982b), which continued to report a generally low state level of participation in the oversight of board and care housing. The emerging strategy includes: (1) the partial withholding of OAA funds to states that fail to certify that they maintain and enforce safety and quality of care standards as part of their OAA plan; (2) the provision of $400,000 to the National Bureau of Standards to complete development of fire safety standards for board and care; (3) the establishment of a board and care coordinating unit within DHHS; (4) the development of model statutes for dissemination to the states; and (5) the requirement that Medicaid waivers used for board and care be granted only to those states in compliance with the Keys Amendment (U.S. DHHS, 1982a).

While the DHHS plan has attempted to clarify the federal role in ensuring life safety and quality of care for board and care residents, no additional federal funds have been made available to the states to improve enforcement and oversight activities. The onus, therefore, rests with state and local governments to make creative use of existing resources and to design strategies for enhancing their regulatory and monitoring capabilities.

Any action taken by government to expand regulatory oversight of the board and care industry can have immediate effects on the supply and availability of this housing. Furthermore, the financing of this regulatory activity presents its own barriers to implementation. In spite of these problems, states are increasingly attempting to respond to the need for expanding the supply and accessibility of facilities, protecting the life safety and personal rights of board and care residents, and ensuring quality of care.

This chapter briefly discusses the status of current knowledge about board and care housing and its residents; provides an overview of regulatory and financing mechanisms; and examines the barriers reported by, and actions being taken by, state governments to effect changes in the quality and quantity of board and care housing. Much more effort will be needed to establish board and care housing as an important component of the long term care service continuum, but these state actions illustrate the strengths and weaknesses of emerging public policy.

This descriptive review draws heavily upon the findings of a recent study conducted by the Aging Health Policy Center (AHPC; see Stone et al., 1982). The study describes the major policy issues with respect to the regulation and administration of adult board and care programs serving the elderly, the mentally ill, the mentally retarded, and the developmentally disabled in all 50 states and D.C. for the 1981–82 period. The major source of data was telephone interviews conducted with representatives of 92 state agencies involved in licensing, regulating, and monitoring board and care programs. In addition, supporting documents were gathered from each agency where available, including statutes and regulations, statistical reports and directories of facilities, administrative and budgetary information and other data to complete the board and care policy picture. Follow-up interviews were conducted to obtain 1983 information on the supply of beds and facilities and important statutory and/or regulatory changes.

What Is Board and Care?

Board and care housing refers to the provision by a nonrelative of food, shelter, and some degrees of protective oversight and/or personal care that is generally nonmedical in nature (McCoy, 1983). The "personal care and oversight" responsibilities of board and care operators, as established by state regulations (Reichstein and Bergofsky, 1983), usually include assistance with activities of daily living (e.g., eating, bathing, grooming); help with transportation and shopping; supervision of resident's medication; and assistance in obtaining medical and social services.

A variety of terms are used to describe board and care housing. These include residential care facilities, community care homes, personal care homes, domiciliary care homes, supervisory care homes, sheltered care facilities, adult foster care, family homes, group homes, transitional living facilities, and halfway houses. Board and care facilities also vary in terms of size, ownership, resident population, administrative or regulatory auspices, services, and funding sources. For example, a national survey of state regulatory programs for board and care housing (Stone et al., 1982), identified 142 distinct board and care programs administered and regulated by 92 state government agencies. Several researchers have attempted to develop a taxonomy of board and care programs based on such factors as level of care (e.g., foster care, personal care), target population (e.g., children, adults, mentally ill, developmentally disabled, aged), facility size (Dittmar and Smith, 1983), and degree of functional impairment (Rutman, 1981). However, the lack of consensus among either researchers or regulators regarding any one taxonomy or definition continues to be problematic.

The diversity of board and care categories has contributed to a wide variation in estimates of the number of both facilities and residents. A report issued by the Office of the Inspector General (U.S. DHHS, 1982b), estimates that there are approximately 300,000 boarding homes and 30,000 board and care homes in the United States housing between 500,000 and 1.5 million residents. While the vast majority of residents live in unlicensed facilities, studies of adults in licensed homes give some indication of the size of the population currently served by board and care providers. According to a study completed at the Center for Residential Community Services at the University of Minnesota (Lakin, Bruininks, Hill, and Hauber, 1982), there are approximately 90,000 mentally retarded persons in "private community-based" residences. One national survey of group homes for the mentally retarded (Janicki, Mayeda, and Epple, 1982) estimates that 49,000 mentally retarded adults now reside in 6300 facilities of this type. Sherwood and Seltzer (1981) estimate that between 60,000 and 80,000 mentally ill adults reside in board and care homes in the United States, with the largest subgroup housed in foster care facilities. A recent nationwide survey of board and care facilities for the aged (Reichstein and Bergofsky, 1983) identifies approximately 25,000 licensed and 5,000 unlicensed facilities housing a primarily elderly population. Another study (Teresi, Holmes, and Holmes, 1982) estimates the board and care population of persons 65 or older to be about 285,000.

The Aging Health Policy Center (AHPC) nationwide survey of board and care programs serving a variety of dependent adult populations estimates that there were approximately 458,513 board and care beds in 1983 (see Table 8.1). Table 8.2 presents a more detailed distribution of the residential care bed supply for mentally disabled and aged populations. The wide variation in number and distribution of beds among the states reflects not only demographic characteristics, but also the influence of such factors as differential statutory and regulatory policies, as well as definitional ambiguities and variations in the quality of information reporting systems.

Regulation and Administration

Formal regulation involves a number of activities, including the licensing and/or certification of board and care facilities, the enforce-

TABLE 8.1 Number of Licensed Adult Board and Care Beds by Type of Facility, 1983

State	Residential Care[1]	Adult Foster Care[2]	Apartments[3]	Unclassified
AL	684	987	0	0
AK	325	16	25	226
AZ	3,641	0	1,369	0
AR	1,098	0	0	169
CA	91,853	0	0	0
CO	693	656	322	235
CT	4,390	441	109	0
DE	446	402	86	0
DC	—	—	0	2,518*
FL	38,092	3,643	16	0
GA	424	1,248	496	1,480
HI	3,956	0	0	0
ID	1,941	0	0	0
IL	133	0	0	9,084
IN	1,653	862	0	0
IA	17,565	100	0	100
KS	370	0	0	850
KY	8,227	1,388	0	149
LA	545	100	128	0
ME	3,294	732	0	0
MD	4,183	218	128	0
MA	8,856	99	2,096	2,607
MI	25,909	8,497	0	0
MN	3,222	0	0	1,686
MS	462	0	58	0
MO	12,417	314	90	0
MT	662	187	0	0
NE	3,366*	450	—	0
NV	815	94	0	0
NH	1,493	0	0	0
NJ	13,682*	40	438	1,878
NM	1,794	0	0	0
NY	33,225*	1,800	0	6,451
NC	14,589*	2,942*	8	0
ND	2,111	0	0	53
OH	3,150*	—	0	2,756
OK	2,102*	0	0	—
OR	3,687*	1,526*	231	0
PA	15,074	0	0	9,780
RI	300	63	312	0
SC	3,471*	0	28	0
SD	1,119	320	137*	0
TN	5,106	0	0	1,250
TX	15,466	0	0	0
UT	969	98	0	0
VT	2,398	0	209	0

TABLE 8.1 Continued

State	Residential Care[1]	Adult Foster Care[2]	Apartments[3]	Unclassified
VA	14,495	135	19	0
WA	–	–	–	–
WV	1,554	1,250	91	0
WI	6,930	0	0	0
WY	270	30	0	0
Total	382,207*	28,638*	6,396*	41,272*

SOURCE: Adapted from AHPC (1984).

–Indicates data unavailable at time of survey.
*Indicates incomplete data.
1. Residential Care Facilities include a broad array of settings (e.g., community care homes, personal care homes, domiciliary care homes, supervisory care homes, sheltered care homes, family homes, and group homes).
2. Adult Foster Care refers to a specific program, usually licensed or certified by the state, which allows individuals to provide board and care services in their homes to a limited number of nonrelatives.
3. Apartments refer to free-standing facilities in the community which include units licensed to provide board and care services.

ment of explicit rules and regulations through both formal and informal sanctions, and the monitoring of these facilities to ensure that operators adhere to the regulations. All states have some type of statutory authority and regulations addressing board and care concerns, but states vary tremendously in the level of effort invested in licensing and regulation (ABA, 1983). In addition, standards frequently vary by type of facility within and between states. Some states use general licensing standards for all board and care facilities, while others have promulgated different standards by size and type of facility, with special requirements for each target population.

The regulatory process and administrative structure of board and care programs nationwide form a continuum from total control of residential care programs (in which both the supply of and demand for facilities are determined by state policies) to a pure market model in which supply and demand are subject to competition and choice (Harmon, 1982; Stone et al., 1982). Programs targeted specifically for the mentally retarded adult tend to be the most formally and strictly regulated, with state and local agencies controlling recruitment and financing of providers as well as placement and oversight of

TABLE 8.2   Number of Licensed Beds in Adult Residential Care Facilities by
by Target Population, 1983

State	Mentally Disabled[1]	Aged and Adult[2]
AL	0	684
AK	84	241
AZ	3,641	0
AR	301	797
CA	31,869	59,984
CO	293	400
CT	933	3,457
DE	42	404
DC	—	—
FL	4,279	33,813
GA	424	0
HI	0	3,956
ID	490	1,451
IL	70	63
IN	1,653	0
IA	1,521	16,044
KS	211	159
KY	112	8,115
LA	545	0
ME	0	3,294
MD	260	3,923
MA	2,004	6,852
MI	0	25,909
MN	0	3,222
MS	142	320
MO	2,899	9,518
MT	632	30
NE	740*	2,626
NV	84	731
NH	534	959
NJ	10,689	2,993*
NM	135	1,659
NY	3,580*	29,645
NC	782*	13,807*
ND	962	1,149
OH	—	3,150
OK	—	2,102
OR	652*	3,035
PA	0	15,074
RI	107	193
SC	735*	2,736*
SD	592	527
TN	2,208	2,898
TX	15,466	0
UT	336	633
VT	66	2,332
VA	629	13,866

TABLE 8.2 Continued

State	Mentally Disabled[1]	Aged and Adult[2]
WA	–	–
WV	156	1,398
WI	1,485	5,445
WY	0	270
Total	92,343	289,864

SOURCE: Adapted from AHPC (1984).
–Indicates data unavailable at time of survey.
*Indicates incomplete data.
1. Facilities provide residential care for a distinct mentally retarded and/or developmentally disabled population, a distinct mentally ill population, or a combination of the three target populations.
2. Facilities provide residential care for a distinct aged (over 65) population or a mixed population of aged and nonaged mentally or physically disabled.

residents. Board and care programs for the mentally ill that are part of the state mental health system also appear to be heavily controlled by state policy.

Board and care facilities housing the elderly and/or a mixed adult population have been traditionally subject to minimal regulation and oversight. However, the past decade has witnessed a variety of state initiatives to formalize board and care programs and strengthen state regulatory and oversight functions. Reichstein and Bergofsky's (1983) nationwide survey of 118 state-administered board and care programs serving the aged or a mixed population identifies three common functions performed by a single state agency or combination of agencies: (1) regulation of facilities; (2) case management or placement of residents; and (3) financial functions including eligibility determination and reimbursement.

Board and care policy research points to the existence of a two-tiered system of board and care programs (Sherwood, Mor, and Gutkin, 1981; Stone et al., 1982; Dittmar and Smith, 1983). Residential care facilities for the mentally retarded and, to a lesser extent, the mentally ill, are usually small group homes with a strong therapeutic orientation. In contrast, facilities housing the elderly or a mixed adult population tend to be larger and institutional in character with little attention paid to rehabilitation or services. Data from an analysis of 31 sets of board and care regulations (Sherwood and Seltzer, 1981) indicate that as compared with regulations addressing facilities for the mentally retarded, standards focusing on board and care for the elderly emphasize maintenance rather than rehabilitation or training. Moreover, Dittmar and Smith (1983) argue that the goals of deinstitutionalization are being met to a much higher degree with the mentally retarded than with the elderly, and that the care being provided to the latter population is really just a form of "reinstitutionalization."

Financing Mechanism

The primary source of public reimbursement for board and care programs is the federal Supplemental Security Income (SSI) program (Title XVI of the Social Security Act), which provides a guaranteed minimum income to persons who are aged, blind, or disabled. States have the option of supplementing these federal payments through State Supplemental Payments (SSP). The SSI benefit levels are established nationally and provide uniform minimum payments in all states. The maximum benefit levels in 1982 were $264.70 for an individual and $397.00 for a couple. The SSP income is more varied with different possible income levels depending on household size, housing type, and whether the person is aged, blind, or disabled. Thirty states provide SSP specifically for persons receiving some form of personal care or supportive housing. Twenty-nine states offer SSP to individuals living independently. Twenty states offer SSP benefits to both independent living and supportive housing populations, while nine states do not offer SSP benefits to either subpopulation (U.S. SSA, 1982).

The income levels provided through the SSI/SSP program operate as a direct income supplement to the low-income aged, blind, and disabled population. Recipients can use these funds to help pay the rent in board and care housing. This approach, especially for the aged, relies largely on a "market" approach to influencing the supply, rent levels, and demand for board and care housing. A few states have adopted procedures which more directly affect the supply and access to this type of housing. Such procedures are most commonly used to purchase board and care services for low-income clients who are not eligible for SSI (e.g., New Jersey) or for residents of states that do not offer optional supplementation payment. Washington state, for example, does not provide an SSP benefit to board and care residents, but pays for these placements directly by contracted arrangements using other state and Social Service Block Grant funds.

Barriers to Effective Regulation and Oversight

Formal standards and regulations have been promulgated in each state; yet the 1982 AHPC survey found that implementation has been extremely problematic for most regulatory agencies. A variety of major barriers were identified by state agencies (Stone et al., 1982).

LACK OF FUNDING AND PERSONNEL

Perhaps the most pervasive problem is the failure of the states to committ adequate resources to regulatory and monitoring activities. The AHPC survey of state agency officials (Stone et al., 1982) found that 75 percent of the agencies reported inadequate funds or personnel to license, inspect, or enforce regulations. While all state agencies are usually required to inspect facilities at least annually, several states noted that budget cuts and reduction in staff have seriously curtailed visits to many board and care homes. An earlier survey by Ruchlin (1979) suggests that states have understaffed their regulatory programs for some time.

WEAK STATUTORY AND ENFORCEMENT AUTHORITY

Statutes governing board and care programs are generally regarded as weak. While requirements for the inspection and regulation of the physical plant are usually explicit, the language regarding the monitoring of quality of care is ambiguous (Stone et al., 1982; ABA, 1983). In addition, the absence of intermediate sanctions, especially civil penalties and fines not subject to lengthy administrative and judicial review, impedes the enforcement capabilities of state agencies.

THE ENCUMBERED LEGAL PROCESS

The lenghty and costly formal procedures involved in revoking a license or closing a facility have been found to impede effective regulation and enforcement (Ruchlin, 1979). Such drastic measures are rarely used because inadequate funds usually preclude this expensive course of action. Another factor operating to reduce enforcement is the judicial protection afforded for owners' property rights over residents' rights to quality of care. Even when the operator of a facility has been convicted of a felony, and the state actively attempts to remove the operating license, legal obstacles and appeals can prevent or delay the facility's closing.

INADEQUATE DATA BASE TO FACILITATE
REGULATION AND OVERSIGHT

Few state and local resources have been made available to support the maintenance of adequate records regarding changes in bed supply, client placement and turnover, and enforcement actions (Reichstein and Bergofsky, 1983). Consequently, there are no mechanisms for ensuring accountability or for assessing the impact of state discretionary policy changes on the supply, availability, or accessibility of board and care facilities.

FRAGMENTATION OF AGENCY RESPONSIBILITY

Compounding other barriers to effective regulation and oversight of board and care programs is the fragmentation of administrative and regulatory responsibility. These responsibilites are frequently spread among a number of agencies, encouraging duplication of effort and allowing clients and facilities to become lost in a bureaucratic maze. For example, local as well as state departments of health are often responsible for sanitation and other physical environment considerations. Furthermore, state and/or local health and social service offices may share responsibility for programmatic review. The division of authority between state and local government, and among categorical service populations (e.g., aged versus mentally retarded), helps contribute to fragmentation. Most states lack formal intergovernmental coordination mechanisms. Informal coordination usually depends upon such factors as proximity of agencies and the degree to which a "problem" facility or program is perceived as a common threat.

INADEQUATE KNOWLEDGE AND SKILLS
AMONG REGULATORY OFFICIALS AND OPERATORS

Board and care housing inspectors have been described in many states as having little knowledge of the unique problems of the elderly or disabled target populations and of not being specifically trained to evaluate the quality of care in board and care facilites (Ruchlin, 1979; Stone et al., 1982).

Many board and care operators have been found to lack the administrative skills and/or substantive understanding of the needs and concerns of their residents to provide adequate and appropriate care (U.S. DHHS, 1982b; Harmon, 1982). "Mom and Pop" operators, in particular, are frequently unskilled in such areas as bookkeeping and records management and are often confused by the intricacies of state and local regulatory changes (Dittmar and Smith, 1983).

INADEQUATE REIMBURSEMENT POLICIES

The current reimbursement method for board and care housing, which relies primarily on SSI/SSP benefit levels, has been described as an inadequate mechanism for encouraging the expansion of supply and the upgrading of facilities to meet life safety and quality of care standards (U.S. GAO, 1979; U.S. DHHS, 1982b; Stone et al., 1982). One particularly important consideration is the ability of low-income (publicly subsidized) persons needing board and care to compete with private (non-subsidized) individuals seeking such housing. Access to this care is especially problematic in situations where there is a high demand from private payers and a limited bed supply. Without public subsidies that are high enough to compete with private payers, low-income persons can be expected to have limited access.

While no study has investigated how reimbursement levels affect supply and access on a national scale, the experience of Washington state (Peguillan-Shea, Wood, and Newcomer, 1983) illustrates the potential interaction between reimbursement levels and access. Rather than providing an SSP benefit to board and care residents, this state pays for these placements by contracted arrangements using other state and Social Service Block Grant funds. The Washington State Department of Health and Human Services views these reimbursement rates as low in comparison to private market rents. In 1980 there were 16,000 licensed supervised housing (i.e., board and care) beds within Washington meeting an estimated 59 percent of the need for this housing. Because of the relatively low reimbursement level, less than one-third of these beds were occupied by SSI-eligible persons; the balance were occupied by residents who pay privately.

Alternative State Strategies

Recognizing the various obstacles to regulation and enforcement, several states have begun to explore nonregulatory alternatives to expanding the supply and availability of facilities and ensuring life safety and quality of care. These strategies make use of existing resources and attempt to provide low-cost, less threatening mechanisms to facilitate provider compliance. Recent reports (U.S. DHHS, 1982b; Harmon, 1982; Stone et al., 1982) have identified some of these activities as "best practices." Following are examples of ways in which state and local governments might address their board and care problem. Given the newness of most of these programs and the myraid changes and reorganizations occurring in state agencies, formal evaluations have not been conducted.

COORDINATION AMONG AGENCIES

The lack of coordination among agencies involved in regulating and administering board and care programs has been addressed by policies requiring all agencies responsible for licensing, inspection, placement, and monitoring activities to share information (Stone et al., 1982). Several states (e.g., California, Oregon, Minnesota) have developed formal information-sharing agreements among the appropriate agencies. New Jersey has even used a state statute to mandate the establishment of a formal communication network.

CONSULTATION/TECHNICAL ASSISTANCE

Recognizing that a purely adversarial approach to noncomplying board and care operators may result in unnecessary reductions in the availability of needed beds (Harmon, 1982), many state agencies have adopted technical assistance strategies to encourage operators to comply with standards and to upgrade physical plant and quality of care (U.S. DHHS, 1982b; Stone et al., 1982). While most of the state regulations include, at best, minimal training requirements, a number of state agencies have instituted formal training programs in issues such as financial management, home improvement, cardiopulmonary resuscitation, and nutrition. A few states offer formal courses for operators to receive certification. Curriculum for operators is also being tested to include accessing community resources, establishing case management, and handling medications. While these activities reflect an increasing recognition of the benefits of formal training, this strategy requires a strong financial commitment from the state in order to be successfully executed.

FINANCIAL INCENTIVES

The provision of financial incentives beyond board and care reimbursement rates is another major nonregulatory device for encouraging the supply of board and care facilities while simultaneously ensuring quality of care and life safety among residents. Among a few states, these incentives have taken the form of low-interest loan and grant programs to assist operators in upgrading their physical plants. This upgrading can include the installation of sprinklers and smoke alarm systems or more elaborate remodeling. One state has even appropriated funds to help finance the upgrading and new construction of facilities for the developmentally disabled and the mentally ill, as well as for conversion of motels into group homes.

ESTABLISHMENT OF COMPLAINT OFFICES

Several states have attempted to capitalize on informal existing sources to strengthen state enforcement efforts. These include encouraging the general public, through advertising in the mass media, to report complaints. Another state operates a 24-hour hotline with complaints investigated within 24 to 72 hours and results reported to county welfare agencies for action. A Central Referral Bureau to control placement and monitoring of any individual receiving board and care assistance represents an even more stringent attempt by a state agency to improve life safety and quality of care oversight.

States have also utilized their Nursing Home Ombudsman programs to strengthen monitoring activities. Though most of these efforts are still on an ad hoc basis, at least three states require their ombudsmen to investigate all complaints related to board and care facilities.

EXTERNAL PARTICIPATION
IN INSPECTION AND MONITORING

The use of provider and consumer groups represents a low-cost strategy for inspecting and monitoring board and care facilities. Provider organizations have begun to assume some responsibility for enforcing standards in several states. These include offering bimonthly training sessions for operators and monitoring the quality of care in member facilities. In addition, some provider groups have begun to help the state identify unlicensed facilities.

**INTEGRATION OF BOARD AND CARE
WITH THE CONTINUUM OF CARE**

Several states, committed to the dual goals of cost containment and the provision of appropriate levels of care, have attempted to incorporate board and care into their broader long term care strategy (Sherwood et al., 1981; Harmon, 1982; Stone et al., 1982). This has been done by provider recruitment and training, direct control of placement by restricting SSI and/or other state funds to clients determined eligible by the program agency, formal needs assessment, case management, and linkages to community services (Harmon, 1982).

Conclusion

State and local governments have been hindered by a number of serious barriers in their policy attempts to encourage the expansion of supply and accessibility to board and care facilities while at the same time ensuring life safety and quality of care for board and care residents. To date such diverse factors as the definitional ambiguities surrounding the concepts *board and care* and *quality of care,* insufficient state and local resources for programs, weak statutory authority and an encumbered legal process, fragmentation of responsibility, and an inadequate data and knowledge base have impeded effective regulation and oversight of the board and care industry.

Several states have attempted to overcome these barriers by expanding their statutory authority and/or by promulgating stricter and more explicit regulations. Others have begun to explore alternative strategies to strengthen their administrative and oversight capacities. The development of financial incentives for board and care operators and the expansion and upgrading of technical assistance and formal training programs for providers and licensing and inspection personnel represent two promising approaches. Formal evaluations of these innovations are needed, however, to assess the impact of these activities and to ascertain the feasibility of replicating them.

Particular attention must be paid to the costs of alternative strategies and their potentially adverse effects on the supply of licensed beds. For example, one course of action might require the licensing of all group housing facilities, but would also increase the regulatory costs for state and local governments. A countervailing strategy might entail federal, state, and local government experimentation with alternative reimbursement policies beyond the SSI/SSP benefit levels. Options would include tax incentives, subsidized construction, and bond issues.

Regardless of the approach adopted, the AHPC review of board and care programs (Stone et al., 1982) suggests two factors which will help to determine the relative success or failure of state strategies. One is that the future of board and care policy depends, in large part, on the level of financial commitment from state and local governments to support the development and coordination of board and care programs. In addition, the design and monitoring of effective policy requires more complete national and state data documenting client and facility characteristics, changes in board and care regulations and standards, enforcement activities, and utilization patterns. In spite of the presence of these problems, states have shown innovativeness in their attempts to establish greater administrative oversight of this industry. Although board and care services potentially have a key role to play in the long term care service continuum, it is apparent that approaches to financing and regulating this industry need to be reformulated. Without such action, it is likely that state and local government will continue to have problems ensuring availability, accessibility, and quality of care in board and care housing.

References

Aging Health Policy Center (AHPC). Unpublished telephone board and care survey. San Francisco, CA: AHPC, University of California, 1984.

American Bar Association (ABA). "State Laws and Programs Serving Elderly Persons and Disabled Adults." *Mental Disability Law Reporter,* 7, No. 2 (March–April 1983), 158-209.

Dittmar, N. D., and G. P. Smith. *Evaluation of Board and Care Homes: Summary of Survey Procedures and Findings.* Denver, CO: Denver Research Institute, 1983.

Harmon, C. *Board and Care: An Old Problem, A New Resource of Long Term Care.* Washington, DC: Center for the Study of Social Policy, 1982.

Janicki, M. P., T. Mayeda, and W. A. Epple. *A Report on the Availability of Group Homes for Persons with Mental Retardation in the United States.* Albany, NY: New York State Office of Mental Retardation and Development Disabilities, 1982.

Lakin, K. C., R. H. Bruininks, B. K. Hill, and F. A. Hauber. *Sourcebook on Long-Term Care for Developmentally Disabled People.* CRCS Report No. 17, Minneapolis, MN: University of Minnesota, 1982.

McCoy, J. L. *Overview of Available Data Relating to Board and Care Homes and Residents.* Unpublished memo. Washington, DC: U.S. Department of Health and Human Services, 1983.

Mellody, J. F., and J. G. White. *Service Delivery Assessment of Boarding Homes.* Technical Report. Philadelphia, PA: U.S. Department of Health, Education, and Welfare, Office of the Principal Regional Official, DHEW Region III, 1979.

Peguillan-Shea, V., J. Wood, and R. Newcomer. *Washington: State Discretionary Politics and Services in the Medicaid, Social Services, and Supplemental Security Income Programs.* San Francisco, CA: Aging Health Policy Center, University of California, 1983.

Reichstein, K. J., and L. Bergofsky. "Domiciliary Care Facilities for Adults: An Analysis of State Regulations." *Research on Aging,* 5, No. 1 (March 1983), 25-43.

Ruchlin, H. S. "An Analysis of Regulatory Issues and Options in Long Term Care." In *Reform and Regulation in Long-Term Care.* Ed. V. La Porte and J. Rubin. New York, NY: Praeger, 1979, pp. 81-125.

Rutman, I. D. "Community-Based Services: Characteristics, Principles, and Program Models." In *Planning for Deinstitutionalization.* Human Services Monograph Series, No. 28. Ed. I. D. Rutman. Rockville, MD: Project Share, 1981.

Sherwood, C. C., and M. M. Seltzer. *Task III Report—Board and Care Literature Review, Evaluation of Board and Care Homes.* Boston, MA: Boston University School of Social work, 1981.

Sherwood, S., V. Mor, and C. E. Gutkin. *Domiciliary Care Clients and the Facilities in Which They Reside.* Boston, MA: Hebrew Rehabilitation Center for Aged, Department of Social Gerontological Research, 1981.

Stone, R., R. J. Newcomer, and M. Saunders. *Descriptive Analysis of Board and Care Policy Trends in the 50 States.* San Francisco, CA: Aging Health Policy Center, University of California, 1982.

Teresi, J., M. Holmes and D. Holmes. *Sheltered Living Environments for the Elderly.* New York, NY: Community Research Applications, 1982.

U.S. Administration on Aging (AoA). Office of Program Development. *The Long Term Care Ombudsman Program: Development from 1975-1980.* Washington, DC: Department of Health and Human Services, 1981.

U.S. Department of Health and Human Services (DHHS). *HHS News,* April 21, 1982a.

U.S. Department of Health and Human Services (DHHS). Office of the Inspector General. *Board and Care Homes: A Study of Federal and State Actions to Safeguard the Health and Safety of Board and Care Home Residents.* Washington, DC: U.S. DHHS, 1982b.

U.S. General Accounting Office (GAO). *Identifying Boarding Homes Housing the Needy Aged, Blind, and Disabled: A Major Step Toward Resolving A National Problem. Report to the Congress by the Comptroller General of the U.S.* Washingron, DC: U.S. GAO, 1979.

U.S. House of Representatives. Select Committee on Aging. Hearing: *Fraud and Abuse in Boarding Homes,* June 25, 1981, No. 97-295. Washington, DC: U.S. Government Printing Office, 1981a.

———. Hearing: *Oversight Hearing on Enforcement of the Keys Amendment,* July 28, 1981. Washington, DC: U.S. Government Printing Office, 1981b.

U.S. Social Security Administration (SSA). Unpublished data. Washington, DC: U.S. Department of Health and Human Services, 1982.

CHAPTER 9

COMMUNITY-BASED LONG TERM CARE

A. E. Benjamin, Jr.

Care in the home and community, rather than in institutions, has historically been the traditional form of care for most elderly and disabled persons in this country. The advent of general hospitals, mental hospitals, nursing homes, and other institutions is a relatively recent occurrence, but one that has come to dominate public spending for health care. The policy pendulum is now beginning to swing back to community-based care, and in the last several years a number of important developments have occurred. Because long term care policy is formulated within a federal system, the roles of both the federal and state governments must be examined if the breadth and complexity of these developments are to be appreciated.

While the federal debate regarding long term care policy continues to be halting and uncertain, at least in part because it is believed the costs of action outweigh those of inaction, more certainty emerges in the federal conviction that state discretion in the design of innovative approaches to long term care should be increased. Most long term care policy activity is now occurring at the state level, as in fact it has for the past decade. It is the purpose of this chapter to consider shifts in federal policy that have stimulated new developments in long term care, to suggest the range of state policy initiatives in this area, and to highlight what seem to be the most interesting and promising among them. While movement toward the development of community-based long term care has often been tentative and indecisive, this

Author's Note: The research on which this chapter is based was supported in part by grants from the National Center on Health Services Research (No. HS04042) and the Pew Memorial Trust.

area clearly represents the most challenging and innovative sector of health care policy, particularly with respect to Medicaid as the primary public payer of long term care services.

Changing Policy Environment

Recent state policy efforts in long term care have been encouraged both by increases in state discretion authorized by federal law, most notably the Omnibus Budget Reconciliation Act (OBRA) of 1981 (U.S. PL 97-35), and by the convergence of several economic and political trends of major consequence for state governments. Section 2176 of OBRA grants the Secretary of the Department of Health and Human Services the authority to waive existing Medicaid requirements in order to permit the states to finance noninstitutional long term care (LTC) services. This waiver authority, designed to support services for Medicaid-eligible persons who otherwise would require nursing home care, constitutes a major change in federal policy, which until 1981 had been heavily biased toward institutional services (Greenberg, Schmitz, and Lakin, 1983). Section 2176 specifies seven services that states may offer under their waiver programs: case management, homemaker, home-health aide, personal care, adult day health, habilitation, and respite care.

The extent of state response to this waiver opportunity is evidence of its timeliness and potential significance. As of July 1983, 44 of the 50 states had submitted 86 waiver applications, of which 45 waivers from 35 states had been approved and only 6 had been denied (Greenberg et al., 1983). Under the additional flexibility granted the states under OBRA waiver provisions, states are freed from the requirement that services be offered to all Medicaid recipients statewide. This has had important consequences, for states may provide a new combination of services to a limited population before considering more comprehensive efforts. As a result, few state waiver programs are statewide and, while no data is yet available, it is certain that the numbers served will be quite modest. Still, the almost universal participation of the states indicates that state interest in the development of community-care systems is widespread and growing. The increased incentives for hospitals associated with Medicare financing on the basis of DRGs (diagnosis-related groups) to move patients into the community will serve only to multiply state interest in community care.

Changes in federal law have been accompanied by other trends that have altered state perspectives on community care. A demographic revolution involving dramatic increases in the number (and proportion) of elderly persons in the population is driving the demand for long term care services. This increase in demand varies among the states, but has become a demographic and political reality in all. In addition, the population distribution within the over-65 age group continues to change in policy-significant ways (See Chapter 2). By the year 2000 it is expected that half of the elderly will be over age 75, and that the numbers of those over 85 will increase even more dramatically (Vladeck and Firman, 1983).

The political environments in which states are making long term care policy also have changed in important ways. Many states have experienced sharp declines in revenues since the late 1970s, along with a shift in the willingness of their populaces to bear the costs of support for public programs. The result has been that state budgets are no longer able, as they seemed to be during the earlier years of the 1960s and 1970s, to absorb the rapidly growing costs of long term care. At the same time, as state resource growth has slowed, levels of federal assistance to the states for medical and social services have been reduced. Growing costs, increasing demand, and curtailed state and federal resources have forced many state governments to confront complex issues of long term care policy, willing or not (Estes, Newcomer and Associates, 1983). Some states have seemed quite willing.

Learning from the Past

While recent changes in federal law have increased substantially the latitude available to the states to develop new approaches to financing long term care, at least some states had been planning for that day for some time. Many states have become increasingly sophisticated about how to provide community care. Earlier Medicare and Medicaid waiver-projects; the activities of selected Older Americans Act agencies; and, in a few cases, dogged state determination outside of the waiver process have produced a body of experience and knowledge about community care that did not exist ten, or even five, years ago.

Growing political support also seem to have emerged in many states for doing something about the "nursing home problem." States seem to fall into three groups in this respect: the states where commitment and funding are available (e.g., Massachusetts); states where some commitment is present but funding is not (e.g., Connecticut); and states where next steps still are being discussed.

Federally funded long term care demonstration projects represent one important source of state experience and expertise with respect to community care. In the context of debates regarding federalism, it is important to note that federal programs supporting demonstrations and experiments are the result of state innovations and state demands as well as federal imagination and planning. Federally supported demonstrations, primarily under the auspices of the U.S. Health Care Financing Administration (HCFA), have emphasized new approaches to community care in three areas:

- The coordination and management of an appropriate mix of health and social services directed at individual client needs with the goal of reducing institutionalization and costs without sacrificing quality of care;

- Medicare and Medicaid coverage of long term care services in which payment for certain quasi-medical services, or changes in the location of services, may reduce the overall costs of long term care; and

- Innovative reimbursement methods that test whether costs are reduced without adversely affecting patient outcomes (Hamm, Kickham, and Cutler, 1983).

The primary thrust of federal demonstration efforts has involved issues of the coordination and management of care. The concepts of organized community care and the personal care organization stimulated an early long term care demonstration in Wisconsin in 1974, called the Community Care Organization (CCO) Project. This and subsequent demonstrations have implemented variations on core case management functions, including centralized intake/screening, client assessment, care planning, and follow-up. While the evidence has been mixed regarding the extent to which community care involves cost savings when compared with institutional care, these projects have provided important experience regarding basic organizational and policy issues in community care (Hamm et al., 1983).

Following early demonstrations in Wisconsin, Georgia, Oregon, and elsewhere, Congress appropriated funds in 1980 to support the National Long-Term Care Channeling Demonstration Program. Channeling projects in twelve states are providing a range of health and social services to long term care clients. The primary elements of the channeling concept are outreach/case finding, screening, client assessment, and case management.

Other demonstration efforts are designed to alter Medicare and Medicaid coverage in order to include nonmedical services for long term care clients in programs that are primarily medical. A national hospice demonstration is the most significant of this type of program, and is considering the impact of additional service coverage for the costs and quality of care. Several efforts to test alternative reimbursement systems have also been initiated under HCFA auspices. Hospitals in several rural states have been permitted to provide long term care using the "swing-bed" concept of care, under which beds can alternatively be used (and reimbursed) for acute and extended care. In social/health maintenance organizations (S/HMO) project, Brandeis University is testing the concept of providing a continuum of medical and social services to the elderly through a health maintenance organization, or prepaid group practice (Luft, 1981). This three-year project involves development, implementation, and evaluation of the S/HMO concept at three sites and represents a promising new approach to bridging the gap between acute and long term care through a single service mechanism (Hamm et al., 1983).

In addition to supporting the testing of new forms of service delivery, federally funded demonstrations are designed to permit states to address problems associated with program boundaries. Separate funding streams for long term care (i.e., Medicaid, Medicare, Social Services Block Grant, Older Americans Act, and others) traditionally have meant profound administrative difficulties in providing a set of services across programs in a coherent fashion. Federal waivers and state determination have increased the possibility of merged funding streams for long term care, although years of administrative groundwork often must be laid before such arrangements are developed. This work is one of the most important challenges confronting the states.

Generally, the states have been enthusiastic in applying for federal Medicaid waivers, in establishing interagency planning bodies to recommend reforms in long term care, and in some instances eager to propose comprehensive solutions to the long term care problem. One such state recommendation is to create a special long term care fund that would accumulate money now (from general revenues or special taxes) and disburse the funds when the baby boom children reach nursing home age. Significantly, however, in the actual design and development of long term care programs, most states have been quite cautious. Because many states are trying something to improve financing for long term care, there are a number of new developments on which to report. In most states, however, comprehensive change still awaits alterations in federal policy. In a few states, on the other hand, efforts to change the mix of long term care services financed and the methods of financing have been determined and imaginative.

Alterations in state financing and design of long term care can take various forms. In fact, much current innovative state activity is less concerned with directly altering funding levels or methods of payment than with other aspects of state community care policy.

Dimensions of State Innovation

An examination of the range of recent state approaches to long term care, reveals a series of policy questions to which these approaches are addressed:

- Who gets into the long term care service system and, more importantly, where in that system do they enter?
- How can traditional modes of community care, including self-care and family care, be reinforced and supported?
- How can present payment methods be altered to reduce the costs of community care?
- How can the fragmentation be reduced among the various public funding streams that support long term care services?
- How can the level of resources available for community long term care services be increased?

ENTRY

Both the remarkable growth in Medicaid nursing home costs and the growing body of evidence that many nursing home residents either do not belong there or do not need the level of care they are receiving have persuaded many states to develop preadmission screening programs for Medicaid patients prior to their entry into nursing homes, i.e., mechanisms by which the decision to place someone in a nursing home is reviewed formally by the state before admission occurs. In a few states preadmission screening has been extended to all persons considered for nursing home care, whatever the source of payment. In the context of long term care, these programs reflect the assumption that it is preferable to divert persons from entering nursing homes than it is to return nursing home residents to community settings (Knowlton, Clauser, and Fatula, 1982). While all states have been required to have utilization review (UR) programs for nursing homes (i.e., often perfunctory reviews of the appropriateness of placement done regularly during nursing home stays), most evidence suggests that review takes place after admission, and at that point return to the community is difficult, if not impossible. A majority of the states have established some form of preadmission screening program. Efforts in Minnesota, Connecticut, New Jersey, and Maryland are among the more ambitious.

State approaches to controlling entrance to nursing homes have involved hospitals as well. Virtually any discussion with knowledgeable state officials responsible for long term care turns eventually to the traditional role played by the hospital—specifically, by hospital discharge planners—in channeling the elderly and others into nursing homes rather than community care. Increasingly, officials maintain that state efforts to do preadmission screening without specific, formal inclusion of hospital discharge planners are unlikely to be successful, since about one-third of nursing home residents go there directly from hospital stays. Some emphasis has been placed on establishing interagency agreements between county governments, or other bodies responsible for screening, and all hospital discharge planning units. In states like Oregon and Wisconsin, the first priority in nursing home/long term care screening has been given to persons in hospitals. Indeed, virtually all nursing home eligible persons diverted to community care services in the first year of Wisconsin's Community Options Program were hospital-based, producing complaints from elderly advocacy groups and resulting in a six-month moratorium on hospital-based admissions to the community-care program (McDowell, 1984).

Informal Supports

In addition to controlling the supply and utilization of institutional services, many states are considering (and some are implementing) initiatives to reinforce and support traditional forms of support for the chronically ill. A number of states have some sort of family support programs, although most are limited in purpose and scope. For example, many provide training and group support rather than more tangible resources. In some states, such as Maine and Maryland, more ambitious efforts have been made to pay family members or neighbors who provide care (Mick, 1983). Concerns about cost and about paying for care that otherwise would be free underlie state reluctance in this area.

More promising in the near future as a possible source of funds for long term care seems to be the reverse-equity mortgage plan, now being considered in many states. Since more than half the elderly own their own homes, their property provides the basis for a system of state financial support designed to improve the changes that older persons can afford to live at home longer, thus delaying the need for institutional care. For example, Connecticut is currently considering a plan that begins with a six-million-dollar state fund from which monthly support payments are to be drawn. This fund would be replenished by repayments from the elderly or their estates when the homes are sold (Mahoney, 1984).

Private health insurance, another potential source of funds for long term care, is receiving public attention in a number of states. Maryland is among the most active states in this regard; a 1982 statute mandated that all health insurance policies providing coverage for inpatient hospital care also provide coverage for home health care benefits. Maryland also became the first state to require health insurance companies and health maintenance organizations to provide health care coverage of hospice services as an option to all policyholders. By mid-1983 all health insurance carriers in West Virginia were required to make available supplemental insurance coverage for continuum of care services at rates considered by the state to be reasonable (Intergovernmental Health Policy Project, 1982). Whether state-mandated community-care insurance can play a significant role in the community-care market remains to be seen.

PAYMENT METHODS

Among the important federal changes in long term care in the past three years has been an increase in the flexibility that states have in reducing nursing home rates. All in all, few additional states have taken advantage of this new authority (Holahan, 1983; see also Chapter 6). This is probably due to current state concerns about hospital reimbursement issues, as well as to the extent of attention given to nursing home policy in the past. It is widely perceived, moreover, that both access to care for Medicaid recipients and quality of care may suffer as a result of further constraints on Medicaid payments (Feder, 1983; Vladeck, 1981). Where changes in methods are occurring, as in Vermont, the direction is from retrospective to prospective methods.

The rapidly rising cost of home health care has become an issue at both the federal and state level, although the absolute level of spending remains relatively small (i.e., around 500 million dollars, or less than 2% of Medicaid program costs). More than half the states have adopted methods other than traditional Medicare cost-based reimbursement for Medicaid home health benefits. The Health Care Financing Administration is funding a demonstration (to begin in 1984) of prospective reimbursement methods for home health care services under Medicare and Medicaid in 5-10 states. Current data already suggest that, under Medicaid, states using Medicare cost-based methods have had greater rates of increase for home health expenditures than have states using modified cost-based methods or variants of prospective payment (Benjamin, 1984). This is no surprise in light of evidence that Medicaid (retrospective) reimbursement contains no incentives to control costs (Holahan, Spitz, Pollack, and Feder, 1977). Important recent provisions under federal law permit states to substitute inexpensive homemaker services for more expensive home health services under Medicaid. Indeed, the rapidly rising costs of home health visits are of great concern to supporters or community care in many states.

FUNDING COORDINATION

Fragmentation of programs and funding sources has been among the various problems plaguing the provision of community care services. Models of service have always begun with income status, which defined funding category, which in turn determined the types of services "needed" (i.e., available through that category). With the increased Medicaid waiver flexibility available to the states to buy services (e.g., homemaker, personal care, and respite care) once confined to other categorical programs programs (e.g., Older Americans Act; U.S. PL 89-73) and Title XX (U.S. PL 93-647) states are now able to contemplate a new model of service provision. This model begins by utilizing assessment and screening procedures to determine which services are needed, and then considers several sources of payment available to pay for similar and related services. States like Oregon, Wisconsin, Florida, and Connecticut have established statewide community care networks providing services with Medicaid, Social Service Block Grant, Older Americans Act, and general revenues under various state titles. That states have been paying for services under several health and social service programs is not new, but that single administrative mechanisms have drawn programs and services together into increasingly coherent and unitary service systems is an encouraging innovation. One early consequences that some harsh light has been shone on available choices between medical and social services. For example, case managers and policy elites are becoming familiar with the decision to buy services from a home-health aide or a homemaker and finding a substantial difference in cost between the two.

New Resources

Because the fear is widespread among officials at all levels of government that the latent demand for community care is enormous, because it is widely believed that some portion of the estimated 80 percent of community care (U. S. HCFA, 1981) that is provided through informal support systems (i.e., family, friends, and others) would withdraw in the face of publicly provided services, and because of the various economic and political constraints, the level of resources available for community-based long term care remains very small. The Medicaid (Section 2176) waiver process makes available to states funds that were not before available to finance community-based services (U.S. PL 97-35); the actual amount of "new money" for community-based services remains a matter of conjecture. Still, in many states, waivers represent a significant increase in resources for community care. Not surprisingly, there is significant variation among the states in terms of intended waiver efforts.

In a period of budgetary caution, most states are more concerned with controlling the costs of public programs, particularly Medicaid, than with expanding commitments to community care. A few states, however, have appropriated relatively substantial amounts of new state funds under state titles to community care, although the levels are paltry when compared to nursing home expenditures. Florida, Illinois, and Oklahoma have recently committed 20–30 million dollars in new state resources (annually) to community-based programs, with an emphasis on in-home and related services. Seven or eight other states have appropriated much smaller sums (1–2 million dollars) under new state titles, again with primary emphasis on home-based services (Mick, 1983). Various states also report some recent success in squeezing more resources out of the Community Services Block Grant and Older Americans Act programs for community care; these successes, combined with Medicaid waiver opportunities, mean that there are probably new resources available for community-based long term care. These increases, however real, remain much too small—relative to the needs of the elderly, disabled, and others—to stir much excitement yet. Some encouragement can come, instead, from what some states are attempting to do with the tiny piece of the long term care pie represented by community-based services.

Conclusion

States like Wisconsin, Connecticut, Oregon, Florida, Minnesota, and Massachusetts are establishing statewide networks of agencies responsible in various ways for managing or monitoring hospital discharge planning for the elderly and others who are chronically ill, preadmission screening for nursing homes, case management, and the funding and coordination of community-based services. A number of common themes emerge when community care programs in these six states are examined.

In each of these states, planning and development of new approaches to community-care predated 1981 federal legislation that expanded Medicaid waiver opportunties. In each state the program began with a demonstration or pilot project (often funded by the state rather than federally funded) that was expanded to a statewide effort over periods ranging from one to seven years. Most began with some state legislation and some state funding commitment. All involve multiple funding streams. Most have utilized existing local coordinating bodies, frequently Older Americans Act agencies, as the locus of local assessment, screening, case management, and service contracting activities.

Each of the states active in community care has devised strategies for individuals to gain access to services before they become poor enough to be Medicaid-eligible and before they are steered to terminal nursing home care. This willingness to challenge categorical program funding and eligibility boundaries is accompanied by an effort to integrate health and social services in sensible and cost-conscious ways.

All of these states also have challenged in various ways the boundaries between acute and long term care, although the intensity of this effort varies (e.g., it seems stronger in Connecticut than in neighboring Massachusetts). At its simplest, this effort involves timely and informed discharge planning and the prescreening of anyone with the slightest change of landing in a nursing home. It means selective short stays in nursing homes and hospital inpatient and outpatient care as needed, but with community care representing the core, or foundation, of required services. In Oregon, where there is an 18-day limit on hospital care under Medicaid, hospital discharge planners were reluctant to become involed in the community care process (Ladd, 1984). But they learned quickly—even before DRGs—that planned timely discharge was probably to the advantage of patient and hospital alike.

Resistance by hospital planners to involvement in community care networks is not unusual; hospitals are clearly facing some new challenges to standard ways of doing business. In Wisconsin, for example, hospitals are part of the current debate on a proposed long term care block grant. Under this proposal, the state would determine the size of appropriations to each county for long term care services, and the counties would decide how to allocate these funds. Hospitals and nursing homes alike are opposed to this plan, for at least two reasons: first, they do not want to deal with county governments, especially since there are 72 of them; and second, they do not want to compete with other providers for health care resources. For example, in this scheme, a hospital that wanted twelve swing beds would have to compete with home health agencies and other providers for the needed funds. If a proposed county long term care block grant worries institutional providers in Wisconsin, the prospect of Medicaid capitation for both acute and long term care in Minnesota certainly causes alarm (whether appropriate or not) among hospitals in that state. In fact, state officials are convinced that capitation can work for acute care, but only nervously hopeful regarding long term care. To what extent such a capitation scheme will encourage the shifting of resources from acute to long term care (or the reverse) remains unclear.

Another theme that emerges in all of the states with strong community care programs is the growing health-care activism of aging interest groups. In states like Minnesota and Wisconsin, independent groups of senior citizens are negotiating with hospitals to accept Medicare assignments. At hospitals in Minneapolis and Milwaukee, contracts have been signed that assure acceptance of assignment and coverage by the hospital of a portion of the Medicare deductible, in exchange for a guaranteed enrollment by group members. Aging groups are also negotiating with physicians in those states; half of the physicians in one county have agreed to accept the Medicare rate for individuals and couples under specified income levels. Some rural hospitals with low occupancy rates in communities with many elderly citizens are planning to seek such agreements as a means of ensuring access to heavy users of medical care.

Aging activism clearly has not been confined to community care issues. It is directed at the range of resources and services related to the health and social needs of older persons, whatever the setting of care. Organized political activity by the elderly probably represents an essential leavening for efforts by human service professionals and others now dealing with various administrative and policy issues in community care, like those described in this chapter. It is those administrative and policy issues related, for example, to melding social and health services across bureaucratic structures and funding streams, as well as political issues involving the extent of public commitment to financing long term care for the elderly, that represent the primary barriers to further development of statewide systems of community care. Federal initiatives and state innovations have now provided policymakers with much of the technical expertise and experience essential to such community care development.

References

Benjamin, A. E. "On Understanding Patterns of Growth in Medicaid Home Health Expenditures." Working Paper. San Francisco, CA: Aging Health Policy Center, University of California, 1984.

Estes, C. L., R. J. Newcomer, and Associates. *Fiscal Austerity and Aging.* Beverly Hills, CA: Sage, 1983.

Feder, J. "Effects of Changing Federal Health Policies on the General Public, the Aged, and Disabled." *Bulletin of the New York Academy of Medicine,* 59, No. 1 (Jan–Feb. 1983), 41-49.

Greenberg, J. N., M. P. Schmitz, and K. C. Lakin. *An Analysis of Responses to the Medicaid Home and Community-Based Long-Term Care Waiver Program.* Washington, DC: National Governors' Association, 1983.

Hamm, L. V., T. M. Kickham, and D. A. Cutler. "Research, Demonstrations, and Evaluations." In *Long-Term Care: Perspectives From Research and Demonstrations.* Ed. R. J. Vogel and H. C. Palmer. Washington, DC: Health Care Financing Administration, 1983.

Holahan, J. "The Medically Needy and Needy." *Bulletin of the New York Academy of Medicine,* 59, No. 1 (Jan–Feb. 1983) 59-68.

Holahan, J., B. Spitz, W. Pollack, and J. Feder. *Altering Medicaid Provider Reimbursement Methods.* Washington, DC: Urban Institute, 1977.

Intergovernmental Health Policy Project. *State Health Notes,* 29 (September 1982), 2-6.

Knowlton, J., S. Clauser, and J. Fatula. "Nursing Home Pre-Admission Screening: A Review of State Programs." *Health Care Financing Review,* 3, No. 3 (Winter 1982), 75-88.

Ladd, R. Telephone interview with Richard Ladd. Office of Elderly Affairs, Department of Human Resources, State of Oregon, January 31, 1984.

Luft, H. S. *Health Maintenance Organizations: Dimensions of Performance.* New York: John Wiley, 1981.

Mahoney, K. Telephone interview with Kevin Mahoney, Department of Aging, State of Connecticut, February 2, 1984.

McDowell, D. Telephone interview with Donna McDowell, Director, Bureau of Aging, Department of Health and Human Services, State of Wisconsin, January 25, 1984.

Mick, C. *A Summary of Recent Long Term Care Initiatives in the 50 States.* Tucson, AZ: Arizona Long Term Care Gerontology Center, 1983.

U.S. Health Care Financing Administration (HCFA). *Long Term Care: Background and Future Directions.* Washington, DC: U.S. Department of Health and Human Services, 1981.

U.S. Public Law 89-73. *Older Americans Act of 1965* (as Amended). Washington, DC: U.S. Government Printing Office, 1983.

U.S. Public Law 93-647. *Social Services Amendments of 1974* (as Amended). Washington, DC: U.S. Government Printing Office, 1975.

U.S. Public Law 97-35. *Omnibus Budget Reconciliation Act (OBRA) of 1981.* Washington, DC: U.S. Government Printing Office, 1981.

Vladeck, B. C. "Equity, Access and the Costs of Health Services." *Medical Care* 19 (December 1981), 69-80.

Vladeck, B.C., and J. A. Firman. "The Aging of the Population and Health Services." *The Annals of the American Academy of Political and Social Science,* 468 (July 1983), 132-148.

CHAPTER 10

PRIVATE NONPROFIT ORGANIZATIONS AND COMMUNITY-BASED LONG TERM CARE

Juanita B. Wood
Carroll L. Estes

For more than a decade, national attention has been focused on developing equitable and effective ways of providing and paying for health care and supportive social services to meet the needs of a growing aging population. Many federally funded studies and service demonstrations, along with considerable political rhetoric, have argued for a move away from institutional care supported by Medicare (in hospitals) and Medicaid (in nursing homes) toward the provision of community based care. The goal of such a shift is to enable older Americans to remain in their homes and communities as long as possible. The development of appropriate community-based services has relied on the availability of agencies within communities to provide the services needed. The need to provide more community-based and in-home, noninstitutional care is prompted by the demographic shift that the United States has experienced. Not only is the proportion of the population 65 years and older growing faster than any other segment, but the elderly are living longer and those 75 years and older are increasing at a disproportionately rapid rate (see Chapter 2).

Recent Public Policy Impact
on the Public and Private Sectors

Since 1980, major changes in U.S. federal policy have been underscored by a national mood of austerity affecting the public,

Authors' Note: We wish to acknowledge the able assistance of Patrick Fox and Connie Mahoney in the preparation of this chapter. We would also like to express our gratitude to Brent Roehrs and the Pew Memorial Trust for supporting the research on which the data in this chapter are based.

the private for-profit sector, and the private nonprofit sector. The structure and delivery of community-based health and social support services to the elderly has been affected, as this chapter attempts to show.

PUBLIC SECTOR CHANGES

As noted in Chapter 1, the Reagan administration introduced a broad range of policy changes under the banner of new federalism. These changes were accompanied by a reduction of approximately 25 percent in federal funds for a variety of categorical health and social service programs, and consolidation of programs into a number of block grants. The result was a cutback in state and local monies from federal sources in 1982. These fiscal pressures were exacerbated by state and local revenue problems resulting from the recession and a series of successful taxpayer initiatives limiting both taxing and spending. Consequently, many states and communities did not have the fiscal resources to compensate for federal cuts to health and social service programs.

Coupled with the new federal policy fostering block grants under state administrative responsibility, these state and local reductions compounded the fiscal problems being experienced in the public sector. The initial response of state and local governments in 1982 was to impose across-the-board reductions rather than to target particular programs or populations for cuts (Swan, Estes, Wood, Kreger, and Garfield, 1982). The impact on programs and populations was differentially experienced, however, as opposed to being absorbed uniformly. Social service recipients experienced severe cutbacks, particularly in terms of those services assisting recipients of the Aid to Families with Dependent Children (AFDC) and General Assistance programs. In health services, Medicaid coverage was reduced through tightened eligibility criteria (particularly for the medically needy), new limitations were imposed to constrain service utilization, and many states invoked reimbursement policy changes (see Chapters, 3, 4, and 5). The initial impact of these cuts was far more severe on the working poor, particularly AFDC and Medicaid-eligible women with small children, than on the elderly or the disabled.

As the programmatic cuts stemming from the 1981 policy changes began to occur, a general impression was that trade-offs were occurring between children and families and the elderly, and that the elderly were being given preference for funding. The elderly were viewed as being part of the "deserving" poor who were included in the "safety-net" group. However, the Aging Health Policy Center's study of the early period following these cutbacks (Swan et al., 1982) demonstrated that the availability of services for the elderly actually declined as fiscal conditions worsened. While the elderly appeared to be relatively better protected *when* states and communities had available resources, cutbacks in aging programs as well as in other health and social services programs were occurring even prior to the Reagan administration's new federalism policies. The 1981 reductions in federal support for the community-based human services and programs placed states and cities in the unenviable position of having to cut services or personnel, or both (Swan, Estes, and Wood, 1983).

PRIVATE SECTOR CHANGES

Part of the dramatic change in policy ushered in the Reagan administration was a massive tax cut that, based on supply-side economic theories, was designed to stimulate the economy and create jobs. Ironically, the nation experienced the worst recession in more than forty years. The private sector was receiving mixed signals. The private sector was immediately asked to share the burden of financing community and voluntary services heretofore considered the responsibility of the public sector. Initial private sector reaction was to deny a capacity for "filling in," and to contend that the responsibility did not appropriately belong to the private sector.

PRIVATE NONPROFIT SECTOR CHANGES

The private nonprofit sector has been placed in a difficult position. These organizations, which were established as private corporate entities to provide a public service and were thus not profit-making, grew rapidly in the 1960s and became the primary recipients of federal funds for a host of federally funded categorical programs, including aging services, many health programs, community development, and job training.

In essence, the private nonprofit sector became the service delivery arm of government, particularly the federal government. This sector expanded in response to government funding, particularly in education, health, and social services; for example, between 1975 and 1980, the private nonprofit sector grew faster than the economy as a whole (Smith and Rosenbaum, 1982). As of 1982, government funding to the private nonprofit sector exceeded that portion received from private funding; in local health and social services, government funding of private nonprofit agencies exceeds private funding by two to three times (Salamon and Abramson, 1982).

The bind in which private nonprofit services agencies now find themselves is a result of two factors: (1) their intense reliance on government funds (primarily federal), which are being cut back; and (2) their tradition of not being competitive with for-profit agencies. Private nonprofit organizations are now forced to compete with state and local governments for federal funds and with each other for the limited available private funding from corporations, private foundations, and individuals. Further, many federal programs have changed their guidelines for funding, requiring competitive bidding open to both for-profit and nonprofit agencies for service delivery grants or contracts.

What then is likely to be the state of the community-based system for long term care of the elderly under these changing conditions? What is the impact, individually and in the aggregate, on the private nonprofit community-based service providers and upon the private for-profit and private nonprofit funders of these community services?

The authors' research (Wood, Estes, Lee, and Fox, 1983) in eight states and 32 urban communities in these states permits a preliminary assessment of the 1982–1983 period.[1] Half of the communities studied are among the 50 largest U.S. cities, and the sample states in which they are located represent large states in eight federal regions. These urban sample sites include the greatest proportion of the elderly population.

Funding Reductions and
Service Delivery Restructuring

The picture emerging from nine different types of community long term care providers (health and social service) and umbrella agencies (e.g., Area Agencies on Aging and United Ways) in 1983 is not the one of the across-the-board cutbacks earlier reported by many agencies and government units in 1982 (Swan et al., 1982). Instead, the federal cutbacks reported for 1983 were less severe than for 1982 for most of the programs funded through block grants and categorical federal programs. Even though the recession affected state and local public revenues and their ability to support programs, the impact on private nonprofit providers was not as marked as in fiscal year 1981.

More important, what appears to be occurring in 1983 is the beginning of a restructuring of the health and human service delivery system of which private nonprofit service providers are a part. An important caveat, however, is that, with the exception of community health centers, it is not known exactly how many service agencies have not survived the major human services reductions initiated in 1981. Community health centers report that cutbacks caused the closing of 200 centers nationwide last year (almost 20 percent of the total prior to that time). Other service agencies studied reported increased caseloads due to the closing of similar agencies, but further research is required to determine the extent of this phenomenon.

Although cutbacks continue and budget shortfalls are still reported by policymakers, the central finding of the research reported in this chapter is that a subtle but profound reshaping is occurring in the community-based human service delivery system. Initially following the cuts, both government units and service agencies attempted to maintain systems in place but in attenuated form; and the pervasiveness of the early across-the-board cuts were one attempt to spread reductions over the whole system in a way that would shrink, but ultimately protect, the overall structure.

More recent data for the 1982-1983 period (Wood et al., 1983) indicate that the shifts now taking place are changes in the nature and structure of the system, in contrast to those formerly designed to assure protection of the system as it existed. The first wave of changes with which agencies had to deal involved adjusting to the budget cuts. The deeper changes resulting from other federal policies are now beginning to be felt in the second wave.

The Context of Current Fiscal Conditions

State and local government fiscal conditions are reflected in a pattern of increased state and county government budgetary shortfalls in 1982 and the beginning of stabilization in 1983 (see Table 10.1).

TABLE 10.1   Percentage of Public Influentials' Reports of
              Budget Surpluses and Shortfalls, 1981-1983

Respondent Category	1981	1982	1983 (Projected)
Mayors (n = 29):			
Surplus	51.7	65.5	34.5
Shortfall	34.5	24.1	34.5
Neither	10.3	10.3	17.2
Don't know	3.5		13.8
County Board of Supervisors (n = 26):			
Surplus	42.3	42.3	42.3
Shortfall	11.5	34.6	15.4
Neither	15.4	11.5	15.4
Don't know	30.8	11.5	26.9
Governors (n = 7):			
Surplus	57.1	28.6	28.6
Shortfall	42.9	71.4	28.6
Neither			28.6
Don't know			14.3
Legislative Budget Analysts (n = 11)			
Surplus	27.3	27.3	45.5
Shortfall	54.5	72.7	36.4
Neither	9.1		
Don't know	9.1		18.2

SOURCE: Adapted from AHPC (1983: Public influentials instrument).

For the city level, however, the mayors' offices present a different experience; for there has been a delayed effect of fiscal tightening. While their 1982 budgetary status showed improvements over 1981 at the city level, reports indicated that city fiscal conditions were worsening in 1983. This time lag in reported fiscal difficulty for cities most likely is the result of fiscal tightening imposed at the state level in 1982 and experienced at the local level in 1983. In contrast to the mayors, the county boards of supervisors report little change, reflecting the counties' different responsibility for service obligation and their less direct dependence on federal funds. The states, in general, reduced program expenditures in both 1981 and 1982 in order to bring revenues and expenditures into balance. This is consistent with the declining budget balances reported by the states (NCSL and NGA, 1983). In addition, there has been a steady decline in state and local expenditures in relation to gross national product since 1978, and in spite of the recession, this trend continued in 1981 and 1982.

Of the nine types of service agencies studied, two-thirds reported being affected by cutbacks or policy changes at the federal level, and over one-half were affected by changes emanating from the state level; only a fraction reported the cutbacks and changes as originating at the local level. However, local governments are expected to assume a more central role as federal funding diminishes and agencies turn to their local communities for support.

An imagery of stabilization both in government units and in the service delivery community would be misleading in that it implies resolution. The situation is complex: not only is a reshaping of the human service system occurring, but also additional changes are anticipated from the federal level that will further affect both government and service agencies. When asked to rate the anticipated effects of federal cutbacks on their governments over the next two years (1984 and 1985), 67 percent of the governors' and mayors' offices reported an expectation that the effects would be moderate, while 22 percent felt they would be severe. Only 8 percent of these officials felt there would be no effects.

Organizational Shifts
in Clientele and Personnel

Community service agencies were much more likely to report increased clientele (66%) than increased budgets (18%). At the same time, important shifts in service provider personnel were also taking place. For example, there is no instance in which the reports of increases in personnel equate the reports of increases in clientele (see Table 10.2). While agencies attempted to avoid cutting services, there were fewer personnel to serve growing numbers of clients. When agencies had to cut services, the number of clients remained the same. The effects of this particular bind affected 44 percent of the 357 service agencies studied in 32 communities.

Three of the nine types of agencies studied (see note 1) reported the largest increases in clientele: community health centers, informa-

TABLE 10.2   Agencies Reporting Largest Increases in Clientele
Contrasted with Increases in Personnel and Service Ability

Agencies*	% Reporting Increased Clientele	% Reporting Increased Full-Time Personnel	% Projecting Increased Service Ability
Community health centers	78.6	35.7	38.7
Information and referral	78.6	35.7	33.3
Home health	70.7	60.4	51.2

SOURCE: Adapted from AHPC (1983: Service delivery instrument).
*The nine service delivery agency types studied were: community health centers, community mental health centers, information and referral, home health, home-maker/chore, adult day/health care, senior centers, nutrition programs, and health departments.

tion and referral agencies, and home-health agencies (see Table 10.2). Of these, only home-health agencies report increased personnel and budget capacity in any major numbers to meet the increased demand for service—a result that is directly tied to Medicare policy and reim-bursement changes made in 1980 for home health. In information and referral and community health centers, demand is growing as a result of increased need, but there are no funding increases to match the demand.

With the exception of home-health agencies, the outlook for agen-cies in the community-based long term care delivery continuum is not bright. As indicated in Table 10.3, senior centers, nutrition pro-grams, and adult day/health care, which are the three aging-specific types of agencies reporting the largest clientele increases, the disparity between increased demand and personnel and service capacity is even greater than for the agencies in Table 10.2.

Nutrition programs report the greatest expectation of increased service capacity; and, again, this is tied to federal policy and the stated federal intention of protecting meals. There is, however, a paring away of the "program" of ancillary services that was instituted under the Older Americans Act. The current concentration on meals alone excludes the additional social support services important to many of the elderly who are receiving meals. The problems reported by

TABLE 10.3   Aging-Specific Agencies Reporting Largest Increases in Clientele
Contrasted with Increases in Full-Time Personnel and Service Ability

Agencies	% Reporting Increased Clientele	% Reporting Increased Full-Time Personnel	% Projecting Increased Service Ability
Senior centers	65.6	19.0	20.8
Nutrition programs	58.8	20.0	33.3
Adult day/health care	57.1	23.8	18.8

SOURCE: Adapted from AHPC (1983: Service delivery instrument).

senior centers, many of which offer nutrition programs, reflect the effects of a similar kind of paring down.

Effects of Changes in Funding Resources

In general, community agencies report that they are attempting to increase income to compensate for funding cuts. More than one-third (38%) of the service providers reported increasing fees and copayments, most often in the community health, community mental health, and local health departments. For aging programs funded under the Older Americans Act, there was pressure from the federal level to increase program income (e.g., "donations" for meals). Further, reports indicate that fees or copayments will be required for all aging services by 1984. Nutrition programs were increasing fees, but varied in their persistence in collecting them. Senior centers were the most reluctant to increase fees.

The agencies that either deliver or fund many of these programs (umbrella agencies) also report reductions. Of the Area Agencies on Aging, almost one-third reported decreases in the number of programs they fund. For the United Way, increases were reported in program funding by about two-thirds of the agencies, but these were primarily in funds being set aside for emergency assistance (e.g., programs for the homeless and the hungry who are without assistance). Such emergency set-asides also reduce the amount of funding available for the usual program areas. Two-thirds of Catholic charities reported reducing or eliminating services. Only Jewish federations, because of their low reliance on government funding, generally did not report program reductions or other major alterations in their organizations.

Both service providers and umbrella agencies placed increased emphasis on private sector funding, generally by philanthropic organizations. Even with a relatively high success rate reported by those who applied, the private funding received was not enough to compensate for the reductions in government funding. Of the foundations studied in the 32 communities, almost eight percent reported funding aging organizations compared with two percent of foundations nationally that the Foundation Center reports as contributing to aging organizations.

Interestingly, in spite of the protestations that the private sector would not and could not fill in for government, foundations indicated that they were, indeed, responding to government cutbacks. Foundations responded to conditions created by current federal policy and the economy in three ways: 40.9 percent reported increasing funding to families and children; 38 percent reported contributing funds to organizations to replace lost government funding, and 30.4 percent reported funding emergency assistance. An important issue is how long foundations can or will continue to respond to increased demands for their support, when 81 percent reported increases in numbers of requests and 51 percent reported increases in the dollar amounts requested between 1981 and 1983.

Service Delivery Restructuring:
Case Examples

Nutrition programs, senior centers, and home health agencies have been selected for illustration because changes in these organizations, resulting from recent federal policy shifts, indicate the subtle but profound restructuring that is occurring with respect to the community-based services. The differential effects of such changes are clear, and they represent the repercussive effects of current policy shifts on the community-based long term care system.

NUTRITION PROGRAMS

The 34 nutrition programs surveyed in the eight states exemplify the tendency for community agencies to shift to a greater reliance on part-time staff and volunteers. Nutrition programs have been replacing paid staff with volunteers particularly in those components of service that deal with supportive services, thus creating greater reliance on part-time staff as core staff.

An important finding is the disruption of the "multi-service" function of nutrition. Staff reductions have resulted in fewer services at the site, even with increased numbers of volunteers. For example, reductions in Title XX funding (U.S. PL 97-35) have affected transportation funding, decreasing access to nutrition programs. When volunteers work in this context, they deliver meals to the homebound rather than transport elders to senior centers or to medical appointments, as was frequently done in the past. Additionally, services such as blood pressure checks, basic health screening, and education or legal services are not always appropriate for assignment to an untrained volunteer.

A major concern is the apparent shifting away from the original intent of the nutrition program to provide a multi-service approach to enhancing the lives of the elderly population, particularly low-income elderly. The shift to a more "cost-effective" format not only eliminates funding, but the concept of need for comprehensive services that do more than meet subsistence requirements. One ramification for nutrition programs is that increasing priority may be given to home-delivered meals over congregate meals. If the current trend continues, volunteers will be drawn into use here under the rationale that they are needed for "basic" services and that costs can be further reduced. However, this clearly would mean the loss of the original intent of the national nutrition program to offer meals in a multi-service setting so that other needs could also be met.

A majority of nutrition programs (59%) that had used Comprehensive Employment Training Act (CETA) workers reported that the elimination of this program had affected their agencies, resulting in the reduction or elimination of services. Examples of this types of support services that were dropped were information and referral, paralegal, housing, and chore services.

Recent federal policy changes that have been particularly troublesome for nutrition programs include the new provisions that contracts may be awarded to for-profit agencies and that agency funding from donations be increased from 13 percent to 20 percent of total program revenue.

Competitive bidding for nutrition contracts between for-profit and nonprofit organizations raises a concern that existing agencies may be at an unfair advantage against larger, wealthier proprietary agencies. A further concern is that this may accelerate the shift in emphasis of the nutrition programs from one that builds on a multi-service base to support the elderly receiving meals, to one that provides meals only. Another concern is the practice of some Area Agencies on Aging of awarding contracts for shorter periods of time so that the ability to plan over the long range is diminished, and the likelihood of cashflow problems is increased.

SENIOR CENTERS

While senior centers vary in the number of functions that they perform, they typify the concept of a coordinated community system. The erosion of their multi-purpose nature illuminated in the 1983 survey of 64 such centers (Wood et al., 1983) will be of concern to those who argue for the necessity of comprehensive, coordinated service delivery approaches. Also of interest is the apparent overall pattern of preference being given in public funding to in-home support services, as opposed to community-based services.

Almost 40 percent of the centers interviewed reported decreases in full-time staffing (40.6% reported no staffing change, and 18.7% reported increases) as a result of state, federal, and local government funding reductions. The most striking personnel shifts were increases in volunteers and in volunteer recruitment, aimed at compensating for staff losses and dealing with demands for information and referral. Additional service reductions were reported by more than half of the centers as a direct result of the loss of CETA workers. CETA workers had been used in such positions as clerical staff, translators in multiethnic centers, recreation program workers, counselors, escort service workers, drivers for transportation services, custodians, and nutrition program workers.

Senior center funding level reductions were usually in response to some federal policy—mostly in Title III Older Americans Act funds both for nutrition and for multi-service senior centers. Local policy changes reported as affecting the centers revolved around shifting local priorities for funding as a result of competing demands for increasingly scarce city and county resources.

In spite of cutbacks, almost half of the centers reported increasing services in response to increased demand despite the fact that less than 20 percent reported full-time staff increases. The senior centers voiced a commitment to serving as many elderly as possible without raising or initiating fees for services, thus most centers (86%) reported neither tightening eligibility, nor initiating fees or copayments. Yet, fully one-quarter of these centers reported that their 1983 budgets would support *less* services than were provided in 1982. Over half felt that their centers would provide about the same service levels as in 1982, and 20 percent felt that their 1983 center budget would provide more services than their 1982 budget.

One-half (59%) of the centers established service priorities, most with nutrition as their highest priority as a result of the continuing federal emphasis on this service. While such prioritizing of "basic" services is based on what is considered a federal funding priority, it may not protect the continuing viability of senior centers. For example, interviews with Area Agencies on Aging indicated their distinct movement away from giving priority to multi-service, commuity-based agencies, particularly senior centers, in favor of an emphasis on in-home services.

Almost two-thirds of the senior centers reported applying for additional funding from private organizations, and of those applying, 75 percent received funds from private sources. However, it must be noted that the total amounts received from private sources were only a fraction of the funding received from governmental sources, and did not begin to replace lost federal funds. Two significant issues are raised: Will the philanthropic sector continue to respond to such agencies requesting funding, and can or will this sector respond to the same degree that government has in the past? Public statements made by representatives of the private sector have consistently denied that it can or will do so.

The fate of senior centers as the ideal type of community-based, multi-service organization is a concern raised by this recent research. The consistency of the general movement away from the concept of the multi-service organization among different types of service delivery agencies raises the question of how important the survival of the multi-service concept is to the prevention of premature or unnecessary institutionalization. It also raises the question of what will result from the reinstitution of the categorically oriented single-service provider as the basis of the community-based long term care system.

HOME HEALTH AGENCIES

Home health care is an area in which the federal government has become more aggressive in an effort to control some of the rising health care costs. Congress has recently authorized an expansion of home health care benefits and has added hospice care as a new Medicare benefit. Home health has never been a major expenditure item of either the Medicare or Medicaid budgets, averaging about one percent or less of the total budget. However, recent changes in federal policy are geared to increase the proportion of public spending in this area.

Visiting nurse associations (VNAs), the first agencies to provide home-health services, are still considered key community agencies in home-health service delivery. Traditionally, VNA services have been supported by philanthropy, private fees, and United Ways. Other organizations have recently moved into this area of long term care service delivery. There has been a long-standing debate over whether proprietary agencies should be allowed into the home health field. The Omnibus Budget Reconciliation Act (OBRA) of 1981 (U.S. PL 97-35), reflecting both the policies of new federalism and of market reform and price competition in health, encouraged the entry of proprietaries into the home health field.

Also significant was the passage of the Tax Equity and Fiscal Responsibility Act (TEFRA) of 1982 (U.S. PL 97-248), which placed a cap on hospital cost increases and specified that Congress approve a payment plan based on a prospectively negotiated rate per case. These changes represent an attempt to create incentives for hospitals to keep costs down. New incentives in the Medicare program, then, are to discharge patients earlier and to provide less intensive hospital care. What this means for the home health industry is an increase in demand for services and for public money in the form of Medicare coverage to pay for these services. Most agencies look to Medicare as their major source of government reimbursement for home health services.

It is in the addition of home health agency staff that the most dramatic changes resulting from the new Medicare policies have occurred. Of the 100 home health providers studied, agencies in all eight sample states reported gains in full-time and part-time staff. In addition, more than half of the agencies contracted out services to cover those for which they did not have permanent staff. Half of these agencies reported an increase in the number of services they contracted out (e.g., physical therapy, speech therapy, and occupational therapy). Contracting out also may be used to make an agency Medicare certifiable by enabling it to offer the required number of mandated services. In contrast to other types of service agencies, the elimination of the CETA program had only a minor effect on home health agencies.

More than two-thirds of the home health agencies reported increases in both the number of clients and the number of older clients, with the largest increases in those 75 years and older. This undoubtedly reflects the relaxed Medicare eligibility regulations, permitting larger numbers of elderly to receive reimbursed home health care. These Medicare changes have almost uniformly increased the demand for services, while supporting the expansion of agency budgets in at least half of the cases.

Medicare coverage has been extended to cover more procedures that can be done at home, such as intravenous therapy, hyperalimentary feeding, and chemotherapy. This, on the surface, seems to be a positive extension of coverage for clients who need these services. However, it also means that these services are extended to care for a client population that can be discharged earlier and sicker than in the past. Legislative changes in Medicare to pay by diagnosis-related groups (DRGs) are designed to shift patient care out of the hospital setting. Home health agencies reported that the influx of sicker patients has increased their need for specialized training in many areas, such as intravenous therapy and hyperalimentary feeding. The agencies express concern about having properly trained staff to perform these skilled services and to meet the demand for a larger number of visits by the sicker clientele. Continued funding will be required to cover these procedures and the necessary number of visits.

While funding through Medicare seems to be enhancing the position of home-health agencies, funding through Medicaid does not. Most home-health agencies reported experiencing either actual cuts in Medicaid reimbursement or anticipation of them. The form was either in the flat rate of Medicaid's reimbursement not being adequate to cover the cost, or in reductions in the number of eligible clients. The VNAs appeared most affected by these reductions since VNAs have a service tradition that militates against turning away low-income clientele.

As Medicaid becomes more restricted, home health agencies will increasingly have to reevaluate whether they can continue to offer service without regard to cost. Some of the changes in Medicaid coverage, such as a reduction in the number of visits covered and patients having to be acutely ill to qualify, place a burden on home health agency resources. The result is the growing reluctance of home health agencies to treat Medicaid patients.

While nearly 60 percent of the respondents indicated increasing services, this has more to do with increasing the volume of existing services (e.g., visiting nurses) than with the addition of new services (e.g., speech therapy). Only a small percentage report the elimination (12%) or reduction (21%) of any services, but these figures mask an important issue for the concept of coordinated services. The services eliminated or reduced were generally homemaker/chore, occupational therapy, or mental health services. A small percentage of the agencies initiated fees or copayments for services and one-third reported increasing fees or copayments, primarily in response to federal requirements.

Concern about program restructuring and the fragmentation of coordinated care focused on the question of how the entry of for-profit home-health agencies would affect the shape of the delivery system—whether such agencies would offer only the services reimbursed by Medicare, excluding the additional support services often funded by federal block grants, United Ways, or other local charities.

This concern about competition is not centered only on proprietaries, but is occurring among nonprofits as well. One specific example in our sample is Texas, where respondents reported that prior to 1981 home health agencies had to go through the certificate-of-need process in order to be licensed by the state. That requirement was dropped by the legislature in 1981, and the number of home health agencies in the state increased from approximately 100 to approximately 300. It is unclear at the moment how the proliferation of home health agencies will affect access, quality of care, or price of services.

Conclusion

While funding cuts and personnel losses have been drastic in many cases, the service delivery restructuring that is occurring is of greater concern. The movement is away from the concept of a system of coordinated community-based care provided by a series of multi-service agencies providing multiple entry points; instead, it is toward the delivery of discrete services. This is most evident in the reductions in the numbers and service components that are a part of nutrition programs and senior centers. A further extension of this trend may result as nutrition and home health services are increasingly provided by proprietary agencies.

Home health exemplifies another type of change—the shift toward the provision of in-home services in place of coordinated community-based services. Supported at the federal level as a means of controlling health costs, increased federal funding for home health combined with decreased funding for support services is promoting the single service concept. Home health agencies have reported not only that their clientele has increased, but that those aged 75 years and older constitute the largest increase.

It is the growth in home health, contrasted with reports of increased donations, fees, and cutbacks in other service areas, that raises an issue of trade-offs. For example, the targeting of services for the frail elderly in the home is likely to create a trade-off in resource allocations between the "young-old" and the "old-old." The "young-old" are being asked to pay for more of their services, while government funding is increasing services for the "old-old." The growth in home health services also appears to mean that community-based services are being traded for in-home services in terms of government financing.

One effect of the single service concept, particularly in services that can be counted (such as meals), is that it is easier to rationalize in terms of "cost-effectiveness" than are multi-services such as information and referral and case management, which are more difficult to document in terms of output and impact. Inasmuch as evaluations can then more easily be made in awarding contracts as to who can deliver the most discrete units at the lowest cost, small nonprofit agencies that have traditionally been the backbone of the human service delivery system may be at a disadvantage in competing with larger proprietary agencies.

Because of federal policy and funding changes, more activity is expected in terms of both the consolidation of agencies and the diversification within agencies. As federal funds are reduced, consolidation of more small agencies in the continuum seems likely, as has already occurred in some senior centers. Agency expansion will be in the area of home health care as long as federal funds remain uncapped. Diversification may also occur in the form of private nonprofit agencies forming for-profit subsidiaries to place themselves in more competitive market positions. Both consolidation and diversification are likely to create problems of access for the elderly clientele. Agency consolidations generally will mean changes in geographic location so that the "community-based" agency may be located far from a client's residence.

The diversion of attention to home health services and away from other types of support services (e.g., adult day/health care and homemaker/chore services) will create problems of access for those who need support services. Should the for-profit agencies continue to expand their share of the home health market, lack of access for low-income clients who cannot pay for service may be exacerbated unless state Medicaid programs increase rates and reduce restrictions. The single service concept, which many agencies have been forced to adopt, will make access to a coordinated program of community-based long term care difficult. At the same time, providers are increasing fees for aging services, which is likely to eliminate access to such services for a significant proportion of low-income elderly.

In sum, government reimbursement policy relative to Medicare has resulted in a trend toward an emphasis on in-home service agencies and a de-emphasis on community-based agencies. This, in conjunction with other funding cuts and the policy of competitively bidding for aging service contracts, has increased the attempt to raise more money through client fees. These conditions create various problems of access for the elderly clientele and promote a movement toward a system of services not simply for the elderly, but for the elderly who can afford to pay.

Note

1. A total of 846 telephone interviews were completed (with a response rate of 94%) with five different respondent types: (1) service providers, (2) umbrella agencies, (3) private foundations, (4) private sector influentials, and (5) public sector influentials. Service providers include: (1) home health, (2) homemaker/chore, (3) adult day/health care, (4) information and referral, (5) senior centers, (6) nutrition, (7) community health centers, (8) community mental health centers, and (9) local and state health

departments. Umbrella agencies interviewed were Area Agencies on Aging, United Ways, Catholic Charities, and Jewish Federations. Private foundations interviewed included community, independent, and corporate foundations in the sample states. Private sector influentials were from state and local Chambers of Commerce. Public sector influentials included governers' offices, state legislative budget analysts, mayors' offices, and county boards of supervisors.

References

Aging Health Policy Center (AHPC). Unpublished private nonprofit telephone survey. San Francisco, CA: AHPC, University of California, 1983.

National Conference of State Legislatures (NCSL) and National Governors' Association (NGA). *The President's FY 1984 Budget: Impact on the States.* Washington, DC: NCSL and NGA, 1983.

Salamon, L. M., and A. J. Abramson. "The Nonprofit Sector." In *The Reagan Experiment.* Ed. J. L. Palmer and I. V. Sawhill. Washington, DC: Urban Institute, 1982.

Smith, B. L. R., and N. M. Rosenbaum. Statement given before the U.S. Senate Committee on Labor and Human Resources, Subcommittee on Aging, Family and Human Resources. Hearing: *Voluntarism in America: Promoting Individual and Corporate Responsibility,* April 22, 1982. Washington, DC: U.S. Government Printing Office, 1982.

Swan, J. H., C. L. Estes, and J. B. Wood. "Fiscal Crisis: Economic and Fiscal Problems of State and Local Governments." In *Fiscal Austerity and Aging.* By C. L. Estes, R. L. Newcomer, and Associates. Beverly Hills, CA: Sage, 1983, pp. 113-132.

Swan, J. H., C. L. Estes, J. B. Wood, M. Kreger, and J. Garfield. *Fiscal Crisis: Impact on Aging Services.* Prepared for the U.S. Administration on Aging under Grant No. 90AR0016. San Francisco, CA: Aging Health Policy Center, University of California, 1982.

U.S. Public Law 97-35. *Omnibus Budget Reconciliation Act (OBRA) of 1981.* Washington, DC: U.S. Government Printing Office, 1981.

U.S. Public Law 97-248. *Tax Equity and Fiscal Responsibility Act (TEFRA) of 1982.* Washington, DC: U.S. Government Printing Office, 1982.

Wood, J. B., C. L. Estes, P. R. Lee, and P. J. Fox. *Public Policy, the Private Nonprofit Sector and the Delivery of Community-Based Long Term Care Services for the Elderly.* Prepared under a grant from the Pew Memorial Trust. San Francisco, CA: Aging Health Policy Center, University of California, 1983.

CHAPTER 11

MEDICAID POLICY CHANGES IN LONG TERM CARE A FRAMEWORK FOR IMPACT ASSESSMENT

Lynn Paringer

The nation's bill for nursing home care totaled 27.3 billion dollars in 1982. Of this total, nearly 50 percent was financed by the Medicaid program and another 44 percent of consumer out-of-pocket payments (Gibson, Waldo, and Levit, 1983). Medicare financed less than 2 percent of nursing home expenditures. Spending on nursing home care has grown more rapidly than spending on any other service during the past decade. Consequently, it has come to account for an ever-increasing share of health expenditures. In 1982, over 40 percent of the Medicaid budget was devoted to nursing home services.

Because the states bear a large share of the burden of financing Medicaid services, they have a major incentive to curtail expenditure growth in this program. Additionally, since a large share of the growth has come from nursing home care, many states have singled out this service as a target of cost control efforts. In defining their Medicaid programs, states have at their disposal a set of discretionary policies. Thus, while the federal government sets minimum standards with respect to a state's Medicaid program, the states have been granted a significant amount of autonomy to exceed the minimum standards. State discretionary policies fall into four general categories: eligibility, service coverage, utilization controls, and reimbursement policy. States may vary their discretionary policies in order to attain a variety of goals for their Medicaid programs, including expanding or limiting access to services and keeping expenditures within budgetary guidelines. That discretionary policies can have a major impact on expenditures and utilization is evidenced by the large variation among states in the number of Medicaid recipients per low-income population and in expenditures per recipient (see Chapter 4).

The effectiveness of a specific policy in altering utilization and expenditures will depend on the magnitude of the policy change and the mix of other policies adopted by the state. For example, limits on the use of physician services may have little impact on expenditures if the state does not also impose limits on the use of clinic or hospital services. In addition, the underlying structure of the market that is affected by the policy may have an important impact on the ability of the policy to achieve a specific goal. For example, expansions in nursing home eligibility criteria may have little effect on nursing home utilization if the state has a shortage of nursing home beds.

To understand and predict the consequences of changes in state discretionary policies, it is important to have a framework for analyzing the policy changes. This chapter sets forth an economic framework for evaluating the impact of changes in states discretionary policy within the Medicaid program (see Holahan, 1975; Feldstein, 1971). The economic framework places the analysis in the context of supply and demand. State discretionary policies affect expenditures and/or utilization by altering either the supply of, or demand for, services. While the chapter focuses primarily on Medicaid nursing home services to the elderly, utilization of, and expenditures for, other services and by other population groups will also be discussed since a given policy cut across service and recipient categories.

Economic Framework

Figure 11.1 presents a simplified conceptual model of the Medicaid market, which incorporates population characteristics, industry characteristics, and state discretionary policy.

Demand

In an economic framework, the demand for services is the number of people who desire to purchase the service at the existing price.

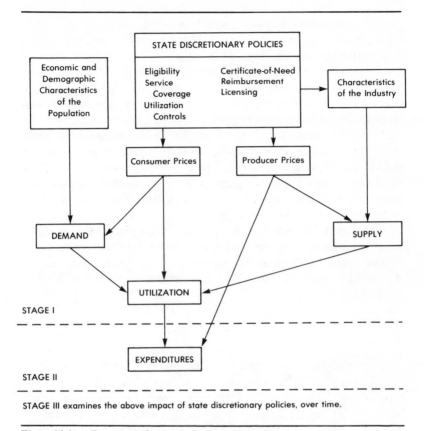

Figure 11.1:   Framework for Analyzing Long Term Care

The quantity demanded of a health service depends, among other things, on the health status and the socioeconomic and demographic background of the individual, the price of the health service, the price and availability of substitute and complementary health services, the amount of resources available to the individual, and the individual's tastes and preferences. By changing any of these variables, state discretionary policies can alter service demand.

For example, if a state decides to liberalize Medicaid income eligibility standards for nursing home care, the effect is to lower the price of nursing home care for some members of the population (i.e., for those who become Medicaid eligible with the state change), thereby increasing demand for nursing home services. Similarly, a state's adoption of a medically needy program lowers the cost of nursing home care, physician services, and other health services by granting Medicaid eligibility to some who previously faced the private price for such services. Conversely, state-level reductions in Medicaid eligibility and the imposition of copayments exert a negative impact on demand for services by raising the price for some people. Changes in state discretionary policies with respect to service coverage, and limits on such coverage, also affect demand for care. Expansion in the availability of home health services under a state's Medicaid program may reduce the demand for nursing home care as some people seek to substitute home health for institutional care. Prior authorization and limits on weekend preoperative stays may reduce demand for hospital services. However, public policies that reduce demand for one type of service may increase demand for substitute services. For example, a state's requirement of prior authorization on physician services may lead to increased demand for hospital services, unless policies are adopted to deal with this likely consequence.

Supply

In an economic framework, the supply of a service is equal to the amount of a service that producers are willing to provide at the existing price. The supply of long term care services depends on the basic structure of the industry (including the average size, ownership, and concentration of firms), the costs of providing services (which are related to labor and construction costs), the technology available to the firm, and federal and state policy (Berki, 1975; Berry, 1976; Davis, 1973). State discretionary policies that affect the supply of services include licensing and certification regulations, certificate-of-need standards, and reimbursement policy. For example, a state's certificate-of-need standards limit the supply of services by limiting entry to the market (Salkever and Bice, 1976). State reimbursement policies are perhaps one of the most important determinants of supply (Pauly and Drake, 1970). All else equal, suppliers will want to provide the services that produce the highest returns. Reimbursement rates represent the price that health care providers can get for providing nursing home care. Increases in reimbursement rates allowable by government can encourage entry into the industry and/or the expansion of existing facilities. For example, increases in Medicaid reimbursement rates may make providers as willing to treat Medicaid patients as their private-pay patients (Paringer, 1980; Hadley and Lee, 1978).

The method of reimbursement may also affect supply of services. The use of retrospective cost-based reimbursement may encourage service supply since providers bear no risk of a loss. In contrast, prospective payment forces the provider to assume some risk and may be negatively related to supply.

Demand, Utilization, and Need

It is important to distinguish between three terms: "demand," "utilization," and "need." As defined previously, the economic concept of "demand" refers to the number of people who wish to purchase a service at the existing price. "Utilization" refers to the number of people who actually consume the service. Only when a market is in equilibrium will demand equal utilization. In terms of an economic framework, "need" is measured in terms of expert clinical judgment as to how many people can benefit from a certain service. It is a subjective assessment and is indepedent of economic conditions. The number of people who "need" a service may be either greater or less than the number who demand the service or the number who actually use the service. This chapter uses concepts of "demand" and "utilization," leaving to experts in other fields the question of whether the "needs" of the population are being met.

Market Equilibrium

The forces affecting demand for services, and those affecting supply, determine the amount of service utilization. When a market is in equilibrium, the amount of services providers are willing to supply at the price they receive just equals the amount of services that consumers are willing to purchase at the existing price. When markets are in equilibrium, factors that increase either demand or supply should result in increased utilization of services; those that lead to reductions in demand or supply should similarly lead to reduced utilization.

It is possible, however, for a market to be in either excess demand or supply. Excess demand occurs when people desire more services at the existing price than are available. One of the consequences of excess demand for services is a queuing up of people who wish to use the services. Excess supply occurs when there is unused capacity within the industry, resulting in low occupancy rates for institutions.

Left to market forces, excess demand or supply should be temporary. In an excess demand situations, prices may be bid up, causing some people (e.g., private-pay or public-pay patients) to drop out of the market for services and, at the same time, inducing providers to increase the quantity of services supplied. Similarly, when there is excess supply, providers may be forced to compete against each other for clients, causing the price of services to fall. Price decreases may encourage more clients to purchase the services.

When excess supply is present, or when the market is in equilibrium, observed utilization of services will equal demand. All those desiring to use a service at the existing price are able to receive services. Under these market conditions, access to care by public beneficiaries is not a problem. However, when excess demand is present, the available supply of the service must be rationed, resulting in a "shortage." Rationing can be based on need, on willingness to pay, or on some other criteria. Providers with the power to ration available services would be expected first to treat those patients from whom they expect to receive the highest return. If the amount they can receive from the private sector exceeds that which they can receive from treating public patients, private patients may be preferred.

The presence of excess demand in a market has serious implications for the impact of state discretionary policies on utilization and expenditures. When excess demand is present, and when providers are financially motivated to prefer private patients to public beneficiares, state policies that alter the demand for a service by public program eligibles (e.g., by increasing accessibility through broadened eligibility standards) are likely to have little or no impact on utilization. For example, if demand for physician services by Medicaid eligibles exceeds the available supply, then utilization of physician services will fall short of demand and some people may go without care. Expansions in Medicaid eligibility that increase demand for physician care will only lengthen the queue of people waiting to receive care, while reductions in state eligibility standards in a state will reduce the length of the queue without exerting any impact on utilization. In contrast, when utilization falls short of demand, policies that expand supply—such as increased reimbursement rates, a reduction in certificate-of-need regulations, or a lowering of licensing standards—can increase utilization of services.

The previous discussion illustrates that understanding market structure is critical to evaluating the impact of state discretionary policy on the utilization of health services by public beneficiaries. Changes in state discretionary policy that reduce utilization when a market is in equilibrium may be ineffective when the same market is in excess demand.

The Nursing Home Market

The market for nursing home services is a unique market in a number of respects: (1) virtually no insurance is available through the private sector, and the public sector finances over 50 percent of the care provided in nursing homes with little support for noninstitutional alternatives; (2) individuals' choices are limited to comprehensive nursing home services even when a more limited set of services might be preferred; (3) there is uncertainty regarding the time period of use; and (4) the structure of the Medicaid program distorts the price of services faced by both public and private consumers of care, leading to market inefficiencies (Paringer, 1983).

From the viewpoint of the nursing home, there are essentially two markets. The private market (including individuals with Medicare coverage) and the Medicaid market. Nursing homes determine the number of patients to be served and the price charged in the private market according to supply and demand. In the Medicaid markets, states determine reimbursement levels. Depending on the level of state-determined Medicaid fees relative to what the facility can receive for treating private patients, Medicaid patients may be more or less desirable than their private-sector counterparts. Nursing homes maximize profits when the incremental revenue received from admitting an additional patient equals the incremental cost of providing the service (Scanlon, 1980; Chiswick, 1976).

The total demand for nursing home care is obtained by summing up the demand by private patients (including Medicare patients, who represent a very small fraction of the market) and Medicaid patients.

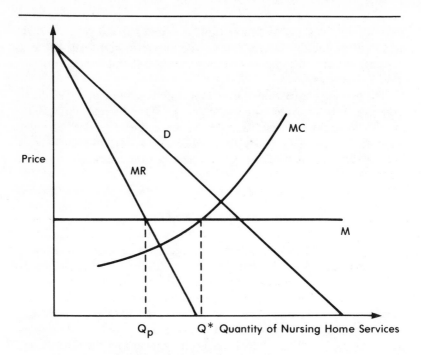

D = private demand for nursing home services

MR = incremental revenue a nursing home will receive for treating
       an additional private patient

MC = incremental cost to a nursing home of treating one more patient

M = Medicaid fee

Q_p = output to the private market

Figure 11.2:   The Nursing Home Market

Demand by private patients depends on the price charged by the nursing home, the price and availability of alternatives to nursing home care (e.g., home health care), the health status of consumers, and their ability to pay for care. Demand for care by Medicaid patients depends on the availability of alternative sources of care but is not affected by the price charged by the facility, since costs to the recipient are not based on facility charges.

Figures 11.2 presents a graphic depiction of the nursing home market. In Figure 11.2, "D" represents the private demand for nursing home services facing an individual facility. The lower the price charged by the home, the greater is the demand for services. Because a nursing home must lower its price to attract more patients, the incremental revenue it receives from treating an additional patient declines as it treats more patients. "M" represents the fee a nursing home can receive for treating a Medicaid patient. This rate is determined by the state as one of its "discretionary" policies. Marginal cost (MC) is the cost to the facility of treating one more patient. As nursing homes expand their services within a given facility, the incremental cost of treating an additional patient will rise. Facilities may need to pay their labor more (overtime) or hire additional personnel at a premium cost to accommodate more patients. There may also be some increases in costs as inefficiencies result from facilities expanding services beyond capacity.

Profit-maximizing nursing homes should accept additional patients as long as the incremental fee received for treating the patient exceeds the incremental cost. A profit-maximizing home should accept private patients as long as the incremental fee from treating a private patient (MR) is greater than the Medicaid fee (M). If the Medicaid patient becomes more lucrative than the private-pay patient, the home is likely to stop taking additional private-pay patients and shift to treating Medicaid eligibles. (According to this graphic model, the profit-maximizing nursing home should provide Qp output (quantity of services) to the private market. An additional Qp-Q* output (quantity of services) will be provided to the Medicaid market since at output greater than Qp, the Medicaid fee (M) is now higher than the additional revenue that can be obtained by treating another private patient (MR). At output greater than Q*, the cost of treating another patient (MC) becomes greater than the Medicaid fee (M) so that, at this point, the nursing home could be expected to stop accepting Medicaid patients also.)

State discretionary policy can have an important effect on the demand for nursing home care. For example, expansions in Medicaid eligibility may increase the demand for services by providing public subsidy, thereby lowering the out-of-pocket price for the new eligibles. Instituting limitations on the use of substitute services (e.g., home health care) under Medicaid may motivate some beneficiaries to substitute nursing home care for the unavailable services rather than pay the private market price. (Both of these changes, which states can make through Medicaid policy, should lengthen the distance Qp-Q* in Figure 11.2 by shifting Q* to the right.)

On the supply side of the market, nursing homes are influenced by the costs of providing services and the payment rates they receive from treating private and Medicaid patients. Because labor costs account for a large share of total costs, the wages and salaries paid to nurses and aides have a significant influence on the supply decisions of facilities. Construction, wages, interest rates, and the availability of internal financing will also affect supply decisions since they impact on the cost of building new homes and expanding existing ones.

State discretionary policy also affects the supply of nursing home services. Regulations that strengthen life and safety practices and increase patient staffing ratios serve to increase costs, thereby reducing investment incentives (Dunlop, 1979). Government underwriting of bond issues and provision of loan guarantees can reduce investment costs and stimulate construction of facilities. The type of reimbursement method (retrospective, prospective class rate, or prospective facility-specific) and the level of reimbursement will affect nursing home profitability and investment. Policies that result in increasing nursing home costs (such as increases in the salaries of nurses) will shift the marginal cost (MC) curve to the left and reduce output. Policies that result in a lowering of costs will shift the "MC" curve to the right and increase output. Increases in Medicaid reimbursement rates will shift up the "M" line, and reductions in reimbursement will lower the line.

To illustrate how a particular policy fits into both the conceptual and empirical model, two policies—changes in the income eligibility standards for nursing home care and changes in nursing home reimbursement—are followed through the conceptual model.

Figure 11.3 illustrates the behavior of a profit-maximizing nursing home. Assume that the quantity of nursing home services desired by Medicaid eligibles is given by the distance "Qp-Q*." The fee which the nursing home receives for treating an additional Medicaid patient (the distance Q*-B) is greater than the incremental cost of providing services (the distance Q*-C). Under these conditions, there is no excess demand, and all Medicaid patients who qualify for and desire nursing home care should receive it. Now, suppose that a state increases the income eligibility standards for nursing home care, thereby making more people eligible and increasing demand for Medicaid nursing home services (from Qp-Q* to Qp-Q**).

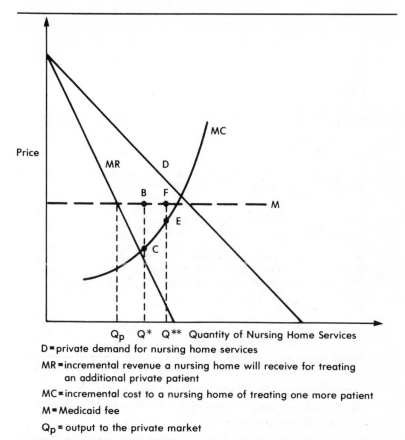

D = private demand for nursing home services

MR = incremental revenue a nursing home will receive for treating an additional private patient

MC = incremental cost to a nursing home of treating one more patient

M = Medicaid fee

Q_p = output to the private market

Figure 11.3:   The Nursing Home Market with No Excess Demand

Under circumstances of no excess demand, services to Medicaid beneficiaries are likely to increase and Medicaid utilization of nursing home services may rise. In contrast, consider Figure 11.4. (Q_p again represents the quantity of services provided to the private market and Q_p-Q^* represents the quantity demanded by Medicaid eligibles.) This time, however, the incremental cost of providing services (Q^*-C) rises above the Medicaid fee (Q^*-B) before demand from Medicaid beneficiaries is satisfied. (Consequently, only Qp-Q output is provided to Medicaid patients while Q-Q^* in additional output is desired, but not supplied.) Under these circumstances, an increase in eligibility may

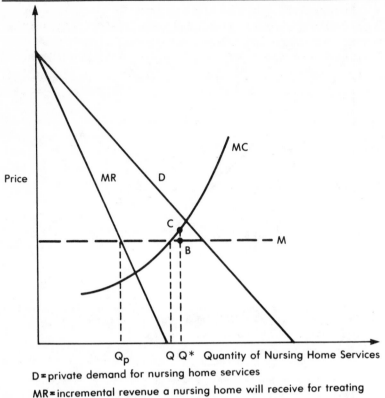

Figure 11.4: The Nursing Home Market with Excess Demand

merely increase the number of people who desire services without increasing utilization by Medicaid eligibles. The implications for analytical purposes are that in states with excess demand for care, variations in nursing home income eligibility standards should have a negligible impact on utilization. In states where excess demand does not exist, expansions in Medicaid eligibility should increase utilization of services.

Expenditure consequences resulting from increased eligibility in states characterized by excess demand should also be negligible. However, in states without a nursing home bed shortage, total expenditures for nursing home care should rise as a result of expansions in Medicaid eligibility standards. Per recipient expenditures may decline in these states if the increased utilization is due to cases with a shorter average length of stay being admitted to the nursing home.

Figure 11.5 can be used to illustrate the impact of an increase in Medicaid payment rates on utilization and expenditures. An increase in the Medicaid fee that states pay (from M to M') may make it more attractive for facilities to serve Medicaid patients vis-à-vis private patients. According to the economic framework, facilities are likely to reduce their output to the private sector (from Qp to Q'p). (Prior to the rise in Medicaid fees, facilities were willing to see Qp-Q* number of Medicaid patients. After the increase in fees, their desired level of output to Medicaid patients rises to Q'p-Q**.) Higher reimbursement rates will also result in higher expenditures per patient day. Empirically, then, an increase in rates in a market with excess demand should yield a twofold effect on expenditures, one through changing utilization, and the other through altering expenditures per user.

The above analysis has focused on the impact of changes in state Medicaid nursing home eligibility and reimbursement policy on utilization of nursing home care. However, changes in Medicaid nursing home policy may affect expenditures and utilization for other services as well. For example, a state's expansion in Medicaid nursing home eligibility standards will increase demand for care but may have no impact on utilization if there is a shortage of beds in the state. Under these circumstances, however, there may be an increase in hospital utilization as patients are maintained in acute care facilities while awaiting nursing home placement.

The net effect of a policy change in a particular market will depend on the ability of the market to respond to the change and the ability of other markets to provide substitute services. Increased hospital utilization is a likely response when there is a nursing home bed shortage and there are vacant beds in the hospital sector. If both markets are in shortage situations, it is more difficult for the hospital to respond to the increased demand for nursing home care. Under these circumstances, patients may need to seek other alternatives, perhaps including alternatives not traditionally considered part of the health

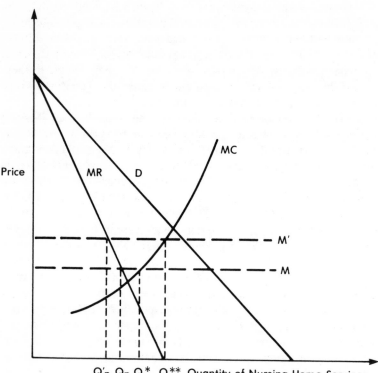

Price

MR   D   MC

M'

M

Q'p Qp Q* Q** Quantity of Nursing Home Services

D= private demand for nursing home services

MR = incremental revenue a nursing home will receive for treating
    an additional private patient

MC = incremental cost to a nursing home of treating one more patient

M = Medicaid fee (old)

M'= Medicaid fee (new)

Q_p = output to the private market before an increase in Medicaid fee

Q'_p = output to the private market after an increase in Medicaid fee

Figure 11.5:   Increasing Medicaid Reimbursement for Nursing Homes

care sector (e.g., board and care, congregate housing) to satisfy their demands for services. Additionally, some patients may go without care.

Virtually any policy change directed at a given medical care market will have spillover consequences in other markets. The total effect of state or other policy changes can only be calculated by summing the effects across all of the affected markets. By focusing policy analysis on only one market, researchers may misinterpret the effectiveness of a program change and may advocate an inappropriate course of action. For example, instituting copayments on physician services may be a very effective method of limiting physician utilization and curtailing expenditure growth for those services. However, if copayments on physician services induce consumers to substitute hospital emergency room care or to wait until an illness has progressed to a serious stage before seeking medical treatment, expenditures in other markets could rise to offset the savings in the physician market. For this reason, it is important to use a systems approach, such as the one outlined in this chapter, in evaluating policy changes. The structure underlying each of the health care markets should be identified and possible spillover effects of policy changes across markets recognized.

For the same reason that state (or federal) Medicaid policy changes directed at the nursing home market may have spillover effects in other markets, policy changes in the hospital and physicians arena may in turn have expenditure and utilization consequences in the nursing home market. Additionally, policy changes in programs outside of Medicaid—such as Medicare and Supplemental Security Income (SSI)—may also affect use of nursing home care by the Medicaid eligible population. Because Medicaid eligibility is closely tied to eligibility for SSI, increases in federal income eligibility standards, or in income eligibility standards for state supplementation, will increase the number of persons eligible for Medicaid (see Chapter 4 for a discussion of Medicaid eligibility policy). All else equal, such changes will result in increased demand for all Medicaid services, including nursing home care.

The SSI policies with an impact on demand for Medicaid nursing home care include the set of living arrangements under which individuals can receive state supplementation of SSI and the level of such supplementation. Currently, individual SSI recipients who seek nursing home care under Medicaid must forfeit their SSI payment except for a 25-dollar-per-month personal needs allowance. If the state elects to provide SSI supplementation to individuals in board and care, congregate, or foster homes, some persons may find it financially viable to stay out of nursing homes—thereby cutting down on demand for Medicaid nursing home services. Thus, how a state shapes its SSI policies—with respect to income eligibility standards, supplementation levels, and the kind of living arrangements that are supplemented—can have a significant impact on demand for Medicaid nursing home services.

In general, states can affect the demand for Medicaid nursing home care by altering any program that provides for the long term care needs of the elderly. Housing subsidies, meals programs, social and recreational services, and utility subsidies all can affect the demand for Medicaid services. Depending on the structure of the market, policy changes in these areas may or may not affect nursing home utilization rates and expenditures for services.

Within the health services sector, Medicare and Medicaid policies in markets outside of the nursing home market (e.g., physician services) will also affect demand for nursing home care. The implementation of the Medicare diagnosis-related group (DRG) system of reimbursement may increase demand for nursing home care for hospitals to attempt to reduce length of stay by transferring patients to long term care facilities. At this point, the impact of this policy change is difficult to predict. If more patients recovering from acute illnesses are discharged to nursing homes and, therefore, more nursing home patients are short-term, average length of stay and hence expenditures per person may decrease. If a nursing home bed shortage exists in the state, and if Medicare reimburses long term care facilities more generously than Medicaid, increased access problems may face Medicaid patients as nursing homes attempt to displace Medicaid patients with more lucrative Medicare patients.

Other state or federal policy changes, in either the Medicaid or Medicare programs, could lead to changes in demand for Medicaid nursing home services. For example, policies that expand the availability of home health services could lead some individuals to substitute in-home services for institutional care. Again, depending on the underlying market structure, such a change may or may not result in changes in nursing home utilization.

Conclusion

The discussion in this chapter underscores the usefulness of an economic framework for analyzing the impact of state discretionary policies on the elderly's use of Medicaid long term care services and on expenditures for these services. Expenditure and utilization outcomes can be importantly affected by the manner in which a state designs its Medicaid program. Equally important, however, are state policies with respect to a whole host of other programs for the elderly and the structure of the health care markets being affected by the policy change. The presence of excess demand in a market may render ineffective any policy that is designed to either expand or decrease utilization by changing demand for services. Only if these interactions between policy and market structure are understood can the states or the federal government begin to predict the expenditure and utilization consequences of altering particular state Medicaid discretionary policies.

References

Berki, S. *Hospital Economics*. Lexington, MA: D. C. Heath, 1975.

Berry, R. "Prospective Reimbursement and Cost Containment: Formula Reimbursement in New York." *Inquiry*, 13, No. 3 (September 1976). 288-301.

Chriswick, B. "The Demand for Nursing Home Care: An Analysis of the Substitution Between Institutional and Non-Institutional Care." *Journal of Human Resources*, 11, No. 3 (Summer 1976), 295-316.

Davis, K. "Theories of Hospital Inflation: Some Empirical Evidence." *Journal of Human Resources*, 8, No. 2 (Spring 1973), 181-201.

Dunlop, B. *The Growing of Nursing Home Care*. Lexington, MA: D. C. Heath, 1979.

Feldstein, M. "An Econometric Model of the Medicare System." *Quarterly Journal of Economics*, 85, No. 1 (February 1971), 1-20.

Gibson, R., D. Waldo, and K. Levit. "National Health Expenditures, 1982." *Health Care Financing Review*, 5, No. 1 (Fall 1983), 1-31.

Hadley, J. and R. Lee. "Physicians' Price and Output Decisions: Theory and Evidence." Urban Institute Working Paper No. 998-8. Washington, DC: Urban Institute, 1978.

Holahan, J. *Financing Health Care for the Poor*. Lexington, MA: D. C. Heath, 1975.

Paringer, L. "Economic Incentives in the Provision of Long Term Care." In *Market Reforms in Health Care: Current Issues, New Directions, Strategies Decision*. Ed. J. A. Meyer. Washington, DC: American Enterprise Institute, 1983, pp. 119-143.

———. "Medicare Assignment Rates of Physicians: Their Response to Changes in Reimbursement Policy." *Health Care Financing Review*, 1, No. 3 (Winter 1980), 75-90.

Pauly, M., and D. Drake. "Effect of Third-Party Methods of Reimbursement on Hospital Performance." In *Empirical Studies in Health Economics*, Ed. H. E. Klarman. Baltimore, MD: Johns Hopkins Press, 1970, 297-314.

Salkever, D., and T. Bice. "The Impact of Certificate-of-Need Controls on Hospital
    Investment." *Milbank Memorial Fund Quarterly/Health and Society,* 54, No. 2
    (Spring 1976), 185-214.
Scanlon, W. "Nursing Home Utilization Patterns: Implications for Policy." *Journal
    of Health Politics, Policy and Law,* 4, No. 4 (Winter 1980), 619-641.

CHAPTER 12

FUTURE DIRECTIONS IN LONG TERM CARE

Carroll L. Estes
Charlene Harrington

Long term care policy in the 1980s will be influenced by the conceptions of the problem, the strength of special interests, and the larger political and economic context of federal and state policy. The major federal policy shifts of reduced social spending, the revival of new federalism and block grants, and the introduction of procompetitive health proposals (Estes and Lee, 1981) provide that context. Long term care (LTC), along with other health and social service programs, is under intense scrutiny at both the federal and state levels, as declarations of fiscal crisis deepen at all levels of government. Fundamental assumptions about basic entitlement programs are being questioned and new policy directions are under consideration.

What began as a limited federal and state government response to a relatively small-scale need for institutional long term care for the aged in the mid-1930s has mushroomed by the 1980s into a multibillion dollar policy problem. Future trends in long term care will be influenced by multiple public policies, particularly those related to such domestic spending issues as income maintenance, health care, social service, and housing. In each of these areas, states will continue to play a key role in outcomes of policy because of the variety of federal laws affecting long term care, particularly Supplemental Security Income, Medicaid, and Social Service program legislation, which

Authors' Note: We are deeply indebted to Philip R. Lee and Lenore E. Gerard for their assistance in developing these ideas and in preparing this chapter. Support for the research on which this chapter is based was funded by the National Center for Health Services Research (Grant No. HS04042), the Health Care Financing Administration (Grant No. 18-P9762019), and the Pew Memorial Trust.

assigns the states major responsibility and affords them broad discretion in carrying out these programs.

The pressures on government are growing with the demand for long term care services. The simple demographic fact that the U.S. population is growing older at a rapid rate is reason enough for national concern about long term care. Demographic factors intersect with social, economic, and cultural factors, augmenting the urgency of an adequate long term care policy. Long term care demand is affected by such factors as the rate of economic growth, the strength of the public and private sector (including the nonprofit or independent sector), and the available human and institutional resources. A new national long term care policy is needed to respond to broad social, economic, and political forces.

Basic Principles of a
Comprehensive Long Term Care System

To develop a national long term care policy, certain principles should be followed. An adequate system of long term care must include four basic elements:

(1) First, it must be comprehensive, including a full range of health and social services covering the long term care continuum from community-based care to institutional care. It must also include preventive and restorative services as well as treatment and illness mnagement. Long term care services must be linked with other health and social services as well as with hospital and physician services.

(2) Second, it must provide incentives for providers to keep costs at a reasonable level, to prevent overutilization, and to promote the use of appropriate services. One way to do this is to put providers at risk under capitated prepayment plans; another is to have an effective system of regulations at the state level that includes all payers for hospital, physician, and nursing home services.

(3) Third, it must have a financing system that provides protection from impoverishment to individuals who need long term care and that allows for combining private and public resources to assure protection for individuals before they become ill

(4) Fourth, it must ensure access to those who need the services regardless of financial ability to pay or other characteristics. Clients must have access to the services regardless of age or disability. While long term

care is predominantly used by older individuals, it is a system for those of all ages who are disabled. In our view no adequate rationale can be made for age segregation in long term care. Age integrated services are essential.

A Comprehensive and Integrated Service System

In addition to basic acute care, ambulatory care, drug coverage, and other health services, older and disabled individuals should have access to a comprehensive service program. A full range of long term care services should include the following:

Institutional care (licensed health facilities):
    rehabilitation
    skilled nursing services
    intermediate care services
    psychiatric services

Residential care (homes without nursing care):
    group homes
    family homes
    personal care
    boarding care
    foster care
    congregate living

Community services:
    hospice care—for terminally ill
    respite care—short-term care to relieve caretakers
    day health care—health and rehabilitative services
    day care—social programs without health services
    sheltered workshops—supervised work settings
    community mental health
    legal services
    protective services
    information and referral
    transportation
    case management—coordinator of care
    home health nurse/aide

homemaker chore services
meals
housing
combination of the above programs

Health promotion and disease prevention are also important components of long term care. The burden of a number of chronic conditions common among the aged such as hypertension, heart conditions, diabetes, dental diseases, and osteoporosis can be lessened through a variety of preventive approaches including diet and exercise. Much work needs to be done to inform consumers and providers about health-promoting behavior and the available health care resources. Even more can be done to let consumers know about the cost, quality, and availability of services (e.g., whether or not physicians accept Medicare assignment and what they charge for their services).

It is not difficult to agree on the elements of a comprehensive LTC benefit package. The difficulty is in agreeing on how many and what type of service providers are needed, who is going to pay for the services, and how the system will be organized and financed. If these are the essential components to a service delivery system, each geographic area must first determine how it stands in developing the range of services needed. In the urban and rural areas, most states do not have a full network of LTC services. While states are beginning to develop such programs as foster care and adult day health care, the growth rate is slow. The rate of development of community-based services does not appear to be sufficient to meet the growing LTC needs of the nation. Congressional proposals that would expend the development of community-based service programs would be desirable. Many states have developed programs through the community-based Medicaid demonstration projects (described in Chapter 9), which show great promise in making services more comprehensive. Incremental approaches at the state and federal level for expanding community-based long term care options are important. Other means of providing federal funds to states for these efforts could speed the growth and development of needed programs, particularly in rural areas and in underdeveloped states.

Achieving the full range of services need not always mean an increase in direct total public expenditures. In many cases, expansion of services could be possible by *shifting* resources away from one service area to another. In spite of a lot of rhetoric about the efficacy of shifting resources away from hospitals and nursing homes, most states have permitted an expansion of acute care services and nursing home beds at the expense of developing noninstitutional services. Since there is little evidence that greater numbers of nursing home beds are needed (Vladeck, 1980), states could limit expenditures in this area and direct limited public and private resources toward developing those services that are *not* available or that are *inadequate.*

In the authors' view, new long term care programs should ideally be community-based, either public or nonprofit, with community boards. This is a difficult political issue. While proprietary programs sometimes develop more quickly and have more funds for new service programs, past charges of fraud, abuse, and poor quality of care associated with operations (e.g., nursing homes and home health agencies) and the questions of their true cost effectiveness (Relman, 1984) support this preference for growth in the public and nonprofit programs, rather than in the proprietary facilities.

Chronic illness and disability services cannot easily be *separated* from acute and primary care services. Those with chronic illnesses and disabilities not only need the LTC services that have been described, but also many occasionally or even frequently need hospital, ambulatory medical, drug, eyeglass, podiatric, and dental services, along with many others that are not traditionally called LTC services. Access to this full range of services within one comprehensive system is the most desirable. If long term care services are financed and delivered separately from acute care, then individuals and patients may have difficulty obtaining needed services from one system or the other; individuals may not receive necessary services, since providers and agencies may dispute who has the responsibility to provide or pay for needed care.

More important, acute care services are considered to be providing a considerable amount of unnecessary care. For example, estimates are that as much as 25–40 percent of current hospital utilization and costs could be saved through different financing and delivery models such as HMOs (Luft, 1981). If such savings could be accomplished, they could be redirected to financing long term care and ambulatory care services; however, the shifting of funds from acute to chronic care services cannot be accomplished easily if the services are financed and delivered through separate systems.

One proposal at the federal level (Home and Community-Based Services for the Elderly and Disabled Act, Hatch, S. 1539, 98th Cong., June 23, 1983) would establish a block grant to states for home and community services. Other proposals of a similar type have been made in states such as California and by a group of Medicaid directors (National Study Group, 1984). These proposals offer the disadvantage of further fragmenting the financing of health care and the delivery of care. By prohibiting expenditures for inpatient coverage even for respite care, such proposals could further add to the problems of continuity of care. The proposals do not facilitate integration of acute and long term care services and would not permit savings from acute care utilization to be transferred to long term care programs. Further, block grants provide an easy vehicle to limit the total expenditures from the federal government, but do not ensure that states will develop cost-effective service delivery programs. States may continue traditional fee-for-service payment systems (described in Chapter 6) that lead to serious cost escalation and to overutilization of services. Such proposals should be reexamined for methods of combining the financing and delivery of all health and long term care services through organized delivery systems at the local level.

A variety of incremental proposals have been made that would expand the development of community-based services. These include: capping federal Medicaid expenditures for institutional care, providing higher federal matching rates for Medicaid community-based services than for institutional services; expanding Social Service and Medicaid coverage of in-home services; eliminating the one-third reduction in SSI payments when a recipient lives in the household of another, and other proposals (U.S. HCFA, 1981). The problem with most of the proposals to expand long term care benefits is that additional funds would be required at a time when neither the federal nor state governments are willing to incur additional costs.

Only those proposals that show cost containment or shifting of public funds are likely to be given consideration. Other proposals (such as the one made by Vladeck, 1983b) would reorganize existing programs using strategies such as combining Medicare and Medicaid at the federal level to increase administrative efficiencies and to provide a full set of benefits to all elderly and disabled. This approach is financially viable since it would use existing resources, but politically sensitive because of fears that Medicare might be viewed partially as a welfare program, jeopardizing popular support for existing benefits in the Medicare program.

Controlling Costs

Because there is general agreement that the rapid rate of increase of health care costs must be reduced, high priority is being given to hospital cost containment through altered reimbursement policies. Congress altered Medicare hospital reimbursement substantially in the Tax Equity and Fiscal Responsibility Act (TEFRA) of 1982 (U.S. PL 97-248) and in the 1983 Social Security Amendments (U.S. PL 98-21). In addition, the administration has proposed further dramatic increases in patient cost sharing. While this piecemeal approach may reduce hospital expenditures in the Medicare program in the short run, many expect it will result in cost shifting to private third parties unless policies are adopted to prevent that practice by hospitals. It is also likely to diminish access or quality of care for the elderly *unless the Medicare cost containment policies are part of a cost containment effort that includes all payers.*

Unless the rising costs of health care are contained—across the board for hospitals, physicians, nursing homes, and for all payers (individuals, Medicare, Blue Cross, commercial insurance, Medicaid, and other third parties)—there will be a continued reduction of Medicare trust funds. This will result in continued rising costs in services and the shifting of these costs to the aged. Medicare cannot be saved by incremental "Medicare only" reforms, no matter how desirable. An "all-payer" hospital reimbursement system has been adopted in four states—New York, New Jersey, Massachusetts, and Maryland. All-payer systems are those that regulate the amount that can be charged for hospital services regardless of whether the payer is Medicare, Medicaid, private insurance, or private individuals. Each state has taken a different approach to regulating hospital payments (e.g., New York has established a per diem rate; New Jersey, a per admission rate). This has proved to be more effective in controlling costs than the legislation adopted by Congress requiring effective cost containment at the state level. If cost containment measures at the state level are not accomplished, then federal regulatory policies would be put into effect.

An example of a method of all-payer regulation that reaches beyond Medicare-funded services is global budgeting, in which the government sets limits on the annual hospital expenditure increases to a predetermined amount. Canada's experience illustrates what an effective method global budgeting can be in controlling hospital costs. Since the early 1970s, with the exception of the U.K., Canada has been more effective than any other Western industrialized country in controlling health care costs. Prior to 1971, when Canada's publicly funded medical and hospital insurance program was fully implemented, health care expenditures had been rising more rapidly in Canada than in the United States (Marmor, 1982; Simanis and Coleman, 1980). Since 1981, however, Canadian health care expenditures have been contained to a remarkable degree. In 1971, 7.5 percent of the Canadian GNP was attributed to all health care expenditures; in 1981, this figure was only 7.9 percent. By 1982, Canadian health expenditures were approximately 8.2 percent of GNP. In the United States during the same period, health care expenditures rose as a percent of GNP from 7.8 percent in 1971, to 9.8 percent in 1981 and 10.5 percent by 1982. Canada has controlled these costs by instituting global hospital budgeting and negotiated fee schedules for physicians (on a fee-for-service basis) at the provincial level.

HOSPITAL AND PHYSICIAN COSTS

One proposal for controlling hospital costs is a plan for all-payer regulation of hospital expenditures introduced by Kennedy and Gephardt *(Health Care Cost Control Act,* S. 814, 98 Cong., March 15, 1983 and *Medicare Solvency and Health Care Financing Reform Act,* H.R. 4870, 98th Cong., Feb. 21, 1984). This approach would encourage states to develop their own plans to keep costs below levels set by the federal government. States would be required to regulate hospital and physician payments, choosing among the options of prospective payment, competition, or voluntary efforts—or a combination of these mechanisms so long as state costs remain under the federal cost ceilings. This approach would require states that fail to control costs to adopt a federal all-payers prospective payment plan familiar to the one already in place for Medicare. Hospitals would be paid on a prospective basis by diagnosis-related groups (DRGs) for the entire hospital stay including physician fees, which the hospital would pay. The sponsors of the plan claim the government could save 30 billion dollars and the private sector 74 billion dollars over five years, and this would assure the financial solvency of the Medicare hospital trust fund.

Many other approaches could reduce hospital costs; for example, by altering the current Medicare reimbursement regulations that allow hospital payment for capital costs for depreciation and interest expenses. Hospital mergers and acquisitions are increasing the costs of Medicare and Medicaid since the government allows hospitals to refinance the costs of mergers and acquisitions and to increase the depreciation and interest costs to government (U.S. GAO, 1983). Medicare officials have estimated the government pays 2.7 billion dollars for such costs and another 200 million dollars in special allowances for profits. Profits have been an area of particular controversy concerning why the government should pay for such profits. If these types of costs were eliminated from reimbursement under Medicare and Medicaid, the government could experience a significant savings.

NURSING HOME COSTS

Since the enactment of the new Medicare payment system for hospitals, there has been considerable discussion of whether nursing homes should also be paid on the basis of resource utilization groups (RUGs) or some type of case-mix approach for Medicare. As noted in Chapter 6, Medicaid reimbursement for nursing homes is determined by state policies, which are primarily prospective payment systems. Four states are using systems that link case mix to reimbursement (Zahn, Schlenker, and Johnson, 1984; Spitz, 1981; Spitz and Atkinson, 1982). While this approach may improve access for Medicaid patients, those states that have attempted to use such systems have found the approach may increase administrative costs when reimbursement is tied to the actual level of care for individual patients. Further, this type of approach promotes traditional fee-for-service rather than newer efforts to encourage prepayment through organized delivery systems. The fee-for-service systems, in which facilities receive high reimbursement for patients who have higher levels of dependency and illness, tend to encourage facilities to promote illness rather than to reward reductions in the level of dependence and illness. Such perverse incentives may increase the utilization of nursing home services and the dependency of vulnerable patient populations in nursing homes. Adoption of systems that link reimbursement to case mix should be seriously studied because these approaches may only increase the utilization of institutional services and the costs to government without any appreciable improvements in quality of care or access to less costly noninstitutional in-home or community-based services.

While state Medicaid programs have adopted more stringent controls on nursing home reimbursement rates, most state programs only focus on controlling Medicaid rates, while private rates are not controlled. All-payer regulation of nursing home payments would have benefits in controlling the increases in costs and protecting individual consumers from excessive price increases. Contract bidding for nursing home services by Medicaid programs is another approach that would ensure access to nursing home services (and could be established using the contract bidding model designed by California Medicaid for hospital services).

Effective controls on the demand and costs for nursing homes probably cannot be without moving away from fee-for-service payment models. By changing the financing for long term care so that payment is made on a capitation basis for a package of services including institutional care, as proposed in the social health maintenance organization (S/HMO) models, providers would be given incentives to control both cost and inappropriate utilization.

ALTERNATIVE APPROACH: PREPAID CAPITATED PLANS

In designing health and long term care systems, public policymakers should carefully consider the various models that can be used to provide incentives to control costs. The greater use of prepaid health plans where providers are placed "at risk" for the provision of services, would change the incentives for providers. "At risk" is the term for the concept that providers would pay for additional costs incurred *above those* allowed for the reimbursement rates. This structure gives providers incentives to control costs and to reduce the utilization of services.

Prepaid plans and health maintenance organizations (HMOs) are means of placing providers at risk and changing incentives. Prepaid, capitated systems permit rates to be established in advance of service provision for each individual enrolled rather than on the units of service delivered. They are designed to ensure that providers keep costs below the rate paid. This has been a key feature of health maintenance organizations, which generally have been able to reduce costs to the states where they have been utilized.

The elderly and disabled have not generally sought enrollment in HMOs and prepaid plans. In part, this has been because of a lack of knowledge about some of the benefits that HMO enrollments may provide, including a wider range of benefits covered, reduction of paperwork and bill-paying for enrollees, reduction in copayments and deductibles, and access to physicians who take Medicare as payment in full. In part, HMOs have not marketed themselves to or reached out to attract new, older enrollees given the uncertainty of the costs of a potentially less healthy population than the typical (younger) HMO enrollee. Further, HMOs, like private insurance, provide minimal long term care benefits. HMOs have been selective in the types of patients enrolled in the program to avoid high-cost patients such as the aged and disabled.

To solve some of these problems, new prepaid plans are now being developed on a model that includes long term care services as well as acute and primary care services. These social health maintenance organizations (S/HMOs) have potential for redesigning both the delivery and financing of long term care. The S/HMO combines a comprehensive delivery system with a financing system (prepayment) that controls costs (Diamond and Berman, 1981). S/HMOs are financed with a payment system based on capitation rates (fixed in advance per individual) like the payments for HMOs. Clients enroll voluntarily, and payments for enrollment may come from a variety of sources including Medicare, Medicaid, and private sources. Four initial S/HMO demonstration projects have been developed by the Health Care Financing Administration and Brandeis University using a combination of public and private funds.[1] In spite of the initial barriers to development, this new model is one of the most promising approaches, and recently introduced legislation would establish more S/HMO demonstrations.

*Financing System that Provides
Protection from Improverishment*

The current financing system for long term care does not provide protection from impoverishment. Both private insurance and Medicare provide little long term care coverage. As noted in Chapter 1, of the total nursing home expenditures in 1982, only 1.5 percent was paid by private insurance; 54.5 percent was paid by public programs (largely Medicaid); and 44 percent was paid out-of-pocket by the elderly and their families (Gibson, Waldo, and Levit, 1983).

Because of inadequate coverage of long term care, many individuals and families face *impoverishment* over the expenses for chronic illness when hospitalization or nursing home care is required for an extended period of time. When a chronic illness lasts over a period of time, many middle-class elderly individuals and families soon exhaust their resources and are forced to use public resources from Medicaid to pay for expensive care. The number of individuals unable to pay for long term care will most likely continue to increase as social, economic,and political pressures increase demand. This will be a certainty without a new long term care policy and reforms in the financing and delivery of care. How many aged persons can afford to pay the 70 dollars a day, or 26,000 dollars a year in costs for nursing home care for any extended period of time without losing their homes and other assets? Individuals should be able to purchase protection against the possibility of such impoverishment.

From government's perspective, the best system would allow for a combination of public and private financing that would reduce the state and federal financial burden of the Medicaid program. A financing system for long term care should also spread the financial risks across the broad range of enrollees. Since less than 34 percent of the aged Medicaid recipients account for more than 82 percent of the total Medicaid expenditures for nursing homes, it is important to enroll as many of the elderly as possible to share the enrollment costs of a comprehensive health system among a wide enrollment pool (U.S. HCFA, 1984). In addition, if individuals of all ages pay into the financing system for long term care, this would broaden the coverage and spread the risk to the entire population. While the elderly use most long term care services, all age groups are subject to injury and disability and may also use long term care services. A combination of public and private financing provides a stronger financial base and spreads the financial support to the broader community. The entire population could then share in the costs—costs that would otherwise fall largely on the chronically ill and disabled. If *only* those who are disabled are enrolled in the system, it would be extremely expensive, and would lose its value as an insurance or indemnity arrangement.

One approach would be to develop private long term care insurance. Obstacles to developing long term care insurance are: insurance industry fear of open-ended liability; absence of reliable data for making estimates of utilization and costs; regulation of insurance; lack of demand by the elderly who do not understand that Medicare and Medi-gap policies do not include long term care; and limited income by the elderly to purchase additional policies. Meiners (1983) makes a convincing case that there is a market for long term care insurance and that policies can be developed that are reasonable in cost and profitable to the insurance industry (see Meiners' prototype policy). Government would have a substantial interest in promoting private insurance policies to reduce the financial burden on Medicaid for long term care services for those who lose their assets and cannot pay for services. Tax breaks and other incentives can be developed that would encourage the development of an enrollment in long term care insurance. Private insurance programs could be developed voluntarily, but states could also mandate that any health insurance company operating within their boundaires would have to offer an optional plan for long term care services.

Another approach to financing long term care would be to establish publicly financed plans. This type of approach could be accomplished at either the federal or state level, and could be financed with a variety of funds including tax dollars, premiums by employees and employers, and/or private premiums. Such programs could be administered jointly with current programs such as Medicare or established separately (U.S. HCFA, 1981). One modification of this approach at the state level would be to establish long term care benefits under the worker's compensation program or a similar program where employers and workers could pay into a fund that would provide protection for long term care. This approach would have the advantage of involving payments from employers and all age groups that could build protection for benefits that are more likely to be used in later years. The publicly funded and administered plans would remove the costs of administration and profits that would be incurred if private insurance companies developed long term care insurance plans, but would have the same benefits as the insurance arrangement described above.

Another option for financing would be to develop prepaid long term care plans. Prepaid long term care plans and S/HMOs allow individuals to use private funds to purchase a comprehensive benefit package that includes long term care. One recent congressional proposal (*The Health Care Coordination Act,* Heinz, S. 1614, 98th Cong., July 13, 1983) would expand the development of S/HMOs. This proposal would establish 20 demonstration projects in the country using the model described above, facilitating the rapid development of S/HMOs with both Medicare and Medicaid funds, while allowing private individuals to purchase such plans. States could also use this approach for Medicaid financed long term care services, by developing contract arrangements with prepaid plans or HMO services to offer long term care in addition to basic health benefits. This model could have immediate cost saving advantages and encourage more appropriate delivery and financing of care than do current models.

There are other proposals that would employ more private financing of long term care by individuals and families based on the tax system, without redesigning the existing financing system. Such proposals are more incremental and probably less effective in providing protection. Current estimates are that 80 percent of existing long term care services are provided informally by families and friends (U.S. HCFA, 1981). As these resources are strained, individuals needing care turn to formal services provided by government. Existing informal care by families and friends should be interfaced with assistance that assures independent living whenever feasible. For example, proposals may include tax reforms to allow greater deductions for dependent care or respite care. Although in the short run costs may increase, such proposals may prevent greater costs to government.

EQUITY AND ACCESS

Despite an enormous investment of public resources in health care, serious problems still exist in the equitable distribution of these resources. There continue to be class, racial, and regional disparities in the benefits of the publicly financed health care system (U.S. President's Commission, 1983). The Medicare program is an example of a broad entitlement, but one in which inequities occur. While most aged are eligible for Medicare, research has shown that Medicare benefits have been provided disproportionately to the upper and middle classes and to whites rather than to the lower classes and blacks, who suffer a greater burden of illness and disability (Davis, 1975). In the southern region of the United States, where 56 percent of the nation's aged nonwhites reside, the disparities between white and nonwhite Medicare beneficiaries are present (Ruther and Dobson, 1981). Furthermore, upper and middle-class aged can afford to supplement these benefits with private health insurance, and they are better able to meet the increasing costs of copayments and deductibles under Medicare than are the lower-class aged.

The Reagan administration and Congress have adopted policies in the Omnibus Budget Reconciliation Act (OBRA) of 1981 (U.S. PL 97-35) and the Tax Equity and Fiscal Responsibility Act (TEFRA) of 1982 (U.S. PL 97-248) that have cut Medicare and Medicaid and increased the hardship of medical expenses for the poor elderly. Recent policy changes have increased the fiscal hardship of millions of near-poor and poor elderly who are being called upon to hear the growing burden of their health care costs—costs that constitute 17 to 29 percent of the elderly's budget (except for older white men) and that now exceed 1,430 dollars per capita in out-of-pocket expenses (Davis, 1982, p. 25). Out-of-pocket health care expenses are disproportionately borne by older blacks and women. The burden is especially high for the poor and the near-poor who are sick. These costs are sobering in view of the fact that the median income for individual elders in 1982 was 6,593 dollars (U.S. Bureau of the Census, 1984) and that the poor and minorities tend to the sicker.

The effect of the most recent policy shifts in the United States (efforts to slow the growth in federal Medicaid costs, shifts to block grants, and reduce social spending) will be to increase existing inequities in programs for the poor across the states. The block grants of the 1970s and 1980s have eased the contraints of categorical funding and of federal requirements, resulting in increased discretion for state government decision making in multiple programs that affect the most economically disadvantaged and vulnerable elderly. Reductions in the federal share of Medicaid, as well as fiscal cutbacks at the state and local levels of government, have resulted in a number of restrictions on services and eligibility in the Medicaid program. State Medicaid programs have widely varying eligibility criteria that are influenced both by political attitudes toward welfare and fiscal capacity (Bovbjerg and Holahan, 1982). Because of the relationship between state welfare criteria and Medicaid eligibility, even before the first Reagan administration cuts in 1981, it was estimated that only about one-half of all individuals living below the poverty level were eligible for Medicaid (U.S. CBO, 1981; Rowland and Davis, 1981).

Medicare deductibles (the base amount one pays before care becomes covered) and copayments (the proportion of total charges payable by beneficiaries) have both increased dramatically in the past two years. The Part A (Hospital) deductible increased 27 percent between 1981 and 1982 (from $204 to $260), more than double the historical increase. Yet another increase has been incurred for 1984 (to $356). The Supplementary Medical Insurance (SMI) program (Part B) is voluntary and provides coverage primarily for physician and physician ordered services not covered by Part A. The annual deductible rose from 60 dollars in 1981 to 75 dollars in 1982. In addition, SMI beneficiaries must pay a monthly premium (adjusted each year) of $14.60 and 20 percent coinsurance of reasonable charges on services rendered.

When applied equally to all Medicare beneficiaries, the differential impact of these flat-rate cost increases becomes clear. As a percentage of income, lower-income elders bear a significantly higher proportionate cost for their health care than do higher-income elders. For example, the Congressional Budget Office has projected that "by 1984, noninstitutionalized persons with household incomes under 5,000 dollars will have medical expenditures totalling 97 percent of their 3,659 dollar average income, 18 percent of which they must pay out-of-pocket. Those in the highest income category...of 58,306 dollars...will pay just over one percent out-of-pocket" (U.S. CBO, 1983, p. 21).

The most serious aspect of increasing copayments and deductibles or shifting costs to beneficiariess is the disproportionate impact on the poor and near-poor aged. The Medicare use of flat fee schedules, rather than a sliding fee schedule, places the greatest on those who are least able to afford them. The Medicaid program pays for the Medicare deductible and coinsurance for individuals who are poor enough to be eligible for Medicaid. However, only 13 percent of those on Medicare are also covered by Medicaid (Feder et al., 1982; Fisher, 1980). The administration's proposal to increase catastrophic coverage would benefit only an estimated two percent of Medicare beneficiaries and thus would not offset the effect of increased cost sharing on the greater majority of beneficiaries.

Voucher proposals have been made for Medicare that appear to be new approaches to financing. Such plans would provide a fixed dollar subsidy to individuals to purchase private insurance or health plans. These proposals are efforts to increase the cost sharing by Medicare beneficiaries in an effort to reduce Medicare costs. These proposals would have the same negative effects on Medicare beneficiaries that other proposals had, which is to increase the share of costs of individuals.

The only current proposals for increasing premiums that would not directly affect the poor elderly and disabled are those proposals that would tax individuals in high income brackets at higher rates. One proposal is to include surtax provisions for the elderly with annual incomes of 25,000 dollars or more to pay for Medicare. This places the burden on the elderly without recognizing that long term care benefits are needed by other groups who become disabled. Some type of surtax on all high incomes to finance long term care of Medicare would be more equitable than the proposals for increases in premiums and deductibles.

The Federal Role

The "national" policy is comprised of multiple, variable, noncomparable policies and programs, each of which vary in different states. A major question is whether particular long term care policy goals and programs should be determined nationally or left to state and local governments. Given the structure of current programs, a complete understanding of the "national" policy on health care for the elderly in general, or for long term care in particular, cannot be obtained without a systematic examination of policies across states. The goal of such an examination should be to distinguish those responsibilities that are logically state and local in nature from those that are so significant and moral in impact that the inequities made possible by decentralized decision making must be prevented through the development of a single national policy.

The myriad state-level cost-saving strategies in health have not led to systemwide reform. The research of the Aging Health Policy Center demonstrates that, on the contrary, savings from direct cutbacks or from eligibility restrictions have not resulted in the transfer of money to social and community-based services (Estes, Newcomer, and Associates, 1983). Often such savings (where they occur) merely enable state and local governments to keep pace with the overall inflation in medical care prices and the pressures on Medicaid generated by unemployment. The research further illustrates the vulnerability of the aged to capricious and complex federal and state health and aging policies, as well as to broader policy considerations, such as cost containment and decentralization of programs from the federal to state and local governments (Estes, Newcomer, and Associates, 1983).

The goal of an equitable allocation and distribution of the nation's health care resources cannot be reached without a vital federal role in health and aging. As state and local governments across the country devise ways to meet the countervailing demands of taxpayers, health providers, and the public needing health care, it has become increasingly clear that long range comprehensive reform will not come about without concerted national leadership.

The Reagan administration's new federalism and decentralization strategies have turned the nation's compass in quite the opposite direction. In framing a long term care strategy, Congress must consider the relationship between state and local government capacity to assume responsibility for the elderly (and particularly for the long term care policies for the near-poor and poor elderly) and the fiscal context within which state and local governments are operating; in interrelationship between state and federal economic conditions, policies; and the real (and growing) revenue disparities among states and geographic regions.

Numerous proposals have been advanced concerning the need for a uniform national policy on long term care. The private out-of-pocket money spent on long term care in addition to the Medicaid national long term care dollars and the Medicare dollars spent on acute care represent an enormous sum. If these separate public and private resources were to be combined, a truly national health protection plan for older people in this country could be developed (Vladeck, 1983a).

In conclusion, Congress must take the lead in developing a national policy that will provide to all citizens of the United States the same kind of universal comprehensive health insurance, including long term care, that is already enjoyed by our less affluent but equally hard-working neighbors to the north—the Canadians. Congress took a major step in enacting Medicare and Medicaid in 1965; it now needs to go the rest of the way.

Note

1. Waiver approval for using Medicare funds has been subject to blockage by the Office of Management and Budgets because of their concerns about Medicare paying for long term care services.

References

Bovbjerg, R. R., and J. Holahan. *Medicaid in the Reagan Era: Federal Policy and State Choices.* Washington, DC: Urban Institute, 1982.

Davis, K. "Equal Treatment and Unequal Benefits: The Medicare Program." *Milbank Memorial Fund Quarterly/Health and Society,* 53, No. 4 (1975), 449-488.

———. "Medicare Reconsidered." Paper presented for the Duke University Medical Center Seventh Private Sector Conference on the Financial Support of Health Care of the Elderly and the Indigent, Durham, NC, 14–16 March 1982.

Diamond, L. M., and D. E. Berman. "The Social/Health Maintenance Organization: A Single Entry, Prepaid, Long-Term Care Delivery System." In *Reforming the Long Term Care System.* Ed. J. Callahan and S. S. Wallace. Lexington, MA: Lexington Books, D. C. Health and Co., 1981.

Estes, C. L., and P. R. Lee. "Policy Shifts and Their Impact on Health Care for Elderly Persons." *Western Journal of Medicine,* 135, No. 6 (December 1981), 511-518.

Estes, C. L., R. J. Newcomber, and Associates. *Fiscal Austerity and Aging.* Beverly Hills, CA: Sage, 1983.

Feder, J., J. Holahan, R. R. Bovbjerg, and J. Hadley. "Health." In *The Reagan Experiment.* Ed. J. L. Palmer and I. V. Sawhill. Washington, DC: Urban Institute, 1982.

Fisher, C. R. "Difference by Age Groups in Health Care Spending." *Health Care Financing Review,* 1, No. 4 (Spring 1980), 65-90.

Gibson, R. M., D. R. Waldo, and K. R. Levit. "National Health Expenditures, 1982." *Health Care Finacing Review,* 5, No. 1 (Fall 1983), 1-31.

Luft, H. S. *Health Maintenance Organizations: Dimensions of Performance.* New York, NY: John Wiley and Sons, 1981.

Marmor, T. R. "Is Health Care Better in Canada than in the United States? The View from America." Unpublished paper. New Haven, CT: Yale University, 1982.

Meiners, M. R. "The Case for Long-Term Care Insurance." *Health Affairs,* 2, No. 1 (1983), 55-79.

National Study Group for State Medicaid Strategies. *Restructuring Medicaid: An Agenda for Change*. Washington, DC: The Center for the Study of Social Policy, 1984.

Relman, A. S. "The New Medical-Industrial Complex." In *The Nationa's Health*. Ed. P. R. Lee, C. L. Estes, and N. B. Ramsay. San Francisco, CA: Boyd & Fraser Publishing Company, 1984.

Rowland, D., and C. R. Davis. "Medicaid Eligibility and Benefits: Current Policies and Future Choices." Paper presented at the 1981 Commonwealth Fund Forum, Lake Bluff, IL, August 9-12, 1981.

Rowland, D. and C. R. Gaus. "Medicaid Eligibility and Benefits: Current Policies and Future Choices." Paper presented at the 1981 Commonwealth Fund Forum, Lake Bluff, Illinois, August 9-12, 1981.

Ruther, M., and A. Dobson. "Equal Treatment and Unequal Benefits: a Re-examination of the Use of Medicare Services by Race, 1967-1976." *Health Care Financing Review*, 2, No. 3 (Winter 1981), 55-83.

Simanis, J. D., and J. R. Coleman. "Health Care Expenditures in Nine Industrialized Countries, 1960-1976." *Social Security Bulletin*, 43, No. 1 (January 1980), 3-8.

Spitz, B. *Medicaid Nursing Home Reimbursement: New York, Illinois, California Case Studies*. Baltimore, MD: U.S. Health Care Financing Administration, 1981.

Spitz, B., and G. Atkinson. *Nursing Homes, Hospitals and Medicaid: Reimbursement Policy Adjustments, 1981-1982*. Washington, DC: National Governors' Association, 1982.

U.S. Bureau of the Census. "Money Income of Households, Families, and Persons in the United States, 1982." *Current Population Report*, Series P-60, No. 142. Washington, DC: U.S. Government Printing Office, 1984.

U.S. Congressional Budget Office (CBO). *Medicaid: Choices of 1982 and Beyond*. Washington, DC: U.S. CBO, 1981.

———. *Changing the Structure of Medicare Benefits: Issues and Options*. Washington, DC: U.S. CBO, 1983.

U.S. General Accounting Office (GAO). *Hospital Merger Increased Medicare and Medicaid Payments for Capital Costs*, by the Comptroller General of the United States. Washington, DC: U.S. GAO, 1983.

U.S. Health Care Financing Administration (HCFA). *Long Term Care: Background and Future Directions*. Washington, DC: U.S. Department of Health and Human Services, 1981.

———. Medicaid Program Data Branch. *National Medicaid Statistics: Fiscal Years 1975 to 1982*. State 2082 Tables data tape. Baltimore, MD: U.S. Department of Health and Human Services, 1984.

U.S. President's Commission for the Study of Ethical Problems in Medicine and Biomedical and Behavioral Research. *Securing access to Health Care: A Report on the Ethical Implications of Differences in the Availability of Health Services*. Vol. 1: Report. Washington, DC: U.S. Government Printing Office, 1983.

U.S. Public Law 97-35. *Omnibus Budget Reconciliation Act (OBRA) of 1981*. Washington, DC: U.S. Government Printing Office, 1981.

U.S. Public Law 97-248. *Tax Equity and Fiscal Responsibility Act (TEFRA) of 1982*. Washington, DC: U.S. Government Printing Office, 1982.

U.S. Public Law 98-21. *Social Security Amendments of 1983*. Washington, DC: U.S. Government Printing Office, 1983.

Vladeck, B. "Long Term Care: What Have We Learned." Paper presented at the Western Gerontological on Health and Aging, San Francisco, CA, November 1983a.

———. "Two Steps Forward, One Back: The Changing Agenda of Long Term Care Reform." *Pride Institute Journal of Long Term Home Health Care.* 2, No. 3 (Summer 1983b), 1-7.

———. *Unloving Care: The Nursing Home Tragedy.* New York, NY: Basic Books, 1980.

Zahn, M. A., R. E. Schlenker, and J. L. Johnson. *Overview of Medicaid Nursing Home Reimbursement Systems: An Analysis of Long-Term Care Payment Systems.* Denver: Center for Health Services Research, University of Colorado Health Sciences Center, March, 1984.

NAME INDEX

SUBJECT INDEX

ABOUT THE AUTHORS

A. E. BENJAMIN, Jr., Ph.D., Adjunct Assistant Professor, Department of Social and Behavioral Sciences, is Associate Director of the Aging Health Policy Center, University of California, San Francisco. Dr. Benjamin has completed a study of health planning and the elderly and has written on health planning, income assistance, and long term care for the elderly. His current research interests include home-health care under Medicare and Medicaid, state systems of community care, and policy trade-offs among vulnerable populations.

MARJORIE P. BOGAERT-TULLIS, B.Sc.N., Research Assistant, Department of Social and Behavioral Sciences, Aging Health Policy Center, School of Nursing, University of California, San Francisco, is a master's candidate in nursing at the University of California, San Francisco. She has been involved in numerous research projects studying the elderly, nursing homes, and long term care, both in Canada and the United Kingdom.

CARROLL L. ESTES, Ph.D., Professor of Sociology, is Chairperson of the Department of Social and Behavioral Sciences in the School of Nursing and Director of the Aging Health Policy Center, University of California, San Francisco. Dr. Estes conducts research and writes about aging policy, long term care, and the effects of fiscal crisis and new federalism policies on public policy, the private nonprofit sector, and the elderly. The author of *The Aging Enterprise* (1979) and *The Decision Makers: The Power Structure of Dallas* (1963), and coauthor of *Fiscal Austerity and Aging* (1983) and *Political Economy, Health and Aging* (1984), and coeditor of *Readings in Political Economy of Aging,* Dr. Estes is past president of the Western Gerontological Society and the Association for Gerontology in Higher Education.

CHARLENE HARRINGTON, R.N., Ph.D., Adjunct Associate Professor, Department of Social and Behavioral Sciences, is Associate Director of the Aging Health Policy Center and Codirector, Gerontological Nurse Training Grant, Department of Family Health Care Nursing, University of California, San Francisco. Dr. Harrington has had twenty years of active experience in the health care field and has administered state and regional health planning and regulatory agencies. She currently directs research projects examining trends in long term care service expenditure and utilization and has written extensively on nursing homes and long term care.

PHILIP R. LEE, M.D., Professor of Social Medicine, Department of Medicine, is Director of the Institute for Health Policy Studies, School of Medicine, University of California, San Francisco. A former Assistant Secretary of Health in the U.S. Department of Health, Education, and Welfare (1965–1969), and former Chancellor of University of California, San Francisco (1969–1972), Dr. Lee conducts research and writes about a wide range of health policy issues, including long term care for the elderly, prescription drugs, primary health care, and health promotion and disease prevention.

ROBERT J. NEWCOMER, Ph.D., Associate Professor, Department of Social and Behavioral Science, is Deputy Director of the Aging Health Policy Center, University of California, San Francisco. Dr. Newcomer's research includes studies of state health care financing and service delivery, the effect of new federalism policies on aging services, and the issues relating to housing for the elderly. Dr. Newcomer is also Director of the National Policy Center on Health funded by the Administration on Aging and has been responsible for the preparation of a number of reports on health promotion and disease prevention among the elderly. His books include *Community Planning for an Aging Society* (1976) and *Housing an Aging Society* (in press) both edited with M. Powell Lawton and Thomas Byerts, and *Fiscal Austerity and Aging* (1983) coauthored with Carroll L. Estes and Associates.

LYNN PARINGER, Ph. D., Associate Professor of Economics, California State University, Hayward, is Visiting Lecturer, Aging Health Policy Center, University of California, San Francisco. Dr. Paringer teaches health economics and health care financing and conducts research on the impact of public policy changes on utilization and expenditures for publicly financed health services.

IDA VSW RED, M.A., M.S.L.S., Senior Public Administration Analyst, Department of Social and Behavioral Sciences, is Resource Director, Aging Health Policy Center, University of California, San Francisco. Ms. Red manages the AHPC research library, investigates funding opportunites, chairs the publications committee, and edits and disseminates AHPC publications. She was coeditor of the first edition of *The Nation's Health* (1981) and coordinating editor of *Fiscal Austerity and Aging* (1983).

DOROTHY P. RICE, B.A., D.Sc. (hon.), Professor in Residence, Department of Social and Behavioral Sciences, Aging Health Policy Center, University of California, San Francisco, is a former Director of the National Center for Health Statistics, U.S. Public Health Service (1976–82), with thirty years of federal service in the Public Health Service and Social Security Administration. She is involved in research on the burden of chronic diseases and has written extensively on the delivery and financing of health care services, cost of illness, and health statistics.

CAROL E. SATTLER, B.A., Staff Research Associate, Department of Social and Behavioral Sciences, Aging Health Policy Center, School of Nursing, University of California, San Francisco, has been involved in a project studying the impact of state policies on expenditures for, and utilization of, publicly financed long term care. She is currently a doctoral student in economics at the University of Maryland, College Park.

ROBYN STONE, M.P.A., Research Associate, Aging Health Policy Center, University of California, San Francisco, is involved in research in the areas of older women's health and board and care housing for the elderly. She has served on the staff of the Department of Health and Human Services Offices of Human Development Services and is currently a doctoral student in public health at the University of California, Berkeley.

JAMES H. SWAN, Ph.D., Adjunct Assistant Professor, Department of Social and Behavioral Sciences, is Senior Research Associate, Aging Health Policy Center, University of California, San Francisco. Dr. Swan directed a project with Dr. Estes assessing the impact on aging services of fiscal crisis at the state and local levels.

JUANITA B. WOOD, Ph.D., Adjunct Assistant Professor, Department of Social and Behavioral Sciences, Aging Health Policy Center,

University of California, San Francisco, is Project Director of the nonprofit sector study and also teaches a graduate seminar in field research in the School of Nursing, University of California, San Francisco.